A Republic of Law

The rule of law is a valuable human achievement. It is valuable not only instrumentally, but also for its own sake as a significant aspect of social justice: only in a society that enjoys the rule of law is it possible for people to regard one another as fellow free citizens, with no one the master of anyone else. Nevertheless, the rule of law is poorly understood. In this book Frank Lovett develops a rigorous conception of the rule of law that is grounded in legal positivism, and offers a civic republican argument for its value in terms of freedom from domination. Bridging persistent methodological gaps that divide legal philosophy, social science, and political theory, Lovett demonstrates how insights from all three can be united in a single powerful theory. This book will appeal to anyone interested in the rule of law, including scholars, legal officials, and policy makers.

FRANK LOVETT is Associate Professor of Political Science and Director of Legal Studies at Washington University in St. Louis.

A Republic of Law

FRANK LOVETT

CAMBRIDGE
UNIVERSITY PRESS

CAMBRIDGE
UNIVERSITY PRESS

University Printing House, Cambridge CB2 8BS, United Kingdom

Cambridge University Press is part of the University of Cambridge.

It furthers the University's mission by disseminating knowledge in the pursuit of education, learning and research at the highest international levels of excellence.

www.cambridge.org
Information on this title: www.cambridge.org/9781107130647

First published 2016

A catalogue record for this publication is available from the British Library

Library of Congress Cataloguing in Publication data
Names: Lovett, Frank.
Title: A republic of law / Frank Lovett.
Description: Cambridge : Cambridge University Press, 2016. | Includes bibliographical references and index.
Identifiers: LCCN 2016011213 | ISBN 9781107130647 (Hardback) | ISBN 9781107576568 (Paperback)
Subjects: LCSH: Rule of law–Philosophy. | Legal positivism. | Sociological jurisprudence.
Classification: LCC K3171 .L68 2016 | DDC 340/.11–dc23 LC record available at http://lccn.loc.gov/2016011213

ISBN 978-1-107-13064-7 Hardback
ISBN 978-1-107-57656-8 Paperback

For Henry

Contents

Acknowledgments   *page* ix

1 Introduction   1
   1.1 Existing Accounts of the Rule of Law   2
   1.2 A Better Account of the Rule of Law   9
   1.3 The Rule of Law and Positivism   17

Part I   Legal Statics   27

2 Social Rules and Norms   29
   2.1 Habits and Personal Rules   30
   2.2 Social Rules   41
   2.3 Social Norms and the Practice Theory   51
   2.4 Conventions and Social Order   61

3 Legal Systems   63
   3.1 Law and Public Coercion   65
   3.2 The Possibility of Law   79
   3.3 Law and Authority   90
   3.4 Conclusion   96

4 The Rule of Law and Its Value   100
   4.1 Defining the Rule of Law   100
   4.2 Value of the Rule of Law   113
   4.3 Rule of Law Principles   126
   4.4 Conclusion   135

Part II   Legal Dynamics   137

5 Adjudication and the Realist Challenge   139
   5.1 Realism and the Rule of Law   140
   5.2 The Efficacy of Law   144
   5.3 Legal Indeterminacy and Hard Cases   152
   5.4 Adjudication and Legal Office   160
   5.5 Conclusion   174

6   Legislation, Administration, and Discretion   176
    6.1 The Rule of Law and Legal Change   177
    6.2 Designing Legislative Authority   185
    6.3 Discretion and Economic Justice   192
    6.4 The Rule of Law and the Modern State   200

7   Conclusion   203

Appendix A: The Principles of Legality   209

Appendix B: Measuring the Rule of Law   212

Bibliography   219

Index   229

Acknowledgments

It has taken me a long time to write this book. The underlying intuition on which it is based – namely, that the strongest and most compelling theory of the rule of law and its value would be one built on the foundation of legal positivism – occurred to me more than fifteen years ago, in the course of my first serious introduction to jurisprudence. That introduction was due to Jeremy Waldron, who also encouraged my initial efforts to develop the intuition. In the event, my views about the rule of law have turned out rather different from his. It is thus only proper that, even as I express my appreciation for his having initially inspired this project, I also absolve him of any responsibility for its contents.

Various parts of the manuscript have been presented at meetings of the American Political Science Association, the Midwestern Political Science Association, and the Association for Political Theory; at the Workshop in Politics, Ethics, and Society at Washington University; and at the Washington University Law School Faculty Workshop. I am grateful to the organizers, chairs, and discussants at these events, and also for the many interesting puzzles and challenges posed by audience members. Significant portions of Chapter 5 were previously published as "A Republican Theory of Adjudication," in *Res Publica* 21 (2015): 1–18. The editors and anonymous reviewers at that journal helped strengthen my arguments considerably, as did the excellent anonymous referees at Cambridge University Press. I am also grateful to Charlie Kurth, Chad Flanders, and especially Brian Tamanaha, each of whom read the manuscript in part or in whole: their invaluable feedback and advice not only deepened my understanding, but also saved me from numerous errors. Jacob Montgomery supplied important assistance with respect to Appendix B. Numerous conversations with colleagues – Randy Calvert, Clarissa Hayward, Ian MacMullen, John Patty, and Maggie Penn, in particular – helped clarify my thinking on many foundational issues.

largely achieved through the state's monopoly on the legitimate use of violence, which more or less effectively denies ordinary citizens the means to employ coercive force against one another. The domination people might experience at the hands of a state, however, is no better – and, indeed, can be much worse – than any domination they might experience at the hands of other ordinary citizens. Hence, we may also speak of the rule of law in a narrower sense: in this narrower sense, the rule of law exists roughly to the extent that all public uses of coercive force are effectively controlled and regulated by the rules and procedures embodied in a legal system. The rule of law alone, in either sense, certainly does not guarantee that any specific individual will lead a flourishing life; nevertheless, as one necessary condition (among others) for the achievement of human flourishing, the rule of law constitutes a significant part of social justice. Only in a society enjoying the rule of law in some measure is it possible for people to regard one another as fellow free citizens, no one the master of any one else. In the traditional language of the classical republicans, such a society would be an "empire of laws and not of men."[4]

The previous paragraph expresses, in highly condensed form, roughly what I plan to argue in this book. Much of my argument will involve developing a robust conception of what counts as the rule of law. Given that so many have tried to define the rule of law already, however, one might be tempted to conclude with Brian Tamanaha that proposing yet another definition "in the hope that it would win the day would be redundant and naïve."[5] Thus it is perhaps incumbent on me to explain at the outset why, in my view, none of the existing attempts is entirely satisfactory. That will be the principal aim of this introductory chapter. Part and parcel with this explanation will be a discussion of the approach and method we must adopt if our theory of the rule of law and its value is to succeed.

1.1 Existing Accounts of the Rule of Law

Suppose we want to argue that the rule of law is a good thing. It is worth considering at the outset how our argument might fail. The most

---

[4] This expression is most famously associated with James Harrington 1656, p. 161, and it derives from a creative rendering of a passage in Titus Livy's history of the Roman republic.

[5] Tamanaha 2004, p. 114.

obvious way it might fail is if it turns out to make no practical difference – that is, if it gives us no reasons for doing or avoiding anything in particular. Of course, this is not the only consideration relevant in judging the success or failure of theories, and others may be pressed into service as the occasion warrants. It is a necessary consideration, however. Whatever else its merits, a theory that cannot make a practical difference is a pointless theory.[6]

In order to make a practical difference, a theory of the rule of law must to begin with not be too demanding, on the one hand, nor too permissive, on the other. At either extreme, it will not matter what we do. In the former case this is because even our best efforts will be insufficient for success, whereas in the latter case it is because success will come whether we exert much effort or not. Surprisingly, many well-known accounts of the rule of law fail to meet even this minimum requirement. For example, in a famous passage from the *Spirit of the Laws*, Montesquieu says that judges should be

... no more than the mouth that pronounces the words of the law, mere passive beings, incapable of moderating either its force or rigor.[7]

Similar sentiments have been expressed many times, by many different authors. Chief Justice John Marshall, for instance, once asserted that:

Judicial power, as contradistinguished from the power of laws, has no existence. Courts are mere instruments of law, and can will nothing.[8]

These passages might be interpreted loosely, of course, as the metaphorical expression of a certain reasonably plausible ideal. Interpreted literally, however, they advance a deeply naïve view concerning what legal systems are, or even could be. If our theory demands that the laws govern in the literal sense that Montesquieu and Marshall suggest, then the rule of law would be impossible to achieve. Such a theory would fail to make a practical difference.

---

[6] For the purposes of this book, I will regard this assertion as axiomatic; if pressed to defend it, I would refer to Charles Sanders Peirce and the other American pragmatists. Of course one might believe a theory can have other merits: for instance, it might lead us to think differently about the world. Merits of this sort lie outside the scope of my concern here.

[7] Montesquieu 1748, I.11.48: p. 159.

[8] See *Osborn v. Bank of United States*, 22 U.S. 738 (1824), p. 866.

On the other side, there is also a tradition of defining legal systems merely as the system of order imposed by states on their populations, whatever character that order happens to have. Hans Kelsen, who himself held something like this view, clearly recognized the consequence for our idea of the rule of law:

If the state is comprehended as a legal order, then every state is a state governed by law (*Rechsstaat*), and this term becomes a pleonism.[9]

The same thought is expressed even more emphatically by a less well-known author, Wolfgang Friedmann, as follows:

... the rule of law simply means the "existence of public order." It means organized government, operating through the various instruments and channels of legal command. In this sense, all modern societies live under the rule of law, fascist as well as socialist and liberal states.[10]

Kelsen's conception of the rule of law is discussed in greater detail later (in Chapter 4). Here the point is simply to observe that if we accept either his or Friedmann's view, then the rule of law would be too easily achieved. States could hardly fail to observe the rule of law, so understood, and again our theory would make no practical difference.

Of course, there is no truth in definitions per se. Everything depends on what we want a definition to do. Thus, depending on our aims, it might be perfectly reasonable to define the rule of law in such a way that the concept will perform no substantive work. In some theories, for example, a concept's role might simply be to organize or summarize other ideas, or to represent one aspect of a more general idea. If we want to argue that the rule of law is a good thing, however, it is best not to doom our project from the start, but rather at least aim to develop a theory that navigates between the two extremes we have considered. In this way, it is at least possible that our argument might make a practical difference. Nothing ensures we will succeed. It might turn out in the nature of things that the rule of law can only be given coherent sense as either an impossible ideal or else a pointless triviality.[11] In that case, our project will ultimately fail, but at least that failure will not have been preordained.

[9] Kelsen 1960, p. 313.   [10] Friedmann 1951, p. 281.
[11] Here I assume for pragmatic reasons that we want a definition of the rule of law to bear at least some resemblance to our intuitive sense of what the term means in common usage: obviously, it would be easy enough to meet the requirements

Most of the better-known contemporary discussions of the rule of law avoid the two extremes indicated above; that is, they aim to present a conception of the rule of law that is neither impossible nor too easy to achieve. Nevertheless, it is my view that they also fail, and that their failure is largely due to the way in which they approach the task at hand. Since the difficulty is more subtle, however, it will require a somewhat more detailed discussion.

It is standard, in the contemporary literature, to characterize the rule of law not as a single idea, but rather as a bundle of normative requirements or virtues. Often these are called the "principles of legality."[12] Alas, there is little agreement on what this bundle includes. According to some, the relevant principles can be stated with relative dispatch: "a legal system satisfies the requirements of the rule of law if its commands are general, knowable, and performable," write William Eskridge and John Ferejohn.[13] Indeed, even this relatively short list might be longer than necessary. "Stripped of all technicalities," says Friedrich Hayek, the rule of law only "means that government in all its actions is bound by rules fixed and announced beforehand"; and on the view of Justice Antonin Scalia, it means simply "a law of rules" rather than of discretionary standards.[14]

Others, however, tend toward lengthier lists. For example, Richard Fallon enumerates five principles of legality: first, people "must be able to understand the law and comply with it"; second, the "law should actually guide people, at least for the most part"; third, the "law should be reasonably stable, in order to facilitate planning and coordinated action over time"; fourth, the "law should rule officials, including judges, as well as ordinary citizens"; and fifth, courts "should be available to enforce the law and should employ fair procedures."[15] Joseph Raz and John Finnis find even this somewhat longer list insufficient, each proposing no fewer than eight distinct principles, though not the same eight. Both agree that all laws should be prospective and that the laws and the process of legislation should be reasonably clear, public, and stable. Finnis adds, but Raz does not, a requirement that laws not command the impossible or contradict one another; whereas

of practical utility if we permitted ourselves to give the term any meaning we chose, without such a constraint.

[12] This term is due to Fuller 1969, p. 41 and *passim*.
[13] Eskridge and Ferejohn 1994, p. 265.
[14] Hayek 1944, p. 80; Scalia 1989, p. 1187.   [15] Fallon 1997, pp. 8–9.

Raz insists that there exist an independent judiciary with powers of review, whose courts are readily accessible. Raz then rounds out his list with requirements that "natural justice" be observed, and that discretion in the criminal justice system be restrained so as to not "pervert the law." By contrast, Finnis concludes his list with requirements that officials be "accountable" for their administration of the law "consistently and in accordance with its tenor."[16]

When John Rawls offers his account, he initially seems to adopt a middle-of-the-road approach, identifying four "precepts of justice associated with the rule of law." But this apparent parsimony is deceptive, since most of these turn out to have many sub-clauses. First, there is the "precept that ought implies can." This has three sub-clauses: the law must "not impose a duty to do what cannot be done," officials "who enact the laws" should do so "in good faith" that is "recognized by those subject to their enactments," and the legal system should "recognize impossibility of performance as a defense." The second precept, "that similar cases be treated similarly," is regarded as clear enough as it stands, but a third, "that there is no offense without a law," is found to have no fewer than five sub-clauses: the laws should be "known and expressly promulgated" and "clearly defined," statutes should be "general both in statement and intent," and in criminal law "severe offenses" should be "strictly construed" and penal laws not "retroactive." Finally, the fourth precept, that "natural justice" be observed, has four sub-clauses: there should be "provisions for conducting orderly trials" and "rules of evidence that guarantee rational procedures of inquiry," "judges must be independent and impartial" entailing that "no man may judge in his own case," and "trials must be fair and open, but not prejudiced by public clamor."[17]

Rawls provides about as detailed an accounting of rule of law principles as one might expect or desire, but neither his nor any of the other mentioned alternatives has emerged as the consensus view. Nor has the well-known account of Lon Fuller, which I discuss in greater detail below. This lack of agreement in the contemporary literature is striking, and also frustrating. One might wonder, however, whether it bars all progress. Could we perhaps make do with a "family resemblance" conception of the rule of law as an imprecise

[16] Raz 1979, pp. 214–218; Finnis 1980, pp. 270–271.
[17] Rawls 1971, pp. 236–239.

ideal loosely associated with a few commonly recurring principles?[18] Unfortunately not. While disagreement at the margin is no doubt inevitable, if we want our theory to make a practical difference – if we want it to guide our actions and decisions – we must in central cases at least be able to decisively identify the rule of law when we see it. Only then can we say with confidence where reform is necessary, what specific measures would help, whether our efforts have succeeded, and so forth. For such purposes, it is necessary that we agree on a specific conception.[19]

How then shall we decide which view is best? Broadly speaking, there are two different approaches to answering this question. Neither is satisfactory, though for very different reasons.[20] On the first, the principles of legality are taken to represent the *form* legal rules should take and not their substantive *content* – especially, not their merit or demerit from an ethical or moral point of view. The correct list of principles is thus supposed to be the one that most accurately captures the formal properties characteristic of law. Unfortunately, legal rules may or may not possess many different formal properties, and it is not immediately obvious which among these are the relevant ones. (Is enforcement by an independent judiciary, for example, an essential formal characteristic of law?) What is worse, formal conceptions have difficulty articulating the value of the rule of law. To be sure, it is widely appreciated that individuals subject to a legal system derive some measure of benefit whenever certain formal requirements are respected: it is easier to plan our lives, for instance, when legal rules are predictable, consistent, and clear. But these benefits seem decidedly limited. Indeed, there is no reason a legal regime of slavery could not perfectly well observe the rule of law principles understood as mere

---

[18] The idea of a family resemblance concept derives from Wittgenstein 1958, §§ 66–69: pp. 31–33. The instances of such concepts have overlapping similarities without any universally shared elements, as for example the sets {A, B, C}, {B, C, D}, and {A, D, E}.

[19] Sometimes it is suggested that agreement is impossible because the rule of law is an "essentially contested" concept: see Fallon 1997, p. 7; and Waldron 2002, pp. 153–159. For reasons that will become clear subsequently, this is not my view.

[20] For the following distinction between formal and substantive accounts of the rule of law, see Summers 1993; Craig 1997; Tamanaha 2004, chs. 7–8; or Waldron 2011.

formal requirements: rules permitting the ownership of human beings can be clear, consistent, published in advance, and so forth.[21]

Thus it has seemed to many that if the rule of law is to be taken seriously as an important political ideal, we must understand its principles substantively – as requiring not only that legal rules take a certain form, but also that they possess substantive merit with respect to their content. Consider, for instance, the principle of generality: interpreted formally, this might simply be the requirement that legal rules not refer to proper names. But many unjust distinctions can be made consistent with such a requirement, as for example a distinction between persons owned (slaves) and persons who own others (masters). To avoid this consequence, we might say that generality further requires legal distinctions to be acceptable to a majority of persons in each distinguished class, thus transforming generality into a substantive principle.[22] So interpreted, the rule of law would certainly be inconsistent with slavery, among many other things. But now we confront a very different problem, clearly articulated by Raz as follows:

> If the rule of law is the rule of good law then to explain its nature is to propound a complete social philosophy. But if so the term lacks any useful function. We have no need to be converted to the rule of law just in order to discover that to believe in it is to believe that good should triumph.[23]

In other words, interpreted substantively, the principles of legality simply represent a view about what sorts of laws it would be good to have – which is to say, a view on the meaning of social justice itself.[24] Since no agreement on the meaning of social justice is soon to be expected, we are unfortunately no closer to determining which conception of the rule of law is best.[25]

Thus following either of these standard approaches found in the contemporary literature, it appears our argument that the rule of law is a good thing will in the end make little practical difference: understood formally, the rule of law is at best a minor ideal, but understood

---

[21] Raz 1979, pp. 221–222, admits this is a feature of his formal conception.
[22] Hayek 1960, pp. 153–154, proposes this standard.   [23] Raz 1979, p. 211.
[24] Dworkin 1985, pp. 11–12, admits this is a feature of his substantive conception.
[25] See Summers 1993, pp. 135–138. Of course, if one's aim is to advance a theory of social justice within which the concept of the rule of law serves to summarize or organize other ideas, this may not be a problem. In effect, this is the strategy proposed by Gowder 2013, who identifies the rule of law with legal equality.

substantively, it is a redundant one. Neither approach, moreover, is much help in settling disagreements regarding the correct principles of legality. Fortunately, there is another way to proceed. As we shall see in the following section, all the various problems bedeviling contemporary discussions of the rule of law stem from the same source, and accordingly have the same solution.

1.2 A Better Account of the Rule of Law

How can we make sense of the intuitively plausible claim that the rule of law is a good thing? Significantly, most contemporary accounts assume that we should understand the rule of law as a virtue of legal systems: thus, it is often said, the rule of law is "one of the virtues which a legal system may possess and by which it is to be judged," or "the name commonly given to the state of affairs in which a legal system is legally in good shape," or "the conception of formal justice … applied to the legal system," or the insistence that certain "moral and political rights be recognized in positive law."[26] From this assumption, these accounts proceed straightaway to an enumeration of what they regard as the relevant virtues or principles. But this is not the best way to understand the rule of law: we should understand it not as a virtue of legal systems, but rather as a virtue of systems of social organization. Let me explain as follows.

1.2.1 Law as a Social Practice

Suppose we begin with the idea of a legal system as one large and complex social formation alongside others, such as a market system, a democratic political system, and so forth.[27] Social formations of this kind are of course interrelated in many significant respects: the law can enhance markets by defining and enforcing contracts, for instance, or democracy by expanding and protecting the rights of citizenship; and these and other social formations can in turn enhance law.[28]

---

[26] Raz 1979, p. 211; Finnis 1980, p. 270; Rawls 1971, p. 235; Dworkin 1985, p. 11.

[27] For this handy expression of law as a "social formation" I am indebted to Galligan 2007, p. 4 and *passim*.

[28] It is sometimes suggested that markets are necessarily constituted by law. This does not seem right to me: as will be discussed in Chapters 3 and 4, markets

Without suggesting that such interrelations between social formations are unimportant, the argument that follows will focus on the differences among them. Each social formation, let us say, is a specific arrangement of practices or ways of doing things – practices, in particular, for managing the expectations and motivating the cooperation of diverse individuals.[29] Their differing approaches to managing expectations and motivating cooperation lend each social formation its own distinctive character. In other words, the way people do things in the context of a legal system is different from the way they do things in the marketplace, and either from the way they do things in the democratic forum. These differences give the experience of participating in each a unique quality.[30]

Next suppose we undertake to develop a good "descriptive sociology" of the various practices constituting each social formation.[31] These investigations would issue in a set of field reports, so to speak: the field report on law, for example, would detail the various characteristic features of legal practices and describe how these distinguish the law from other ways of doing things.

With these field reports in hand, we can easily make sense of the intuitively plausible claim that the rule of law is a good thing. What we mean to say, roughly, is that in some specific set of situations or contexts – perhaps, situations in which some persons or groups wield coercive force over others – it is better to manage expectations and motivate cooperation through the particular bundle of practices characteristic of a legal system than it would be through any of the alternatives. To clarify, this is not the familiar claim that the law's legitimacy derives, at least in part, from its capacity to solve

---

necessarily depend on background social conventions and norms, but not necessarily on law in particular.

[29] This is not to say that it is the *function* of a social formation to manage expectations and motivate cooperation. For one thing, this implies intentional design, which should not be assumed: only sometimes are markets deliberately created, for instance, and then only in the case of specific goods. More importantly, large-scale social formations always serve a multitude of functions. Thus, not only do legal systems solve coordination problems, they also provide security, express community values, and so on. For further discussion, see Chapter 3.

[30] Cf. Elster 1986, who famously contrasts the market and the forum.

[31] This turn of phrase is obviously due to Hart 1994, p. vi, and the connection to his views and those of the legal positivists in general are discussed below.

coordination problems.[32] Of course the law can do this, but so too can market exchange or democratic deliberation. It is entirely possible that the law might claim legitimate authority in some context even when our activities in that context would be better organized some other way, all things considered: this might be the case, for instance, when sub-optimal laws are produced through fair democratic procedures. Likewise, it is entirely possible that even when the law lacks legitimate authority, it is nevertheless better to organize certain activities through law than in some other way (as we shall see in Chapter 4). The relevant claim here is simply a comparative one: given that the different social formations have different characteristic features, it stands to reason that in some contexts it will be better to organize our activities through law, just as in others it will be better to organize our activities through markets, and so on.[33]

Notice that the argument, now properly framed, is clearly positioned to make a practical difference: it is an eminently relevant question which specific bundles of practices are best suited to organizing our activities in which specific situations or contexts. In order to fully succeed, of course, two distinct claims must eventually be vindicated. The first is the claim that the practices characteristic of a legal system are experientially distinct from other practices in ways that matter, normatively speaking. The second is the claim that there are at least some important situations or contexts in which, according to plausible normative criteria, the practices characteristic of a legal system are indeed the best way to manage expectations and motivate cooperation. As it happens, both claims have been denied.

The first claim was most famously rejected by the legal realists of the 1920s – Karl Llewellyn, Jerome Frank, and others. On their view, roughly speaking, our experience of the law is produced by the behavior of judges and their various deputies: to say that the law prohibits theft, for example, is only to say that judges routinely order the

---

[32] Such claims date back at least to Aquinas, if not before; modern versions can be found in Finnis 1980, pp. 351–352; or in Raz 1999, pp. 64, 159, and 2009, pp. 153–154, 158. For critical discussions, see Green 1985 or Dworkin 1986, ch. 4.

[33] The approach taken here might thus be usefully compared with the work of Knight and Johnson 2007, who analogously argue for the priority of democratic practices in certain contexts. Fuller 1969, pp. 168–178, discusses various contexts in which the law is *not* the best mode of operation.

punishment of thieves and that these orders are routinely carried out. The distinctiveness of law thus hinges on the nature of the various determinants of judicial behavior, among which, the realists argued, actual rules of law as such do not centrally figure.[34] Under various guises, legal realism has exercised an immense influence over the past century or so. It has led to various theories we might describe as *reductionist* – that is, theories which aim to reduce the social phenomena we usually associate with legal systems to something else allegedly more concrete or realistic. For example, the critical legal studies authors such as Roberto Unger and Duncan Kennedy generally try to show that legal systems are really ideologically masked authoritarian systems.[35] Similarly, the adherents of the attitudinal model of judicial politics generally try to show that the law (in whole, or at least in part) is really the expression of ordinary policy preferences.[36] Finally, on some interpretations, the so-called law and economics school of jurisprudence aims to show that legal systems are best described in economic terms.[37] If any of these views is sound – that is, if we really can reduce the law to relationships of mere authority, politics, or markets – then my first claim is wrong: there is no bundle of practices characteristic of a legal system relevantly distinct from the practices of these other social formations.

H. L. A. Hart famously argued that what underlies legal realism (and by implication, the various traditions descending from realism) is the assumption of what he called "rule skepticism."[38] Put crudely, rule skepticism is the idea that since one power can be constrained only by another equal or greater power, there is no sense in which we can describe rules as such (and especially, rules of law) as having any real effect, as imposing any real constraint on human behavior. In order to defeat rule skepticism, one needs to show that the distinctive practices constituting a legal system can impose real and meaningful constraints on the exercise of power – i.e., that legal rules are not merely

---

[34] Leiter 2007, p. 16 and *passim*, argues that all the legal realists shared the "core claim" that "in deciding cases, judges respond primarily to the stimulus of the facts" rather than rules of law.

[35] See Unger 1976 and Kennedy 1997.

[36] Segal and Spaeth 2002 are the most influential exponents of this model. Sometimes these models are explicitly restricted to appellate courts or courts of final review.

[37] See for example Posner 2000.   [38] Hart 1994, pp. 136–147.

epiphenomenal justifications or rationalizations for what would have happened anyway. This can be done by showing that rule skepticism is directed against a superficial and naïve conception of social rules, and that when faced with a more sophisticated conception it has little or no force. Hart points the way toward such a response, but in my view does not go far enough. In later chapters (and especially in Chapter 5), I attempt to finish the job.

Although objections to the first claim are more common, the second also has its detractors. To reiterate, this is the claim that there will be at least some situations or contexts in which the way of doing things characteristic of legal systems will turn out to be the best way. Marxists and radicals of various stripes have rejected this claim, though their critiques find less favor today than those of two other groups. The first are the adherents of the law and economics school, now interpreted as a normative project aiming to replace legal practices with market practices so far as possible.[39] The second are some advocates of deliberative democracy, who argue that the practices of law ought to be supplanted to some extent by more democratic procedures.[40] Against objections of this sort, I will argue (primarily in Chapter 4) that once we have a sound descriptive sociology of the practices distinctive of legal systems in hand, we will find that using those practices can in certain important situations carry significant normative advantages.

This is not to say, of course, that the rule of law is a comprehensive political ideal. On the contrary, it is precisely an advantage of the approach outlined here that we can define and delimit precisely the sphere of practical activity for which the practices distinctively characteristic of a legal system are the most appropriate method for organizing our activities. This cannot so easily be done within the framework of the standard contemporary accounts, which identify the rule of law with a mere catalogue of legal virtues. Principles of legality do not themselves address the appropriate scope of law's domain. Imagine a society with a highly articulated legal system answering to all the principles of legality, but whose rules govern only the distribution of honorific titles and not ordinary uses of coercive force. Alternatively, imagine a society with a robust legal system

---

[39] As a characteristic example in this genre, see Posner 2007.
[40] See for example Hutchinson and Monahan 1987 or Bellamy 2007.

answering to all the principles of legality, whose rules do indeed govern the use of coercive force, but only with respect to a small elite. Neither, on my view, would be a society properly characterized by the rule of law. As we shall see in Chapter 4, once we recognize that the rule of law is best understood as a virtue of systems of social organization, the conflict between slavery and the rule of law can be explained without importing a substantive view about what sorts of laws it would be good to have. Roughly speaking, the law of slavery governs only the relations of coercion among non-slaves, leaving the coercion of slaves to the personal discretion of their masters: it represents, in other words, an insufficient extension of the rule of law.

We can also finally settle the debates with which we began regarding the principles of legality themselves.[41] These principles can be seen as conclusions derived from our theory of the rule of law, rather than as the starting point for such a theory. In other words, it is because the practices of law typically have characteristics $L_1, L_2, \ldots, L_n$, whereas the practices of markets (say) do not, that we prefer employing the former rather than the latter when it comes to situations of type S. We can handily summarize this line of reasoning, discussed further in Chapter 4, by framing $L_1, L_2, \ldots, L_n$ as principles of legality. Achieving the rule of law will thus necessarily mean respecting these principles, so defined (though, to reiterate, the converse is not true, since the principles of legality do not themselves delimit the appropriate domain of law). The correct list of principles is thus simply the list that accurately tracks the descriptive features of legal practices we happen to find advantageous. So derived, the principles of legality will have an intrinsic connection to the nature of legal systems, and not be mere substantive criteria of good laws redescribed.

1.2.2 Fuller on the Rule of Law

I have not yet discussed what is probably the best-known account of the rule of law in the contemporary literature, namely, Lon Fuller's

---

[41] This approach to deriving the principles of legality was sketched in Lovett 2002, and has since been independently proposed by Marmor 2010 and by Hadfield and Weingast 2014.

The Morality of Law. Having outlined my own particular approach, it may be instructive to consider the two in explicit contrast.

Fuller begins, promisingly from my point of view, with a discussion of eight distinct ways in which public authorities can fail in "the attempt to create and maintain a system of legal rules."[42] They can fail through relying on ad hoc decisions rather than general rules; through omitting to promulgate whatever rules there are; through issuing rules that are retroactive, unclear, or contradictory; through requiring conduct beyond the powers of ordinary citizens to perform; through changing the rules issued too frequently; or through failing to administer the rules in a manner congruent with the announced intentions of those rules. Corresponding with these potential failures are "eight kinds of legal excellence" – his version of the catalogue of principles traditionally associated with the rule of law.[43] So far, so good. Problems arise, however, when Fuller tries to articulate the exact nature of the failure involved in violating the principles.[44]

Initially he suggests that a "total failure in any one of these eight directions does not simply result in a bad system of law; it results in something that is not properly called a legal system at all."[45] Read literally, this seems to be a purely analytical claim about the meaning of law – about what we mean when we describe something as a legal system. On this view, the eight principles represent conceptual criteria: governments can and do issue retroactive commands and regulations, for example, but whatever these are, they do not count as law, properly understood. There is nothing incoherent about saying this but, as I observed earlier, there is no truth in definitions per se. Fuller surely wants to advance something more than a mere formal definition of law. It comes as no surprise, therefore, when the principles of legality are described in later passages as aspirational virtues of a legal system. Thus, in respecting the requirements Fuller has enumerated, a ruler is "compelled to articulate the principles on which he acts" when issuing a law, which "permits the public to judge of its fairness" more readily.[46] On this view, the eight principles embody a relationship of reciprocity between governments and citizens, dictating how the former must act in order to earn the obedience of the latter.

---

[42] Fuller 1969, p. 38.   [43] Ibid., p. 41.
[44] The analysis that follows is indebted to Waldron 1994.
[45] Fuller 1969, p. 39.   [46] Ibid., p. 159; cf. p. 51.

Most often, however, Fuller seems to regard the principles of legality as pragmatic guidelines for a particular sort of human enterprise – roughly speaking, "the enterprise of subjecting human conduct to the governance of rules."[47] To the extent that we want to engage in this enterprise, it is simply a practical empirical truth that "some minimum adherence to legal morality is essential" for its "practical efficacy."[48] We are thus left to wonder what, fundamentally, is the intended nature of his argument: conceptual, normative, or empirical?

The instability of his account can be seen if we press on any one of its three strands. Suppose we begin with the last strand, for example. The art or craft of lawmaking, let us suppose, is a sort of purposeful activity, like carpentry. In any such purposeful activity, there will be certain instrumental considerations that constrain the form and shape our performance of that activity must assume if it is to be generally efficacious. These constraints are "natural laws" in the straight-forward empirical sense that the material properties of different sorts of lumber are constraints on effective carpentry.[49] If our aim is to subject human conduct to the governance of rules, then we will usually not succeed in our aim issuing rules that cannot be performed, that are retroactive, and so forth. So far so good. But usually is not always. What if, in some particular instance, our aim seems to be better served by violating one of the principles of legality? In an example raised by Fuller himself, the government of the Soviet Union once sought to bring economic corruption under effective legal control by subjecting some individuals to retroactive judgment under new, harsher statutes requiring the death penalty.[50] This clearly violates the principles of legality, but perhaps in a manner instrumentally serving the long-run aim of effectively subjecting human conduct to the governance of rules. To this Fuller might respond by observing that, while the Soviet tactic was effective, it was something other than lawmaking. This response, however, implies a conceptual rather than an empirical claim about what counts as law, to which one might fairly respond: what do we care what we call it? What's at stake? Interestingly, when pressed on this front Fuller seems to answer in normative terms. He argues that "an observance of the demands of legal morality can serve the broader

---

[47] Ibid., pp. 91; cf. pp. 53, 66, 74.   [48] Ibid., p. 156.
[49] Ibid., p. 96, where the comparison to carpentry is suggested by Fuller; cf. pp. 155–156.
[50] Ibid., p. 202.

aims of human life generally," specifically, our aspiration to regard each person as "a responsible agent, capable of understanding and following rules, and answerable for his defaults." From this point of view, we might regard the Soviet strategy, or indeed any "departure from the principles of law's inner morality," as "an affront to man's dignity as a responsible agent."[51] Which, of course, brings us back to the problematic identification of the rule of law with the mere rule of good law.

None of this is to suggest that one could not impose an interpretation on Fuller resolving these ambiguities. Rather, the point is only to further illustrate my earlier assertion that a fully adequate account of the rule of law and its value cannot be found in the literature as it presently stands. As it happens, in the "Reply to Critics" Fuller added to the revised edition of *The Morality of Law* one can find the outline of an account in some ways congenial with mine. Roughly speaking, Fuller proposes contrasting the law as one form of social ordering with another termed "managerial direction." While the eight principles of legality are indeed merely the pragmatic success conditions specific to the former enterprise, normative benefits are now seen to flow from their observance as a sort of side effect, thus explaining why we should prefer law to managerial direction.[52]

This is roughly the correct approach, on my view, but it remains woefully incomplete: the connection Fuller draws between the nature of law and the specific principles of legality is only intuitive; the comparative value of being governed by law is left underdescribed; and the significance of the rule of law in its wider sense – that is, in controlling and regulating the use of coercive force in general, not merely its use by the state – is basically ignored. Instead of persisting in our search for a workable account in the pages of Fuller or anywhere else, why not simply get on with the job of laying out the best theory directly? If we subsequently find that some earlier writers can be interpreted in a manner friendly to our favored conception, so much the better.

1.3 The Rule of Law and Positivism

What ensures that our project will succeed where others have failed? As some readers may have gathered by this point, its potential for

[51] Ibid., p. 162.   [52] Ibid., pp. 207–210.

success hinges in part on our maintaining a strict methodological separation between the descriptive and the normative aspects of the argument. In other words, it relies on a commitment to what is traditionally known as *legal positivism*, broadly construed. Unfortunately, legal positivism has in recent years been pushed by its practitioners in an especially abstract and austere direction, with the result that its insights are increasingly accessible to an insular cognoscenti alone.[53] Taking my cue instead from Hart's earlier-cited characterization of positivism as a sort of "descriptive sociology," I intend to approach the object of this study from a somewhat different direction. Primarily using tools familiar to social scientists (and, especially, the tools of game theory), my focus will be less on analyzing the normative nature of law or the formal attributes of legal validity than it will be on appreciating the actual felt experience of law – on understanding the distinctive social practices characteristic of those legal systems with which we are familiar through historical and contemporary experience. I would argue this is closer in spirit to what Hart was trying to do all along, though of course not all readers will agree and not much hinges on such interpretative debates.

Some inevitable adjustments aside, my approach will reproduce many of the modern legal positivists' core insights, but on firmer grounds open to a wider audience.[54] Ultimately, however, reconstructing legal positivism is only a secondary aim of the project. Its primary aim is to employ the positivist framework to build a better account of the rule of law and its value. For some readers, it may not be obvious that this is the best way to proceed. Let me explain.

Broadly speaking, let us distinguish between setting out to describe the nature of a legal system, and setting out to evaluate its merits or demerits. The former might be called an exercise in *analytic jurisprudence,* the latter an exercise in *normative jurisprudence.*[55] Certainly,

---

[53] Hence the now common complaint that legal positivism has little useful to say about anything we should care about: see for instance Dyzenhaus 2000 or Dworkin 2002. Though understandable, the complaint is in my view unwarranted, as I hope this study will help demonstrate.

[54] Most significantly, Hart's famous "rule of recognition" is provided a somewhat different and, in my view, improved characterization in Chapter 3.

[55] These terms are standard in the literature, though their exact usage varies. Both are here understood as forms of *general*, as distinct from *particular*, jurisprudence – the former being addressed to legal systems in general, the latter to specific legal systems (the legal system of the United States circa 2015, say).

both are important and have their place, but for the moment let us concentrate on the subject of analytic jurisprudence. Suppose our aim is simply to understand the law as a complex social phenomenon. What is its nature? On some views, we cannot properly understand the law without reference to its broader moral or ethical purposes. In other words, part of what it is for something to *count* as law is for it to be part of a purposeful human enterprise directed – more or less perfectly, of course, and sometimes very imperfectly indeed – toward specific worthwhile aims. Thus, a complete understanding of any legal system will necessarily include some reference to the moral or ethical purposes of law. This view is commonly associated with the natural law tradition, according to which unjust laws do not count as laws in the fullest or most proper sense.[56] Of course, this is not merely a version of normative jurisprudence in disguise: those working in the natural law tradition of analytic jurisprudence are still primarily interested in what *counts* as law. Among those purposeful human enterprises directed toward the relevant moral or ethical ends, there may still be interesting and important questions as to which succeed better or worse than others. (Conversely, those engaged in normative jurisprudence need not accept the claim that unjust laws are not laws in the proper sense: they can simply argue that we should have no unjust laws.)

Legal positivism is also a species of analytic jurisprudence, but it rejects the natural law view.[57] Stated somewhat more precisely, legal positivism is commonly identified with two propositions, one affirmative and the other negative. The affirmative proposition – often referred to as the *social fact thesis* – is that the existence and content of law

[56] In contemporary jurisprudence, this school is most prominently represented by Finnis 1980, and Fuller 1969 might be regarded as a fellow-traveler in certain respects. To clarify, on the natural law view specific rules can be legally valid without being just, but they may be imperfectly authoritative and thus deficient instances of law: see Finnis 1980, pp. 363–366.

[57] It is important not to confuse legal positivism, properly so-called, with what is often called *ethical positivism*. Ethical positivists such as MacCormick 1985 or Campbell 1996 argue that it is best to avoid references to morality in law and legal interpretation – perhaps because the law best serves its characteristic purposes or functions when such references are avoided. This view, sometimes also attributed to Hobbes and Bentham, should be understood as a contribution to normative and not analytic jurisprudence.

ultimately depends on social facts.[58] Contrary to the natural law tradition, to understand what counts as law it is sufficient to study those
facts, without reference to the broader moral or ethical purposes legal
systems may or may not serve. In the famous expression of John Austin,
"the existence of law is one thing; its merit or demerit is another."[59]
Positivists have not always agreed as to the character of the relevant
social facts, of course. The classical legal positivists such as Hobbes,
Bentham, or Austin, for example, believed that the relevant facts concerned patterns of habitual obedience in a population to the commands
issued by a sovereign. Hardly any contemporary legal positivist now
accepts this view. Some believe instead that the relevant facts concern
the existence and character of certain kinds of social rules. This is the
view, roughly speaking, of Hart and his followers, and it is also a view
I share and develop one version of in this book. Others, following more
in the tradition of Hans Kelsen than Hart, hold a somewhat different
view, also discussed in subsequent chapters. These issues, however, are
less relevant for our immediate purposes here.

The second, negative proposition commonly identified with legal
positivism concerns the connection between the social facts underwriting law and the criteria of legal validity. Suppose, for example, it is
generally accepted in some legal community that all valid laws must
not only be duly enacted by the designated legislative authority, but
also satisfy certain minimum standards of social justice. In this scenario, the criteria of legality appear to include a moral principle.
(Observe that such cases need not conflict with the social fact thesis,
insofar as the inclusion of moral principles among the criteria of
legality still depends on an underlying social fact – for instance, on
the existence of a conventional agreement that *this* principle count
among the relevant criteria.) Indeed, the legal systems with which we
are familiar in practice often explicitly include moral principles among
their purported criteria of legality.[60] But must the criteria of legality in
any legal system necessarily include moral principles? Positivists

---

[58] Raz 1979, p. 37, and 1985, p. 295; Shapiro 2000, pp. 127–128; Coleman 2001,
      pp. 75, 152–153; Coleman and Leiter 2010, p. 241.
[59] Austin 1832, p. 184.
[60] See for example the Eighth Amendment to the U.S. Constitution, which
      prohibits "cruel and unusual punishments," or even more explicitly the first
      paragraph of Article I of the German Constitution, which states that "Human
      dignity shall be inviolable."

answer no. In Hart's expression, "it is in no sense a necessary truth that laws reproduce or satisfy certain demands of morality."[61] This is often referred to as the *separability thesis*, though the expression is sometimes regarded as misleading.[62]

Since natural lawyers can accept the view that unjust laws count as laws after a fashion (e.g., as deficient laws), they need not reject the separability thesis, though historically many have. Among modern legal theorists and philosophers the separability thesis is most prominently contested by interpretivists such as Ronald Dworkin, or more recently by the moral impact theory of Mark Greenberg.[63] On the former view, the criteria of legality in any community necessarily include (implicitly, if not explicitly) the moral and ethical principles providing the best justification for its legal and political practices. On the latter view, the law in any community is defined as the moral impact of the relevant actions of its legal institutions. Note that on either view, the existence and content of law still ultimately depends on social facts (about existing legal and political practices in the first case, about the relevant actions of legal institutions in the second), so we might plausibly interpret both as accepting the social fact thesis.[64]

Now if our aim is to argue that the rule of law constitutes an important political ideal, and also to derive an account of its principles from the intrinsic nature of law, it may not seem that legal positivism offers the most promising place to start. Would it not make more sense to begin with a theory in which legal systems necessarily possess certain normative merits – either by virtue of their having moral as well as social foundations, or else by virtue of their including moral considerations among their criteria of legal validity?[65] If we insist on operating within a positivist framework instead, will it not be that

---

[61] Hart 1994, pp. 185–186.

[62] Coleman 1982, pp. 4–7; Shapiro 2000, p. 127; Coleman 2001, pp. 151–152; Marmor 2001, p. 71; Coleman and Leiter 2010, p. 228. Many legal positivists now deemphasize the separability thesis on the grounds that it is frequently confused with the (false) claim that there is no necessary connection between law and morality: see esp. Gardner 2001, pp. 222–225 and Coleman 2007, pp. 582–585. Cf. Raz 2009, ch. 6.

[63] See Dworkin 1977, 1985, 1986, and Greenberg 2014, respectively.

[64] Dworkin 1985, p. 17, seems to agree with this assertion, whereas Greenberg 2014, p. 1324, might be read as resisting it.

[65] Notably in this regard, two recent attempts to explicitly connect the rule of law's value to the necessary properties of law – Simmonds 2007 and Waldron 2008 – draw their inspiration from the anti-positivists Fuller and Dworkin, respectively.

much harder to establish significant value for the rule of law? In my view, the best answer is no. Not only is it possible to build a robust account of the rule of law and its value within the framework of legal positivism, this is precisely the best way to do so.

In defense of this claim, I offer two scenarios below. The first is very simple and unrelated to issues in legal theory, whereas the second specifically relates to the problem of legal validity. In light of these scenarios, I then explicitly connect the positivist approach to the account of the rule of law and its value proposed earlier, thus bringing our discussion full circle. One word of caution: the arguments that follow are not intended as a refutation of natural law jurisprudence, interpretivism, or any other approach. Such refutations are beyond the scope of this book. My aim is simply to clarify the basic motivations and assumptions that, for better or worse, underlie my own project.

(a) *Wilderness Preservation.* Suppose we want to argue that wilderness areas are worthy of protection. Our argument, presumably, must take something like the following form:

Wilderness areas should be protected for reasons x, y, and z.

Now I have asserted that to count as successful, an argument must make a practical difference – that is, it must give us reasons for doing or not doing certain things. Suppose we come across a particular track of land such as the Mojave Desert, and wonder whether it specifically should be preserved or not. Consulting our argument above, it should be immediately apparent that the answer depends on whether the Mojave Desert counts as a wilderness area in the relevant sense. So what counts as a wilderness area? Suppose the following definition is offered:

Wilderness areas are those tracts of land relatively free from human interference that have intrinsic natural value.

Consulting this definition, let us imagine there is no problem establishing that the Mojave Desert has been "relatively free from human interference." But what about the second clause? The issue here is not that people might disagree what it means for something to have intrinsic natural value. Indeed they might, but of course they might also disagree on what counts being relatively free from human interference. For the sake of argument we can stipulate that everyone agrees on interpreting "having intrinsic natural value" to mean "valuable for its own sake and not merely for any benefits to human beings." The issue is rather that the second clause proposes an evaluative rather than a descriptive criterion. What does it mean *in practice* for something to have intrinsic value apart from its being a worthy object of our preservation efforts?[66] References to intrinsic value belong on the other side of the "for reasons" clause in our original argument.

Do all tracts of land relatively free from human interference have intrinsic natural value? Perhaps they do, in which case we can substitute the definition above into our original argument as follows:

Tracts of land relatively free from human interference should be preserved for reasons x, y, z, and because they have intrinsic natural value.

We can debate whether this is a good argument or not, of course. The point is only that, despite our attempt to offer a normative account of wilderness, only the descriptive part of the definition ended up on the left side of the argument. What if only some tracts of land relatively free from human interference have intrinsic value? (The wording of our definition seems to suggest this.) Then we are left wondering what additional criterion distinguishes those that do from those that do not. Our argument becomes something like this:

Tracts of land relatively free from human interference that are W should be preserved for reasons x, y, z, and because they have intrinsic natural value.

Alas, we are back where we started, unable to determine whether the Mojave Desert specifically counts. For our normative argument on behalf of wilderness preservation to succeed in the sense of its making a practical difference we must pin down *a strictly descriptive definition of wilderness* – which is to say, we must exclude any evaluative considerations from our definition. Notice the exclusion called for here is simply methodological: far from eschewing normative argument as such, we have found a purely descriptive definition of wilderness is necessary precisely in order to make an effective normative argument about its preservation.

(b) *The Principled Constitution.* Next consider a scenario involving criteria for legal validity.[67] Imagine that in some community, the

---

[66] It is beyond the scope of discussion here for me to defend this view, but roughly I submit that to say something "is good" or "has value" must be shorthand for our having some reason or bundle of reasons for acting in certain positive ways with respect to that thing.

[67] This example is loosely based on *Bowers v. Hardwick*, 478 U.S. 186 (1986).

designated legislative authority has duly enacted a law prohibiting certain private sexual acts. Now suppose two conscientious and law-abiding citizens consult an attorney on this issue. What is the law? they ask. They ask this perhaps because they believe:

People should follow the law for reasons x, y, and z.

According to one view, the attorney's reply should run roughly as follows: "In any legal system, the mere fact that a rule has been duly enacted by the designated legislative authority is not sufficient to establish its legal validity. This is because the criteria of legality for any community necessarily include whatever moral and ethical principles provide the best justification for its legal and political practices as a whole. In order to determine this, however, we must consult moral philosophy, which informs us that the legal and political practices of our community are best justified as reflecting, among other things, a commitment to legal equality. Since the purported law manifestly violates this principle, we may conclude that it is not a valid law."[68] Confident in the advice of their attorney, the two citizens freely disobey the allegedly invalid law. To their shock and dismay, they are arrested and at trail found guilty by a judge who believes the law is perfectly valid. The decision is generally accepted by legal officials and the community at large.

In this example, let us stipulate that the attorney was not mistaken in his analysis of the moral facts: the law does actually violate legal equality, and such a principle does actually provide the best justification for the legal and political practices of the community. Did the attorney give his clients the wrong advice? Of course we might say he gave them *bad* advice, in the strategic sense of giving advice that would have kept his clients out of jail. But if we believe laws must necessarily possess normative merit, his advice was apparently not wrong as to the *legal* facts. This has to be a mistake. The law we are imagining is formally written in the statute books, it has been duly enacted according to appropriate legislative procedures, it is obeyed by most citizens, and it is generally enforced by legal officials. Surely this counts as a law, if anything does! The contrary view would implausibly entail that a great deal of actually existing law is not, in truth, law.

---

[68] Here of course we imagine an interpretivist response to the problem; the scenario might easily be recast using either a natural law or a moral impact conception of law.

This is not to say, of course, that laws cannot have normative merits and demerits. Nor is it to say that the explicit references to moral and ethical principles common in the legal systems with which we are familiar are simply meaningless. It is undeniable that both legal officials and ordinary citizens take such references to be meaningful, and thus any satisfactory theory of the law – positivist or otherwise – must account for their doing so. (Legal positivists, as it happens, disagree on how best to do so, as we shall see in Chapter 6.) The point is rather that moral and ethical principles cannot as such determine what *counts* as law, practically speaking. The injustice of some law may give certain people reasons for doing particular things with respect to that law: depending on one's views, it may give judges a reason to invalidate it, for instance, or (if they don't) it may give citizens a reason to disobey it. To be the object of such practical reasons, however, the law in question must first be a thing we can identify as a descriptive fact.

Now let us apply this reasoning to our present topic, the rule of law. We are interested in making an argument that the rule of law is a good thing, which is roughly equivalent to saying that we have good reasons for promoting the rule of law under certain circumstances.[69] Never mind what the relevant circumstances and reasons are for the moment (they will be discussed later, in Chapter 4). Generally speaking, what must be true of an argument of this sort for it to succeed – for it to make a practical difference? The answer should be obvious. The argument can only succeed if we develop a strictly descriptive conception of what it means to rule by law and not by other means. The rule of law is the concrete thing our reasons, whatever they turn out to be, instruct us to promote.

Of course, I do not mean to claim that our *selection* of a particular descriptive conception will not be motivated by normative criteria. Quite the contrary, our aim will be precisely to develop a definition of the rule of law that fits well with the practical value we ultimately attribute to it.[70] The point is rather that whatever definition we settle

---

[69] See n. 66.

[70] In this sense Krygier 2011, pp. 65–73, is correct to argue that the rule of law is necessarily a "teleological" concept. Indeed, all theories – including all theories of law – are normative in this sense. Hart 1958 and 1994, esp. ch. 9, for instance, insists that there are important advantages to adopting a positivist conception of law. For further discussion, see Waluchow 1994, chs. 2–3.

on, and whatever our motives for settling on it, that definition must be strictly descriptive *in content* if it is to perform its assigned task. This is for the simple reason that, absent any descriptive reference to some concrete thing in the realm of experience, even an otherwise sound and convincing normative argument will leave us wondering what it is we are actually supposed to do.

The standard contemporary discussions of the rule of law, as we observed above, obscure this point, because they approach the problem from the wrong end. They begin with a laundry-list of principles such as generality, prospectivity, stability, and so forth. Often it is unclear what the grounds are for preferring one list to another: each list seems to represent simply the particular author's intuitive sense of the formal or substantive virtues laws should ideally possess. Having stated an opinion on this score, however, we are still left wanting practical direction. Even if we agree that laws should be general, for instance, we still need to know what counts as a general law in the required sense. Is it enough that laws not refer to individuals or groups by their proper names? This does not seem sufficient, since it is too easy to pass this test. Must laws then embody some more robust form of equality? Here the standard discussions become hopelessly mired in the struggle to work out the practical details of their favored principles of legality.

In this book, I aim to develop a theory of the rule of law that approaches the problem in the right way. Part I presents the basic argument in three stages. First, Chapter 2 develops an account of social rules that will serve as the basis for a descriptive conception of law as a hierarchically ordered network of social rules, presented in Chapter 3. Finally, Chapter 4 presents a normative argument for the advantages of law when it comes to particular sorts of problems – specifically, problems arising from the need in any community to make decisions about how to govern the use of coercive force. Having completed the basic argument, Part II addresses some important complications. Roughly speaking, the latter arise from the need for any working legal system to have, first, a method for settling interpretive disagreement, and second, a method for implementing deliberate legal change. Among the main themes of Chapters 5 and 6 are, accordingly, appellate review and legislation, respectively. In both chapters, the challenge will be to show that these complications, contrary to the views of many, do not undermine the basic argument for the rule of law.

PART I

Legal Statics

2 | *Social Rules and Norms*

Consider two simple vignettes. In the first, imagine that Andrea sues Bob for breach of contract. After an attempt to settle their dispute out of court fails, the issue goes to trial. Lawyers representing Andrea and Bob alternately submit motions, introduce evidence, propound arguments, and so forth, at the conclusion of which the court finds for Andrea. Bob's petition for appeal is denied, and he is ordered to pay specified damages, which he subsequently does. In the second vignette, imagine that Carla enters a bank, where she needs the assistance of a teller. The bank is moderately busy, and some other customers waiting for service have already formed a line. Although there are no security guards or other authority figures around, and Carla is in somewhat of a hurry, she joins the line and waits her turn rather than proceeding to the teller booth directly.

How are these series of events different? In my view, they are much less different than they might appear. Both are instances of the same general method for managing the expectations and motivating the cooperation of multiple human agents – what might be called the *method of convention*. There are, of course, many other ways in which the benefits of coordination might be secured. Coordination might be achieved through deference to a settled chain of command, or through a process of deliberation and voting, and so on. Later, in Chapter 4, I discuss some of the advantages and disadvantages of these various methods. Before this, however, my aim will be to show that legal systems – in their central features, at any rate – are best understood as complex, interlocking systems of convention.

The conception of legal systems offered in this chapter and the next represents a variety of legal positivism. All legal positivists agree that the existence and content of law ultimately depends on social, not moral, facts.[1] On one such view, associated especially with the work of H. L. A. Hart and which, broadly speaking, I share, legal systems are best understood as having their foundation specifically in conventional social rules. Hart's account of these social rules has come to be known as the *practice theory*.

Many legal philosophers, including both positivists such as Joseph Raz and Leslie Green, and anti-positivists such as Ronald Dworkin, have criticized the practice theory. Some of their more influential criticisms center on the claim that the practice theory cannot explain a central feature of the law – namely, its characteristic claim to normative authority. This particular criticism will be addressed later, in Chapter 3. My aim in the present chapter is to propose a more robust practice-based conception of social rules, and in the process to answer various other objections that have been raised against the practice theory. In both chapters, my strategy will be to argue that the standard objections to the practice theory are typically directed against an impoverished account of conventional social rules. The richer conception developed here (with the help of some tools drawn from elementary game theory) will help us clear away many of the puzzles and problems that have exercised critics of the practice theory.

2.1 Habits and Personal Rules

What does it mean for human behavior to be governed by a rule? This is not so easy a question to answer as one might imagine. To be sure, casual observation tells us that human behavior often follows patterns. But not every such pattern counts as following a rule in the relevant sense. Suppose we observe Andrea usually taking a walk on Tuesday and Thursday mornings, or Bob usually ordering chicken when he dines out. Does it follow they are following the rules 'always take a morning walk on Tuesdays and Thursdays' and 'always order chicken when dining out' respectively? Not necessarily, as we shall see.

---

[1] In the words of Austin 1832, p. 184, "the existence of law is one thing; its merit or demerit is another." As noted in Chapter 1, this proposition is often called the *social fact thesis*.

2.1.1 *Purposeful Action and Habit*

Let us say that human action is *purposeful* when it is intentionally motivated by some goals or aims the actor happens to have. The phrase "intentionally motivated" here should not be read in any deep philosophical sense. Rather, it is meant only to distinguish the ordinary sort of human behavior from behavior that is exogenously programmed, so to speak – as for example much animal behavior is programmed by natural instinct, or the behavior of a robot by computer code, and so forth. When a person acts purposefully, we simply mean that she acts for some reason – that she tries to do or accomplish something. Her reasons might be good, bad, or indifferent and still count as purposeful; they might be self-regarding or egoistic in the narrow sense, or they might be altruistic, theological, ideological, spiteful, envious, or whatever else you like.

By way of shorthand, let us say that a person *prefers* some path of action if it is the path she would choose from among a set of alternatives known and available to her in a given context. Insofar as much human behavior is purposeful in the very general sense previously described, we can often presume that people choose some paths of action over others because they expect the former to better serve one way or another whatever goals or aims they happen to have.[2] Thus, as economists say, preferences are hypothetical choices and observed choices revealed preferences.[3] The connection between possible paths of action, on the one hand, and our goals or aims, on the other, can assume a variety of forms. Most obviously, an action might serve our aims through bringing about a desired outcome, as for example when we choose an apple from a fruit basket because we prefer having

---

[2] Roughly speaking, we might characterize preference orderings over alternative paths of action as reflecting the joint product of our motivating goals or aims, on the one hand, and our beliefs about the state of the world, on the other. For instance, if I want it to be the case that x and I believe (rightly or wrongly) that ϕ-ing will bring about x, then by assumption I will have a preference for ϕ-ing. Something like this "folk psychology" is defended in Jackson and Pettit 1990. For further discussion see also Lovett 2010, esp. pp. 30–33, 56–61.

[3] Of course the second equivalence will not hold to the extent that some action is strictly spontaneous, reflexive, or otherwise lacking in purpose. Here we may set aside the deeper question of whether the true object of preference is ultimately the choice itself, the state of the world a choice is expected to bring about, or the various qualities instantiated by possible states of the world. According to Pettit 1991, the third view is most plausible.

apples to having other fruits. In other cases, by contrast, we care about the process as much as or more than the outcome, as for example when we choose not to win a game through unsporting means because we prefer playing fair.[4] For present purposes, however, we can abstract from such details.

Although, as we have said, much human behavior is purposeful, purposeful action is not always rational. To count as *rational*, on the standard view, human behavior must satisfy some further conditions. Most importantly, the selection of some particular path of action is fully rational only if it is, to the best knowledge of the actor, the most efficacious or efficient means available for accomplishing her overall goals or aims. The preferences exhibited by rational action, so defined, will have a specific structure we can characterize formally. Without lingering on technical details unimportant for our discussion, we can roughly describe that formal characterization as follows: given a particular set of goals and aims, on the one hand, and a set of available paths of action, on the other, some of the latter must realize better (i.e., more efficiently) and others worse (i.e., less efficiently) the former. It follows that in considering any two possible paths of action, a rational actor must either prefer one to the other or else be indifferent between them. Call this the *completeness* condition of rational preferences. What is more, all of the various preferences of a rational actor must cohere with one another. If Andrea prefers having apples to oranges and having oranges to pears, she must also prefer having apples to pears. Call this the *consistency* condition of rational preferences. Conveniently, when purposeful action meets these (and a few other) conditions, it will be possible to represent that action as if it were an attempt to maximize a cardinal utility function defined over an opportunity set, where an opportunity set is merely the set of possible paths of action available to a given actor in a given context.[5] Formally, then, we can say that a person i will ϕ rather than not ϕ if it is the case that her utility $u_i(\phi)$ for ϕ-ing is greater than her utility $u_i(\sim\phi)$ for not ϕ-ing. If her utility function is relatively stable, then she will ϕ with some regularity. There is much

---

[4] Contrary to what is sometimes believed, game theoretic models can easily capture this diversity of connections by characterizing possible states of the world as history-outcome pairs: see Lovett 2010, pp. 59, 61–62.

[5] The additional conditions are mostly arcane, but include a continuity requirement that rules out lexical preferences.

more to be said on this topic, of course, but the foregoing sketch will be sufficient for the discussion that follows.

This standard view of practical rationality has, of course, been subject to many criticisms. Our present interest, however, is not in debating its broader merits, but rather more narrowly in exploring its usefulness for making sense of the everyday phenomenon of rule-following. Therefore I will merely observe that, properly understood, the standard view is in my view basically sound. Indeed, it is fortunate that this is so, since we rely on it ubiquitously to make sense of the behavior of other human beings.[6] But that is a debate for some other occasion. For the present, let us return to the simple patterns observed in Andrea's and Bob's behavior.

If most human behavior is purposeful in the sense described, then it is reasonable to suppose that many of the patterns we observe in that behavior are easily explained by the existence of stable underlying preferences. In other words, it is possible that Andrea just happens to prefer walking Tuesday and Thursday mornings to doing something else, and that Bob just happens to prefer eating chicken to eating beef or fish. In behaving regularly as they do, they merely act on a relatively stable configuration of preferences they happen to have. Call behavioral patterns of this sort *habits*.

Not everyone will immediately accept this characterization of habit. For some, the very essence of a habit is that it is *not* purposeful, but rather automatic and unreflective. Andrea is only *genuinely* in the habit of taking a walk on Tuesday and Thursday mornings, on this view, if she does so regularly without consciously thinking about it.[7] Undoubtedly, our behavior is often unreflective in this sense, but it is a mistake to conclude that it is therefore not purposeful. Given that our preferences are often relatively stable, we do not always bother deliberately reviewing them at every turn. Indeed we could not, at each and every moment of our lives, try to inventory in detail all the preferences that might bear on what we should next do. That way, madness lies. On any given Tuesday or Thursday morning, Andrea might simply go for a walk without bothering to consult her preferences, on the reliable assumption that they will not change significantly from one day to the next. Her action is nevertheless purposeful in an indirect sense,

---

[6] This point is of course made by Davidson 1980, esp. chs. 2 and 12.

[7] Often Bourdieu 1980, esp. pp. 52–79, is cited in this context.

because it is programmed endogenously, so to speak. In acting on autopilot, she is still acting on preferences she happens to have – she merely does so with greater efficiency.[8]

2.1.2 From Habits to Personal Rules

It is perfectly intelligible to use the term "rule" to describe habits that arise from either direct or indirect purposeful action. For example, we might say that "as a rule, Andrea takes a morning walk on Tuesdays and Thursdays" or that "as a rule, Bob orders chicken when dining out." But in so doing, we are merely describing a pattern, much as when we say that "as a rule, the Alps are snow-covered in May." This is not rule-following in the relevant sense. If Bob simply prefers to order chicken each night, his behavior is not actually *governed by* a rule to that effect: rather, the observed pattern merely emerges from his stable underlying preferences. Nor is the situation relevantly different if the habit in question arises from indirect, endogenously programmed purposeful action. Andrea might employ a rule-of-thumb in deciding whether to take a walk each morning ('if it is Tuesday or Thursday, take a walk'), but her behavior is still not *governed by* a rule in the relevant sense: rather, the rule-of-thumb simply facilitates her acting on a stable configuration of underlying preferences.[9] We should not permit these diverse uses of the term "rule" to confuse the issue at hand.

Our interest lies in what are sometimes called *prescriptive*, rather than *descriptive* rules.[10] Human behavior is governed by a rule in the prescriptive sense only when we can meaningfully say that someone is acting as she does (at least in part) to follow that rule, rather than merely to satisfy an ordinary preference (directly or indirectly). In other words, to count as prescriptive, the rule itself must make a practical difference in behavior. Clearly, rules do sometimes make

---

[8] For an extensive discussion of the many ways in which human beings employ endogenous programming or "heuristics" to better achieve their goals or aims, see Gigerenzer 2008 and Kahneman 2011, esp. chs. 10–18. Curiously, the well-documented use of such heuristics by ordinary people has often been taken to represent a counter-example to the standard view of practical rationality.

[9] Rules of thumb are further discussed by Raz 1999, pp. 59–62, and Schauer 1991, pp. 104–111.

[10] See Schauer 1991, pp. 1–3, 17–22.

a practical difference. We have all had the experience of feeling pulled between a desire to do or not do something, and a contrary commitment to some prescriptive rule we have adopted for ourselves. For example, we might feel pulled between our desire to sleep in, on the one hand, and our commitment to regular exercise, on the other, or pulled between our desire to take the largest piece of cake for ourselves, on the one hand, and our commitment to the rules of etiquette, on the other. The challenge is to make sense of this experience.

Rule-following behavior is not merely habitual behavior under a different description, for the experience we have described does not arise in the case of habits which are, after all, merely descriptive generalizations of our attempts to satisfy stable underlying preferences. If after several months Andrea's preference tilts against morning walks because it has grown cold with the approach of winter, she will simply stop taking them. To be sure, this might take a bit longer if she is following a rule-of-thumb – perhaps a few uncomfortably cold morning walks to nudge the issue back into her conscious reflection.[11] But at no point would she feel pulled in a contrary direction by her commitment to some rule. Contrastingly, if she has adopted the schedule of morning walks as a rule, then she might persist *despite* any changes in the weather. Indeed, it is precisely because rules can have this sort of practical effect that we adopt them in the first place: in adopting the rule, our aim is precisely to constrain our later choices. There would be no point in adopting rules if they made no practical difference.[12]

But why would we want to constrain our later choices by adopting personal rules? This might seem especially puzzling given that, in light of what we have just said, following a rule will sometimes involve acting in ways contrary to our preferences. But actually there are many perfectly sensible reasons. One is to overcome weakness of will: adopting the schedule of morning walks as a rule for herself may help Andrea overcome her momentary desire to avoid bad weather.

[11] This delayed response can sometimes create confusion as to whether someone is following a habit or a rule: see Raz 1999, pp. 60–61, and Schauer 1991, pp. 108–109.

[12] Cf. Shapiro 2008, pp. 133–139, and Raz 2009, pp. 212–215. Schelling 1985, pp. 361–365, further notes that prescriptive rules should be distinguished from mere advanced planning, on the one hand, and techniques for avoiding temptation, on the other: neither results in the conflict between desire and commitment we have described.

We might adopt moral or ethical rules for similar reasons. Perhaps I believe that it is good to contribute to worthy charitable causes, but fear that I will have difficulty parting with large sums of money when the right cause comes along. The solution might be to adopt as a personal rule giving some reasonable fixed sum to a charity every month. Another common reason is to surmount pre-commitment problems. Imagine that Bob can invest a loan from Andrea for a significant profit. Andrea, however, must first decide whether to trust Bob, and the difficulty is that (assuming no third party is available to enforce the agreement) it will be Bob's later preference to abscond with both principal and profit. Knowing this, Andrea will rationally choose not to extend a loan in the first place, which is worse for Bob overall. It would be better for his overall goals or aims to follow the rule 'always repay your loans', even though following that rule is not what he will want to do later on.[13]

There are, of course, many other reasons for adopting personal rules as well.[14] We might adopt dietary rules on religious grounds, for example; we might adopt the rule 'never lie' because we are convinced Kantian ethics is sound; and so on. Our reasons for adopting a rule might include beliefs concerning the moral or legal legitimacy of the rule, though they need not. Indeed, the more serious puzzle might be explaining not *why* we would want to follow rules, but rather *how* we can do so.

2.1.3 *The Feasibility of Rules*

There are at least two reasons we might doubt the feasibility of governing our behavior by rules. One reason is conceptual, the other practical. The former stems from a philosophical worry first raised by Wittgenstein, and it might be described briefly as follows.[15] In order to

---

[13] The weakness of will problem was influentially analyzed by Strotz 1956, and the pre-commitment problem in Schelling 1960. For more recent and wide-ranging treatments, see McClennen 1990 and Elster 2000. Note that adopting a personal rule is not the only possible strategy for responding to these problems, nor even always the best.

[14] Schauer 1991, ch. 7, discusses various additional reasons for rules.

[15] Wittgenstein 1958, esp. §§ 143–242: pp. 56–88; following Wittgenstein, the problem was famously elaborated in Kripke 1982. Radin 1989, pp. 797–810, and Tamanaha 1997, pp. 196–203, explicitly apply the problem to a discussion of the law.

follow a rule, a person must be able to bundle possible paths of action into groups – specifically, those which count as following the rule in the relevant sense, and those which do not. Consider the rule 'always go for a walk Tuesday and Thursday mornings', for instance. Does a short ten-minute stroll around the block count, or must it be longer? What about jogging or biking? In order to avoid having to spell out the rule in painstaking detail, we might simply point to a few illustrative examples, of course. But unfortunately, as Wittgenstein demonstrated, any finite set of examples can in principle instantiate an infinite number of possible rules. To see this, imagine we are away from home on vacation for the first time: what do we do then? Both the rules 'always go for a walk Tuesday and Thursday mornings, even when on vacation' and 'always go for a walk Tuesday and Thursday mornings, except when on vacation' are consistent with all prior examples. Only an infinitely detailed specification, it would seem, can serve as an absolutely reliable guide, and it is implausible to think we could hold such cumbersome objects in our minds, much less employ them in practice. How then can a rule actually govern our behavior?

Some have taken these observations to cast doubt on the very coherence of governing our behavior by rules. This carries the insight too far. Rule-following is a practical *activity*, which should not be confused with our attempts to fully *describe* that activity (to ourselves or others) in propositional language.[16] While it is true that, in principle, any finite series of examples could instantiate an infinite number of possible rules, as a matter of practice human beings tend to respond to particular examples in a very limited number of ways. No one immediately responds to the series 0, 2, 4, 6, 8 as exemplifying the rule 'add 2 until to the number 2000, then add 4 until the number 4000, and so on'. Likewise, it is difficult to believe that Andrea's efforts to implement the rule 'always go for a walk Tuesday and Thursday mornings' would founder on her inability to work out in advance what the rule requires in every possible future circumstance she might face. What then accounts for the relative ease with which people usually follow rules?[17] Part of the explanation, no doubt, lies in natural

---

[16] This distinction is helpfully noted by Schauer 1991, pp. 62–68, in his discussion of the Wittgenstein challenge.

[17] Here I basically follow responses to the problem offered by Pettit 1993, pp. 76–106, and Taylor 1995, pp. 173–179, the former leaning more toward a natural instinct story and the latter toward a background culture story.

instinct. We are simply built to observe and follow patterns – so much so, indeed, that we often seem to find patterns where none exist (and thus require extensive training to fully understand concepts such as statistical significance, standard error, and so forth). Probably just as significant, however, is our shared cultural experience, which fills in gaps and resolves ambiguities with implied background understandings. These factors together guide our practical understanding of rules, and ensure for the most part that rules can be followed without fanfare.

For the most part, though not always, of course: some difficulties of interpretation can always arise, and will figure largely in the case of social rules where common understandings are required, as we shall see below. But these problems should not be so great as to undermine our confidence in the conceptual possibility of governing our behavior by rules. Indeed, it is far more likely that our efforts will be stymied by the simple fact that following a rule may not be what we want to do at the relevant moment.

This brings us to the second reason we might doubt the feasibility of governing our behavior by rules. What supplies the practical motivation for a rational agent to follow a rule when the path of action recommended by the rule diverges from what the agent otherwise wants to do at that moment?

Some have sought an answer in what might be called *second-order preferences*. These are simply preferences about our preferences. For example, we might imagine Andrea's rule 'always take a morning walk Tuesdays and Thursdays' to be bundled with a second-order preference for excluding the first-order preference to avoid cold weather from her decision process.[18] This analysis does not always seem true to experience, however. When we feel pulled between a rule and a preference, we do not usually experience this as a difficulty in excluding the latter: on the contrary, the issue is precisely that the preference has not been excluded, and we are having difficulty sticking to the rule *despite* that preference. Of course, having successfully adopted the rule, Andrea might additionally develop a (second-order) preference that she have a stronger (first-order) preference for talking walks,

[18] The idea of an exclusionary preference here derives from Raz 1999, pp. 58–84. As another example of the second-order preference strategy, Perry 1989, pp. 927–945, regards rules as second-order principles for weighting first-order considerations.

or a (second-order) preference that she have a weaker (first-order) preference for avoiding the cold. If she did have first-order preferences of the later sort, it would doubtless be much easier for her to follow the rule she has adopted. But this is ancillary effect, and it need not be present in all cases. Indeed, we might not always want it to be present: sometimes we experience a greater pride in following a rule when it is more, rather than less, difficult to do so.[19]

What *must* be present for behavior to be genuinely governed by a rule is a distinct first-order preference for following that rule – a preference distinct in the sense that it is not a preference regarding the underlying activity considered on its own immediate merits.[20] This distinct preference might for instance manifest itself as feelings of personal satisfaction whenever one observes the rule and feelings of disappointment or guilt whenever one does not. In effect, prescriptive rules assign additional benefits and costs to the various action classes they define: benefits to those paths of action that count as following the rule, costs to those that do not. On those Tuesdays and Thursdays when Andrea happens to want to take a walk anyway, for instance, her two preferences happily coincide, and it is easy for her to follow the rule she has set for herself. Some other days, however, her two preferences are in tension, and what she will do depends, we might suppose, on their relative strength or intensity. Call the preference for following a rule one's *commitment* to that rule. If some personal rule is in any degree practically effective, this must be because one's commitment to that rule is strong enough to at least sometimes tip the balance against contrary inclination.[21]

---

[19] In my view, what Raz and others call "exclusionary reasons" are merely a by-product of the typical operation of rules in practice. As Schelling 1985, pp. 366–367, points out, rules are likely to be more effective when they clearly partition what counts as compliance from what does not. Inevitably, clear partitions are crude partitions, in the sense that they involve ignoring lots of potentially relevant information. In following the rule, we will thus appear to be "excluding" the latter.

[20] Having a preference for following a rule is often described, following Hart 1994, pp. 56–57 and *passim*, as having "a critical reflective attitude" toward that rule.

[21] Schauer 1991, pp. 112–118, alternatively describes rules as having a "weight" that supplies some "degree of resistance" to the operation of our ordinary preferences. Contrary to Shapiro 2008, pp. 144–150, it does not seem to me that the constraints imposed by rules must necessarily remove options, rather than (in most cases) simply make some more, and others less, costly.

In order for a rational agent to adopt a personal rule for herself, then, she must engage in a bit of endogenous preference manipulation – she must induce some degree of commitment to that rule.[22] There are many ways one might do this. For instance, one might publicly announce to friends and relations one's determination to follow a rule: future deviations will then be accompanied by some embarrassment. Another way to induce self-commitment is by mentally bundling repeated choices. When deciding whether to walk any particular morning, for example, Andrea might convince herself that she is deciding for all future mornings in one go ("if not today, then when?"). This might help combat weakness of will by bringing all the future benefits into present consideration.[23] Yet another method is to build further plans on a stipulated expectation that one will follow a rule. Thus Andrea might plan on listening to an interesting audiobook during her morning walks, effectively raising the stakes for her failing to observe the rule any particular morning.[24]

Notice, in these examples, that our induced preference for following a rule – our commitment to that rule – will be a preference defined over something distinct from the underlying activity considered on its own immediate merits. The likely persistence of our preferences concerning the latter accounts for the familiar experience described earlier: the experience of feeling pulled between a desire to do or not do something, and a contrary commitment to some prescriptive rule.[25]

Given the persistence of our immediate desires, nothing guarantees that endogenous strategies for inducing a commitment to personal rules will succeed. Indeed, it is precisely because we know how challenging it can be for people to adopt rules for themselves that we often engage in *exogenous* preference manipulation. We socialize our children to tell the truth and keep their promises, for example, presumably

---

[22] This is suggested by McClennen 1990, pp. 213–215. Once present to some degree, commitment can be economized on through optimal rule design, as discussed by Schelling 1985, pp. 366–368.

[23] See Elster 1989, pp. 19–23, 102–104.

[24] Bratman 1987, pp. 15–18 and *passim*, discusses our tendency to build plans on plans.

[25] Given our earlier definition of preference, there need be no conflict between the view expressed here and that in Holton 2009. Preferences for following rules may have a phenomenological character different from preferences for deviating from them: in the language of Pettit and Smith 1990, the former "background" desires, whereas the former "foreground" them.

because we think it will usually be better for them if their behavior is governed by these rules. It is beyond the scope of our discussion to speculate as to how much our commitment to various personal rules is or could be due to endogenous, as opposed to exogenous, preference manipulation. The main point is simply that we now have a rough phenomenology of rule-following, presented in terms consistent with the standard view of practical rationality.

2.2 Social Rules

It is important not to exaggerate the significance of personal rules. As mentioned above, endogenous preference manipulation is not always easy, and exogenous preference manipulation (socialization) is not always successful.

The situation is further complicated when we take an interpersonal point of view. In developing our own plans, it is often important for us to know what others are likely to do – for us to have reliable expectations regarding their conduct. It will thus be extremely helpful for us to know when someone else is following a rule, and what rule she is following. Personal rules, alas, are singularly unreliable in this regard. Without knowing much about a person, her language, or her culture, we might of course determine with reasonable accuracy her various *habits* simply by recording the observed patterns in her behavior.[26] But how do we know when a person is following a *rule*? This is much harder to say. Perhaps we would expect a person who has adopted a rule for herself to behave more regularly in that respect than she otherwise would. Unfortunately, we cannot always observe the relevant counterfactual: we can only compare some observed patterns with others. Andrea might set ϕ-ing as a rule for herself, even when she finds ϕ-ing very unpleasant to do (indeed, perhaps precisely *because* she finds it unpleasant, but believes she should ϕ anyway), whereas Bob might have a very strong preference for ϕ-ing, but never bother to set it as a rule for himself (perhaps because he does not need to, in light of his strong preference). In such cases, Bob might ϕ as often, or more, than Andrea. How then can we tell the difference?

---

[26] An exception here might be mental habits: for instance, if a person has the habit of thinking through problems inductively, rather than deductively.

It is true that we might ask them. This is much more complicated than mere observation. Among other difficulties, it requires our understanding the internal meaning of what they report, which may be difficult (especially in cross-cultural circumstances). Another possibility is that we might search for some comparative evidence that would separate the two possibilities. For example, we might think that the presence of rain clouds will affect Andrea's preferences for talking a walk, but not her preference for following a rule she has set for herself. Perhaps Andrea will thus show less weather-variance in her behavior than Bob, who is merely acting on habit. This is speculative, however.[27] At some level, without knowing a great deal about the internal psychology of another person, we will probably not be able to judge their level of commitment to specific personal rules. This can be a serious problem if, for example, we want to form reliable expectations about their future conduct. Fortunately, what we will call *social rules* can to some extent overcome it.

2.2.1 *Social Rules as Nash Equilibria*

Social rules are obviously patterns in the behavior of groups, rather than individuals, but not all patterns in the behavior of groups are social rules. Just as an individual might have reasonably stable personal preferences, giving rise to an individual behavioral habit, so too a group of people might all have similar stable preference configurations, thus giving rise to a shared behavioral habit. Patterns in regional cuisine might be an example.[28] Likewise, we might imagine that some number of people each individually happens to set for him- or herself a similar personal rule, such as the rule of taking a walk Tuesday and Thursday mornings. From the external observer's point of view, the pattern of behavior that emerges might appear to be a social rule: if you happen to observe both Andrea and Bob taking a walk every Tuesday and Thursday morning, you might think they must be following some sort of social rule to that effect. Though often a

---

[27] Hart 1994, pp. 88–90, expresses doubt that pure external observation could alone determine whether a rule is being followed or not.

[28] Though not necessarily. If some cuisines are regarded as strange and others as normal in particular regions, then individuals may feel some pressure to conform their behavior to this view, and local cuisine will turn out to be a kind of social rule. The reason will be clear shortly.

plausible inference, it will not always be correct. The crucial difference here is that, in the case of merely shared habits and shared personal rules, when a given individual's goals or aims change, she can modify her habits or adopt new rules without further consequence. The observed pattern in group behavior exists only as far as, and so long as, the relevant preferences of the participating individuals happen to converge.[29]

Following Max Weber, we might refer to shared habits and shared personal rules together as *customs*.[30] Social rules are not like customs. They arise specifically when the fact that others are behaving in some particular way *itself* gives us an additional extrinsic reason for wanting to behave in some particular way – that is, a reason in addition to our personal baseline preferences with respect to the behavior in question. This additional extrinsic reason can be described as impersonal in a significant respect – namely, in the sense that it is *publicly accessible*. In contrast to private preferences, publicly accessible reasons are reasons we can confidently expect to motivate people across a wide range of contingent circumstances and psychologies. Even without special insight into the private psychology of a particular individual, we can usually be confident they will want to observe a social rule. The following discussion will, I hope, sufficiently clarify why this might be so.

Let us first consider some very simple examples, such as conventions of language. It is obvious that the meanings of words are, at some level, perfectly arbitrary. It does not matter whether we use the word "cat" to refer to cats or dogs or whatever; what matters is only that we *all* use the *same* word in the *same* way. Situations like this can be represented as in Table 2.1. In this table, we see that it does not matter to either speaker how the word "'cat" is used, provided only that if Speaker II uses it to refer to cats, Speaker I will want to do likewise, and vice versa. This example illustrates what might be called a symmetric pure coordination convention. It is *symmetric* in that all participants want to be doing the same thing, and it is *pure* in that neither has an underlying personal preference as to which of the possible conventions is settled on.

---

[29] Coleman 2001, pp. 89–91, makes a similar point.
[30] Weber 1922, p. 319, defines custom as "a typically uniform activity which is kept on the beaten track simply because men are 'accustomed' to it," and not because observance is "'required' in any sense by anyone"; cf. what Elster 1989, pp. 104–105, terms "tradition."

Table 2.1

		Speaker II	
		C	D
Speaker I	C	1, 1	0, 0
	D	0, 0	1, 1

No doubt there is an interesting story to be told about how the word "cat" came to refer to cats, but once that reference is settled, no one cares that the word has that, rather than some other, meaning. Another commonly cited example is the convention of driving on the right in the United States and elsewhere. It does not matter particularly which side of the road we drive on, but the fact that others drive on the right gives us a compelling reason to do so ourselves.[31]

Our motivations for observing conventions of this sort are publicly accessible because they are rooted in an interlocking set of mutual expectations robust across a wide range of subjective preferences and local circumstances. Suppose that Bob has a relatively stable personal preference for chicken over beef, other things being equal, and thus is in the habit of ordering chicken when dining out. This is not something another person would necessarily know about him, without some prior knowledge of his subjective preferences or observation of his habits. Even if someone knew Bob fairly well, she still might not know whether his ordering chicken is merely a habit or a personal rule, how robust his habit is (in the former case), or how strong his commitment to the rule is (in the latter case). Bob's various reasons for ordering or not ordering chicken are thus not reliably accessible to others. Contrast this with Bob's reasons for driving on the right. Even supposing he had a baseline preference for driving on the left for some reason or other, others can be very confident he will not do so. This is because there is an expectation that everyone will drive on the right *whatever their subjective preferences and circumstances happen to be*. Without knowing much about his personal preferences, others can reliably assume that Bob has strong reasons for not driving against traffic. This gives social

---

[31] Such pure coordination conventions figure largely in the pioneering work by Lewis 1969.

Table 2.2

		Firm II	
		N	W
Firm I	N	10, 8	0, 0
	W	0, 0	8, 10

rules a degree of reliability and accessibility that shared habits and even shared personal rules usually do not have.[32]

Pure coordination conventions like the examples above are probably rare. Much more common are impure coordination conventions, in which the participants do have underlying personal preferences with respect to the possible conventions. That is to say, some might prefer one, and others another convention "on the merits" as it were. If a social rule exists, however, these merits must by definition have been outweighed by the benefits of coordination. That is to say, each participant must prefer adhering to the rule rather than going at it alone: if they did not, they would not participate, and social rules do not exist without participants. Consider the example of settling on a standard rail gauge width, represented in Table 2.2.

Suppose that Firm I has made some prior investment in a narrower gauge, whereas Firm II has made some prior investment in a wider gauge; both, however, greatly prefer that something be settled on as the uniform standard. In this situation, it is not a matter of indifference to the firms which convention is settled on, though settling on either convention is much better than not. Impure coordination conventions like this are very common.[33] It is significant that any impure coordination problem potentially raises issues of distribution: the choice of an

[32] Similar accounts of social rules, as distinct from customs, can be found in Hart 1994, pp. 51–61; Postema 1982, pp. 172–179; and Elster 1989, pp. 102–105. In realizing that legal systems cannot be understood merely in terms of shared habits (e.g., habits of obedience to a sovereign), modern positivists advanced beyond the classical positivists such as Bentham and Austin.

[33] Less common, but certainly possible, are situations in which *everyone* would prefer convention *A* to convention *B*, and yet (perhaps through historical accident) they have coordinated on *B*. Pareto inferior conventions like this can persist, despite their being universally disliked, because of difficulties in coordinating the transition to a better convention.

Table 2.3

		Camper II	
		W	E
Camper I	W	0, 0	1, 1
	E	1, 1	0, 0

economic system, for example, might be thought of as a vast impure coordination problem with major social implications. (Any settlement of economic entitlements – even socialism, presumably – must be better than a free-for-all. But clearly different persons will fare very differently depending on which particular system is settled on. How are we to choose among the alternatives? This is the fundamental problem of what is called economic or distributive justice.) Thus, even when it is better for all to coordinate than not, it can matter a very great deal which coordination point is ultimately settled on.[34]

It is also important to observe that coordination problems are not always symmetric: often what is important is for people to coordinate on performing *different*, but complementary, actions. If campers must search for firewood, it is less important who searches to the west and who searches to the east; what matters is only that they search in complementary directions. Situations like these can be represented as in Table 2.3. All but the most rudimentary coordination problems involve some sort of division of labor. In order for a social rule to exist, it is not necessary that everyone be doing the same thing, but rather only that whatever each is doing constitutes their best response to whatever the others are doing – that their respective plans for action mesh with one another, so to speak. Social rules thus represent solutions to what game theorists term *strategic situations*. In a strategic situation, what each person wants to do depends, in some measure, on what the others are doing.[35] Formally speaking, a social rule is a Nash

---

[34] While obvious on reflection, this point is significant because it means that the solution to impure coordination problems will decidedly *not* be arbitrary in certain cases. This contradicts the apparent assumptions of some authors: for example, see Marmor 2001, p. 9; Shapiro 2011, pp. 109–110.

[35] Interestingly, this is roughly equivalent to what Weber 1922, p. 26, defines as a "social relationship," namely, "the behavior of a plurality of actors insofar as . . .

equilibrium, that is, a profile of plans for action such that the plan of each participant in the strategic situation represents their best response to the plan adopted by the others.[36]

It is easy to see that social rules must constitute Nash equilibria. Suppose the contrary, that some people could do better – in other words, better realize whatever goals or aims they happen to have – by doing something other than what they are presently doing in observing the social rule. What then prevents them from changing their behavior unilaterally? Of course, we need not assume that people calculate and recalculate their best responses to what others are doing at every moment. Much as with habits, we usually act on autopilot out of convenience, assuming our earlier calculations are still reasonably sound. In the long run, however, it is inevitable that people will reconsider plans for action that are not serving their goals or aims.[37] Once people start to change what they are doing, the social rule must change, or else cease to exist. When existing social rules are robust, therefore, it *must* be the case that observing the rule represents each participant's best response to what the other participants are doing, all things considered.[38]

2.2.2 Participation and Intentionality

The various participants in a social rule might observe that same rule for different private reasons. Consider our earlier example of setting a standard width for rail gauge from Firm I's the point of view, and suppose the convention settled on is wide gauge. At least initially, this is not what Firm I would prefer to do, other things being equal. Its only reasons for participating in this convention are strategic: given that the other firms will be laying wide-gauge track, its best response will be to lay wide-gauge track also. In time, however, Firm I may have laid enough wide-gauge track that its own underlying preferences shift in that direction, and we might be tempted to say that the convention has evolved into a shared habit. This would be a mistake, however.

the action of each takes into account that of the others and is oriented in these terms."

[36] Here I am indebted to Calvert 1995 for recognizing this equivalence.

[37] This point is nicely put by Pettit 1990, pp. 726–727.

[38] We must hasten to add, of course, that the reasoning in this paragraph explains *only* their robustness, not their historical origin.

While it is true that both firms now privately prefer wide-gauge track to narrow, nevertheless both still have compelling strategic reasons to stick with the convention *even if their private preferences subsequently change*.[39] Customs are not like this. If Bob's preference for chicken over beef changes in the future, the mere fact that others also happen to have a preference for chicken over beef gives him no reason to persist in his original pattern of choice. This is important, again, because public expectations built on genuine social rules will be substantially more reliable than those built on mere shared habits or shared personal rules.

That said, it is not entirely irrelevant whether the underlying preferences of Firm I evolve in the direction of wide-gauge track: other things being equal, we might imagine that social rules will be more robust and uniformly observed to the extent that they become habitual. This is because, in such cases, participants will have non-strategic as well as strategic reasons for observing the rule.

Similarly, we might expect social rules to be more robust when their participants adopt that convention as a personal rule for themselves. (As we noted earlier, there are many different reasons – pragmatic, ethical, religious, and so on – for adopting personal rules.) In language familiar to legal theorists and philosophers, we might describe this as the difference between taking an internal versus an external point of view regarding the social rule.[40] People take an internal point of view toward some social rule when they adopt that rule as a personal rule for themselves, and thus (much as in the case of rules that have become habitual) observe the rule at least in part for non-strategic reasons. The internal point of view, so defined, is sometimes confused with the insider or participant viewpoint more generally, as contrasted with the outside observer viewpoint.[41] These are not the same. As we have said, individuals participating in a social rule might observe that rule for many different reasons. Holmes's famous "bad man" who observes

[39] Technological changes, for instance, might subsequently render narrow-gauge track better for both firms; nevertheless, the wide-gauge track convention may persist until a transition can be coordinated (see n. 33).

[40] Following Hart 1994, pp. 56–57, 89–90.

[41] See Dworkin 1986, pp. 13–15, and Tamanaha 1997, pp. 175–178, for example. Of course, this confusion might have been avoided if Hart had used different language to describe the distinction he introduced. Unfortunately, his language has stuck. For a nice discussion, see Shapiro 2006, esp. pp. 1158–1163.

the law only in order to avoid punishment certainly participates in the legal system – but he does so without adopting any of the rules of law as personal rules for himself.[42] In other words, he maintains an external point of view toward legal practice while nevertheless participating in it.

H. L. A. Hart and others have argued that legal systems cannot exist unless at least some individuals adopt certain important social rules as personal rules for themselves – i.e., unless they assume an internal point of view regarding those rules. In Chapter 3, I will argue that this is not correct. For the time being, however, we may simply observe that the Nash equilibrium concept can easily accommodate the distinction between internal and external points of view. This very comprehensiveness may lead to a different worry, however: namely, that the concept is too broad. While every social rule must constitute a Nash equilibrium, perhaps not every Nash equilibrium constitutes a social rule. Specifically, what about competitive equilibria? According to Downsian models of political competition, for instance, in a unidimensional issue space the best response for both political parties is to track the policy preferences of the median voter.[43] Usually we would not describe a competitive equilibrium of this sort as a social rule, properly so-called. Nor would we so describe equilibrium pricing strategies in a perfect market, and so forth.

One strategy for distinguishing social rules from other sorts of competitive equilibria is suggested by Michael Bratman's discussion of "joint intentional activities" and "shared cooperative activities," which has recently influenced a number of legal theorists and philosophers.[44] Roughly speaking, joint intentional activities are defined as situations in which two or more persons both intend to produce a particular outcome through the coordination or "meshing" of their separate plans for action. (Shared cooperative activities are further defined as the special case in which the meshed plans include some provision of mutual support.) Thus, in the example of firewood gathering above, both campers intend an outcome in which lots of firewood has been gathered quickly, and they coordinate their actions

[42] Holmes 1897, pp. 992–994.   [43] Downs 1957.
[44] See Bratman 1999. Among the legal theorists influenced by Bratman's discussion are Coleman 2001 and Shapiro 2011.

by searching in different directions. If we defined social rules as joint intentional activities, competitive Nash equilibria would be excluded. While it is true that the plans adopted by political parties "mesh," in the sense that each represents the best response to the plan adopted by the other, it is not the case that the parties intend the joint outcome produced. On the contrary, it is precisely the aim of each party to defeat the other at the polls.

There are two difficulties with this approach, however. The first is that so defined, distinguishing social rules from competitive equilibria would require our having access to the internal psychology of the participants – specifically, knowledge about their intentional states. Often we lack this knowledge, of course. The second is that it will probably exclude too much, unless we adopt an oddly loose interpretation of joint intentions. (It would be odd to say that using the word "cat" to refer to cats is a joint intention of English speakers.) This second difficulty will be even more apparent later on, when we discuss social norms.

A better (though still not perfect) strategy begins with the observation that social rules, unlike competitive equilibria, characteristically attach extrinsic costs or benefits to general classes of behavior defined in advance – costs or benefits extrinsic to the various actors' baseline preferences with respect to the behavior in that class. Thus, for example, the convention of driving on the right dictates that I too drive on the right, and only on the right: no other sort of driving will do. By contrast, competitive equilibria do not assign extrinsic costs and benefits to specifically defined classes of behavior. Given that one party has positioned itself near the median voter and that a second party wants to maximize its overall vote share, the optimal response for the second party is to position itself near the median voter as well, thus generating an equilibrium. But notice that no particular class of behavior has been prescribed in advance: if the second party develops different aims, or if the median voter changes, etc., nothing attaches the parties to the particular platform positions they previously held. It follows that competitive equilibria can continuously drift in ways that we would not expect with social rules.

While not perfect, this rough-and-ready approach will more than suffice for our purposes. This is because it will later become apparent (in Chapter 3) that for understanding the existence and content of law, little hinges on our ability to draw the distinction precisely.

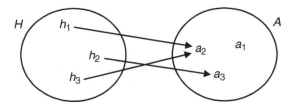

Figure 2.1. The strategy function.

2.3 Social Norms and the Practice Theory

In the examples of social rules discussed so far, we have assumed that people face small, discrete opportunity sets: laying narrow-gauge rail tracks or wide, driving on the right or on the left, searching for firewood to the east or to the west, and so on. Many situations are more complicated than this, however. In order to properly analyze these more complicated situations we must introduce the idea, familiar to game theorists, of a *strategy*.[45]

Formally speaking, a strategy is a function that maps possible histories into possible responses. "Histories" are simply observable events happening prior to a choice, which can thus convey information relevant to making that choice. For example, consider my strategy for deciding whether to take an umbrella to work or not. There are two possible histories – either it is cloudy, or it is not; and there are two possible responses – take an umbrella, or not. My strategy is a sort of plan that assigns to each history a particular response. A very sensible strategy, for instance, might be 'take an umbrella only if it is cloudy'. A less sensible strategy might be 'never take an umbrella'. In either case, we can think of the strategy as a sort of function that assigns particular responses to each possible history. It is called a "mapping" in the sense that, if possible prior histories constitute one set, and possible action-responses another, the strategy function provides a map for getting from one set to the other (see Figure 2.1). Sometimes this is notated as $s: H \rightarrow A$, and sometimes $s(h) = a$. (It is customary to use capital letters to designate sets, and lowercase letters the members of those sets.) Since we usually have several strategy alternatives in a

---

[45] From here my analysis of social rules departs significantly from the familiar practice theory accounts offered by Hart, Postema, and others. The game theory tools employed in what follows can be found in any good textbook, e.g., Gibbons 1992.

given context, we can also refer to "strategy spaces," noted as $S = \{s_1, s_2, \ldots, s_n\}$. A strategy space is the same as what we have referred to as an opportunity set – a group of possible paths of action available to an actor at some point in time. The most important sorts of strategies for our purposes are going to be strategies that contingently respond to the prior actions of other people.

2.3.1 Conditional Strategies and Social Norms

Consider what happens when people arrive at a bank. Let us suppose they all have a preference for being served by a teller as soon as possible. However, were they all to rush to the front, the ensuing confusion would make everyone worse off. It is far better to coordinate on some method of waiting for service in turns. There are several ways they might do this. For example, customers might stand in a single line for the next available teller, or there might be separate lines for each teller, and so on. Suppose at some particular bank, the convention has settled on the single-line approach. Here we have what initially appears to be a simple coordination convention: given that everyone else is standing in line, we might suppose that a new customer's best response is also to stand in line. But on second thought, this cannot be the whole story. If everyone else is standing in line, isn't the best response for a new customer to rush to the front, ahead of the others? Usually we don't expect people to do this, however. Why not?

Suppose for a moment there is no security guard or other authority figure to prevent line-jumping, and suppose the tellers cannot see how the customers come to their window (and thus refuse to serve line-jumpers). It might be, of course, that some people prefer to do what is fair, other things equal, and believe that waiting in line is a fair procedure. These folks will adopt the rule 'always wait your turn in line' as a personal rule for themselves. If many people have done this, then the observed pattern of waiting in line for service is best described as a shared personal rule or custom. While certainly possible, in all likelihood there is more to the observed pattern than this. Specifically, we would probably expect wait-in-liners to get annoyed with line-jumpers, vocally criticize them, or otherwise publicly express their disapproval. Since most of us are sensitive to social disapprobation, this represents an informal sanction on line-jumping that, at least some of the time, makes a practical difference to our own behavior.

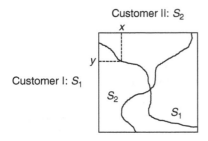

Figure 2.2. Best response correspondences.

Consider what this means in game theory language. Each bank customer has a range of possible strategies to select from in their opportunity set (or strategy space). These include, for example, 'always wait in line', 'never wait in line', 'wait in line and criticize others who don't', and so forth. Now imagine that we line up all the possible strategies for one customer along one axis, and all the possible strategies for another customer along the other (see Figure 2.2). For any given strategy that Customer II might adopt, suppose there is a corresponding strategy for Customer I that represents her best response. If we plot all these best responses, we might get something like the line marked $s_1{}^*$ in Figure 2.2 – what game theorists call a *best response correspondence*. This tells us that if Customer II has adopted the strategy x, for example, the best response for Customer I is given by $s_1(x) = y$. The same can be done for Customer II. Where these two lines cross we have a Nash equilibrium, that is, a situation in which no one can do better by changing his or her strategy, given the strategies others have adopted. Though we have increased the degree of abstraction a bit, it should be apparent with a bit of reflection that Figure 2.2 is not really that different from Tables 2.1, 2.2, and 2.3, except now we are considering complex responsive strategies rather than simple ones, and now the participants have to select among a continuous range of options rather than a few discrete ones.

Back to the bank. What is really going on is probably something like this: among the many possible strategy equilibria, what has been settled on is a social rule in which each customer adopts the strategy 'wait in line and criticize others who don't wait in line'. Given that others have adopted this strategy, no one customer can do better choosing some other strategy unilaterally. It is important to recognize here that the base rule 'wait in line' is not a complete description of the social rule. One reason this is important is because we should keep in mind that any sanctioning behavior also needs to be in equilibrium, so to speak. In other words, supposing that some individual has deviated from the base rule, issuing the relevant sanction rather than not must be the best response to that deviance from the point of view of the sanctioning parties. Otherwise, the threat of sanction would not be credible. In the technical language of game theory, we need a *sub-game perfect* Nash equilibrium: the respective strategies adopted by the players must constitute best responses not only in the game as a whole, but also in the "sub-game" where someone has already departed from the equilibrium path by violating the base rule.[46] The counterfactual possibility of sanctioning in the event of deviance is thus an essential aspect of the equilibrium, even if actual sanctioning is rarely observed. Indeed, if everyone were to conform perfectly to their respective equilibrium strategies, we would *never* observe actual sanctioning, since no one would ever deviate from the base rule!

I shall return to this last point in later discussion. For the moment, it suffices to note that we are now talking about social rules of a rather special sort. Unlike the simpler coordination conventions discussed earlier, the rules we are now considering involve strategies that carry the possibility of conditional responses such as approval or disapproval, praise or blame. Many social rules of etiquette, for example, take this form. The fact that someone else places forks to the left of plates does not *itself* give us a reason to do so as well, any more than the fact that someone else orders chicken rather than beef gives Bob a reason to do so as well. It is our desire to seek social approbation and avoid social disapprobation, however mild, that encourages us to follow the rules of etiquette. Let us call a sanction-supported social rule of this sort a *social norm*, as distinct from a mere coordination convention. This term is not ideal, since norms come in both rule and non-rule varieties (the commands of a revered spiritual leader, for example, might be regarded as normative in some religious communities). However, we will follow the practice standard in much

---

[46] There is a lively debate concerning the rationality of sanctioning: see Elster 1989, pp. 99–100, 132–133; Coleman 1990, pp. 270–273, 282–286; Pettit 1990, pp. 738–741.

social science literature of treating "social norm" as shorthand for "sanction-supported social rule."[47]

As in the case of coordination conventions, social norms can be supported by mixed motives. Many people might prefer to do what a social norm requires anyway, perhaps because they believe it is the morally or ethically right thing to do.[48] In such cases, people take an internal point of view toward the social norm – adopting, as we have said, its base rule as a personal rule for themselves. This does not affect the main point, however. What is important for our purposes is that sanctions increase the robustness of a social rule. Thus social norms generate especially reliable expectations – specifically, expectations that others will observe the norm in a wide range of circumstances, even when we know little about their intentions or personal psychology. Without knowing much about a person's idiosyncratic preferences, we can usually assume they will want to avoid punishment, in part because the sanctioning behavior in a given community will naturally converge on whatever it is that people in that community most commonly want to avoid.[49]

2.3.2 Objections to the Practice Theory

On the view developed here, social rules are constituted by conventional practices of human behavior. This was also the view of Hart, which legal theorists and philosophers generally refer to as the *practice theory* of social rules. According to Hart, a social rule R requiring that we ϕ exists in some community when the following practice conditions obtain, roughly:

(1) people generally ϕ,
(2) people generally criticize those who do not ϕ, and
(3) people generally regard both ϕ-ing, and criticizing those who do not ϕ, as normatively appropriate.[50]

---

[47] E.g., Elster 1989, pp. 98–100, and Pettit 1990, pp. 728–732; cf. Coleman 1990, pp. 243–244, except that he curiously groups personal rules and social norms under the same conceptual head. Social norms are similarly distinguished from mere coordination conventions by Elster 1989, pp. 101–102.

[48] Postema 1982, pp. 177–178, correctly notes this point.

[49] What counts as punishment will therefore vary according to the cultural and historical context: in aristocratic societies, for example, dishonoring someone can be an extremely effective informal sanction.

[50] Hart 1994, esp. pp. 55–57, 85–88.

As noted in the introduction to this chapter, the practice theory has been subject to many criticisms. Fortunately, we can use our conception of social rules as Nash equilibria to improve on Hart, and so answer these criticisms. Specifically, two important objections to the practice theory will be addressed here, while a third is postponed until Chapter 3.

The first main objection is that Hart fails to provide an adequate account of how conventional practices can by themselves constitute social rules in the required prescriptive sense.[51] In other words, how can the mere fact that it is general practice to observe some rule give me a reason to observe it as well? As vegetarians will point out, the general practice of eating meat provides no good reason as such for eating meat oneself. Notice that condition (3) does not supply an answer, for there are clearly instances of rules we regard as normatively appropriate which we nevertheless simply fail to observe. For instance, many people believe that everyone (including themselves) ought to give more money to charity than, as it happens, anyone actually does. Even when people do observe a widely practiced rule they regard as normatively appropriate, it need not follow that they observe that rule *because* it is widely practiced. For example, many people save for retirement, regard it as appropriate to do so, and criticize those who don't. Nevertheless, we would probably not be inclined to say that 'save for retirement' constitutes a social rule. Or consider the conventional wisdom in American football that teams which fail to gain 10 yards in their first three downs should use their fourth to punt. Not only is it the case that coaches usually do call for a punt in such cases, but also that coaches who attempt risky fourth-down conversions are criticized, and that both facts are widely regarded as appropriate. Again, however, it would seem incorrect to say that punting on fourth downs constitutes a social rule.

The difficulty here is subtle, but significant. It seems that on any plausible account of social rules, a genuine social rule must actually make some practical difference: it must actually supply a reason for our doing or not doing something we might not have done *but for* the existence of that rule. On the practice theory, social rules are nothing more than conventional practices. It follows that those conventional

---

[51] Versions of this objection can be found in Raz 1999, pp. 53–56; Green 1999, pp. 37–41; Marmor 2001, pp. 3–7; and Shapiro 2011, pp. 102–105.

practices must themselves somehow supply the necessary reasons. In the examples above, however, patterns in behavior apparently satisfying Hart's practice conditions do not themselves generate reasons. While it is true that many people save for retirement, that is not the reason any one of them does; likewise, while it is true that teams usually punt on fourth down, that is not as such their reason for doing so. In both cases, the relevant reasons are prudential: the reason people save is to secure a comfortable retirement, and the reason teams punt on fourth down is to avoid giving their opponents good field position. Contrast these examples with the rule that a team which fails to advance the line of scrimmage 10 yards in four downs loses possession: here the reason a team loses possession *is* the rule. In other words, *but for* the rule, possession would not change.

In response to this difficulty, some legal theorists have turned to what we earlier termed coordination conventions, and in later work Hart himself apparently embraced this approach.[52] In a coordination convention, the mere fact that others observe a rule such as 'drive on the right' clearly supplies a reason for our doing so as well, thus satisfying the requirement that a genuine social rule must itself make a practical difference. This approach has been roundly criticized on the grounds that many significant aspects of the law cannot be explained as mere coordination conventions.[53] While these criticisms are correct so far as they go, they ignore the existence of what we have called social norms. As discussed earlier, the fact that others wait in line for service at a bank by itself may not supply us a reason to do so as well, but that fact that others wait in line for service *and criticize those who don't* certainly does. As stressed in that earlier discussion, when it comes to social norms, conditional sanctioning behavior must be understood as a part of a complete statement of the rule in question.

In light of our more sophisticated theory, Hart's practice conditions should be amended in two ways. First, we should drop the condition that people regard observance of the rule as normatively appropriate. Social rules can clearly exist even when they are widely regarded as bad, and our version of the practice theory helps us understand how: they can exist as sub-optimal Nash equilibria. (Perhaps most in the

---

[52] See Postema 1982 and Hart 1994, pp. 255–259.
[53] For example, by Green 1999, pp. 41–52; Marmor 2001, pp. 7–10; and Shapiro 2011, pp. 105–110.

European aristocratic classes detested the practice of dueling, but found themselves trapped in equilibrium until eventually the state intervened.) Second, we should add in its place the condition that either a general observance of the rule, or a general observance of the base-rule plus the sanctioning of deviations, must provide a sufficient reason to observe the rule, or to observe the base-rule and sanction deviations, oneself.[54] This is simply to say that the strategies representing the rule ('ϕ and criticize others who do not ϕ', for instance) must constitute a Nash equilibrium. With these amendments, the practice theory can easily explain how conventional practices on their own might constitute prescriptive social rules.

There is a second and potentially more serious criticism of the practice theory, however, which we must consider next. This criticism is most influentially pressed by Ronald Dworkin, and it roughly amounts to the claim that the theory cannot plausibly describe disagreements over social rules.[55] According to the practice theory, social rules are constituted by a particular sort of convergent behavior: where this convergent behavior exists, we have a social rule, and where it does not, we don't. Recall from our earlier discussion of the Wittgenstein challenge, however, that any finite set of behavioral examples might instantiate an infinite variety of possible rules. It follows that two people might falsely believe they are following the same rule when their respective rule-following activities happen to overlap in all cases which have so far arisen. For example, Andrea might be following the rule 'wait in line for service and criticize others who do not,' while Bob is following the rule 'wait in line for service except in when in a great hurry, and criticize others who do not unless

---

[54] Pettit 1990, pp. 730–731, suggests a similar revision to Hart's conditions. Interestingly, it follows on this amendment that fourth-down punting might constitute a social rule after all. Suppose there are some game situations in which clever coaches judge attempting a fourth-down conversion advantageous, even though conventional wisdom would disagree. These coaches might be deterred from acting on their judgment knowing they will be subject to criticism for doing so. If so, then it seems to me that we have a social norm.

[55] See Dworkin 1977, pp. 54–57; 1986, pp. 121–124, 130–135. The objection is also raised by Radin 1989, pp. 801–801, and Kutz 2001, pp. 435–457. Dworkin sometimes refers to versions of his objection as the "semantic sting," on the mistaken view that the practice theory is a semantic theory about the meaning of the concept of law. In replying to the objection here, I try to reconstruct it in a way that avoids this error. For a reply taking the objection more or less at face value, see Raz 2009, ch. 3.

they are in a great hurry'. In what sense can we speak of there being a social rule here? What is the rule they share? According to the practice theory, it would seem, this scenario is properly described as one in which there is a limited social rule governing only those cases in which no one is in a great hurry; elsewhere, there is simply a gap, so to speak, ungoverned by rules.[56]

Unfortunately, this description seems inadequate to capture the reality of how we actually experience disagreement. Suppose the time comes when someone is in a great hurry, revealing the latent disagreement between Andrea and Bob. According to the practice theory, their disagreement must concern how to extend the existing social rule into a previously ungoverned area, and since the existing rule supplies no correct answer to this question, such disagreement is both more or less inevitable, and also unstructured. In actual experience, however, disagreement is not inevitable. Often, people agree on how rules apply in new situations without fanfare. What is more, when disagreement does arise, it is often felt to be a structured disagreement *about what the rule itself requires*.[57] On the practice theory, apparently, that is a mistake: a rule cannot require anything in areas the rule does not (as yet) govern. The challenge for the practice theory, then, is to explain not merely how disagreement is possible, which is easy enough, but further why disagreement is not inevitable, and why, when it does occur, it is often felt to be a disagreement about what the rule requires.

In the game theory language we have been using, this challenge is equivalent to explaining how it is possible for one party in a strategic situation to know which strategy another party has adopted when strategies, as such, cannot be observed. What we observe are discrete actions, and of course any finite series of observed actions can in principle instantiate an infinite number of possible strategies. How

---

[56] Cf. Hart's discussion of the "open texture of law," 1994, pp. 124–136. Note that the response offered by Coleman 1982, pp. 23–25, will not serve. He attempts to deflect the objection by pointing out that there can be agreement on a procedure to resolve disagreements concerning a rule, but this only raises the possibility that the participants might disagree on what counts as following the procedure in the relevant sense. In other words, as Dworkin 2002, pp. 1656–1662, points out in his reply to Coleman, procedures are in effect a sort of rule, and thus subject to the same challenge.

[57] Often, though not always of course. Sometimes the parties to such disputes clearly recognize their dispute as concerning what the rule should be, and not what the rule is. In such cases, their disagreement is straightforwardly political.

can Firm I tell whether Firm II has adopted the strategy 'lay wide-gauge track', or rather 'lay wide-gauge track for ten years, then narrow-gauge track for ten years, and so on'? From a certain philosophical point of view, discussed earlier, it cannot. Nevertheless, it is clear that equilibria in social behavior exist, one way or another. So what accounts for the fact that, first, while confusion always *can* arise, often it does not; and second, *when* confusion arises, it can be experienced as confusion concerning what the relevant strategy requires, and not merely as a dispute concerning which among several possible strategies one should adopt? This is not, of course, how game theorists would tend to view such situations. For the moment, however, we are interested in properly accounting for the authentic felt experience of disagreement, not its optimal theoretical characterization.

Fortunately, an answer to these questions is not hard to find, and indeed was suggested earlier in our discussion of personal rules. While it is true that any finite series of discrete actions can in principle instantiate an infinite number of possible strategies (or rules), in practice our response to examples is heavily conditioned by natural instinct and cultural background. No one responds to the series 0, 2, 4, 6, 8 with the thought that we are adding 2 up to the number 2000, then adding 4 up to the number 4000, and so forth. Conditioning ensures that there will often be convergence in how people respond to examples: witnessing a series of particular actions, people will often tend to agree that those actions exemplify one particular strategy or rule.[58] After several trips to the bank, Andrea and Bob will both almost certainly assume that the general rule is 'wait in line for service and criticize others who do not', rather than 'wait in line for service and criticize others who do not except on Tuesdays', even if neither has ever visited on a Tuesday.

Disagreement or confusion is nevertheless still possible, since no two people are conditioned in exactly the same way or have exactly the same experiences. When disagreement or confusion does arise, since each person has his or her own intuitive sense that the examples exemplify this or that particular rule, their subjective experience will be one of a debate concerning what the rule requires. Thus if Andrea's

---

[58] Interestingly, it follows from this last point that the same set of explicitly enumerated formal rules may yield very different normative social orders in different cultural communities. Herein lies the truth in Cover's 1993, ch. 3, argument that a legal system can arise only through the intersection of formal rules with a determinate lived culture.

experiences have conditioned her toward severity, she might subjectively feel that a natural extension of the rule would preclude exceptions
for those in a great hurry, whereas if Bob's experiences have conditioned him toward indulgence, he might subjectively feel that a natural
extension of the rule would grant exceptions for those in a great hurry.
If pressed to give a philosophical reconstruction of the subjective
experience of disagreement, we might say that disagreements about
rules are disagreements about how unbiased persons from a given
community would respond under favorable conditions to a specific
and finite series of examples in describing the general rule those
examples exemplify.[59] This answer is perfectly consistent with the
practice theory, and plausibly accounts for the common felt experience
of disagreement.

Of course we have only partially responded to Dworkin, who further argues that people sometimes disagree not merely about the
extension of legal rules into some previously ungoverned gap around
the margins, but indeed about the central meaning of law itself in some
fundamental cases.[60] The conclusion of our reply must wait until
Chapter 5, after we have discussed the nature of a legal system.

2.4 Conventions and Social Order

The benefits of human association cannot be secured unless people
manage to coordinate their diverse efforts. Experience suggests that
habit and custom alone are insufficient for this purpose.[61] Fortunately,
as further discussed in Chapter 4, there are many methods available
for managing expectations and motivating cooperation, and nearly
all societies employ a wide variety of them. It is impossible, however,
to imagine a society that did not rely heavily on the method of
convention – that is, on coordination conventions and social norms.
One reason for this is that all the other methods probably rest on
conventional social rules at their base. Authoritarian methods, for
example, rely on an authority-conferring convention; market-based

---

[59] For greater detail, see Pettit's discussion of "fallible readability," 1993,
pp. 90–97.
[60] See esp. Dworkin 1986, pp. 37–43.
[61] Malinowski 1926 famously dispelled the once-popular illusion that primitive
societies are governed by habit and custom alone.

methods rely on conventions of exchange; and so on. Society thus fundamentally depends on conventional social rules.

It is important not to confuse this claim, however, with the claim that such needs *explain* the existence of whatever particular social rules a society happens to have. To make this latter claim would be to engage in dubious functionalist reasoning. Particular social rules arise through complicated historical processes, the explanation of which lies far beyond the scope of this study. In this chapter, I have discussed only how social rules work, and what can make them robust. For the argument that follows, that is sufficient.

3 | *Legal Systems*

At the opening of Chapter 2, we imagined a dispute between Andrea and Bob settled by a court that ultimately found Bob legally liable for breach of contract. What makes this story a story about law and not something else? Many people take it as obvious what the law is. The law is a set of rules, written down in official books of code or statute, enforced by courts and the police. With respect to the dispute between Andrea and Bob, there must have been a rule written down in one of those official books – something like 'perform contracts made'. Since Bob did not do what that rule required, he was held legally liable. If pressed on why the contents of these particular books and not others constitute law, many would go on to describe a process in which some law-making authority (an elected assembly, say, or a king and his deputies) considered and determined what the official rules for the community should be. Thus, the official books of code or statute constitute law in the sense that they record those authoritative determinations.

If these simple answers were true, there would be few puzzles concerning the nature of law. Unfortunately, they are in many ways false. Consider the law of Missouri as an example. What is the law of contract in Missouri? As we would expect, lengthy sections of the official published statutes address the topic of contracts.[1] These sections are curiously circumspect, however. While they discuss in detail such topics as the elements of contract, conditions of performance, possible remedies, and so forth, one is hard-pressed to find any clear explicit statement that citizens of the state of Missouri lie under a general legal obligation to 'perform contracts made'. Can this reticence be explained with reference to some peculiar intentions on the part of the Missouri state legislature? Surprisingly, perhaps, it cannot. This is because, for the most part, the Missouri state legislature did

---

[1] See esp., *Revised Statutes of the State of Missouri* (2000), § 400 and §§ 431–436.

not actually write the relevant part of the statutes. On the contrary, Missouri in 1963 (like most American states around that time) simply incorporated into state law something called the Uniform Commercial Code. The U.C.C. was drafted in the 1940s by a self-appointed group of professional lawyers, judges, and legal academics.[2] In drafting the U.C.C., these authors relied heavily on an earlier document, also produced by self-appointed legal experts, but not explicitly adopted as law in any jurisdiction, called the *Restatement of Contracts*. The *Restatement* was an attempt to summarize in some reasonably coherent form the English and American common law of contracts which, in its turn, was not created through deliberate acts of legislation at all: it was rather the gradual accretion of judicial decisions over several centuries in specific cases of contract dispute, something more akin to custom than to legislation in the familiar sense.

Thus we are left with many questions. Why would a state legislature apparently be so indifferent to the content of contract law as to be willing to adopt wholesale generic code written by an unelected committee? Why is that code so circumspect with respect to our specific legal obligations?[3] And most importantly, perhaps, if we imagine that the law is what is contained in official published books of code or statute, what are we to say about the law of contract in Missouri prior to 1963? Remarkably, when the Missouri state legislature officially adopted the U.C.C., prior statutes were not supplanted. Before that time, the sections of the code governing contracts indicated only that one had to be of a certain age to enter into a contract, that some specified contracts had to be in writing, and a few other incidental details. These brief passages *assumed* that a law of contract existed in the state – as indeed it did – but oddly they did not say what it was.

Neither are such curiosities unique to the Anglo-American common law tradition. One might mention, for instance, the wholesale borrowing of Swiss contract law by Turkey in the 1920s. Or the fact that for centuries, the governing law on many questions in continental

---

[2] Specifically, it was a product of the joint efforts of the American Law Institute and the National Conference of Commissioners on Uniform State Laws. For details, see Gilmore 1977, pp. 68–74, 81–86.

[3] This circumspection is by no means unique to contract law. For example, §§ 565.20–21, 25 of the Missouri code define the various degrees of murder, and indicate punishments appropriate for each, without ever explicitly stating that one should not commit murder!

Europe was the *Corpus Iurius* of Justinian – despite the fact that official pronouncements declaring it a valid source of law were often absent.[4] Clearly, if we are to make any sense of these and other similar puzzles we will need a much more sophisticated conception of law.

Before launching into our discussion, however, one minor word of caution. There are obviously many different uses and meanings for the word "law." From the standpoint of developing an argument about the rule of law, only some of these will be relevant. For example, we may speak of laws of nature, laws of logic or inference, religious and moral laws, the laws of literary success, and so on. In no sense does the conception offered here purport to cover all these possible uses of the term (if indeed it were possible for one conception to do so). When it comes to the rule of law, we are interested in a particular set of social phenomena to which we generally refer using the word in its roughly socio-political sense.[5] It is the distinctive nature and character of those specific social phenomena, and not the proper use of the word "law" in English, that is our topic. Without prejudging the issue, we may initially take contract law, laws against murder, the law of property, and so forth as obvious examples of the particular phenomena we have in mind; less obvious examples will be addressed in the course of discussion when relevant.

3.1 Law and Public Coercion

As a first step in building our conception of law, we will need to introduce a distinction between those uses of coercive force that are public and those that are not. Let us say that one agent employs coercive force against another when the former changes what the latter would otherwise prefer or be able to do through the use or threat of violence, physical restraint, or other like means. Since it is not an aim of this study to provide an analysis of coercion, I will simply assume that the idea of coercive force is reasonably clear and unproblematic. Roughly speaking, coercive force will count as *public* when employed

---

[4] For further discussion, see Watson 2001.
[5] We need not, however, restrict ourselves to what is commonly called "municipal law," i.e., the domestic law of independent sovereign states. This chapter considers some varieties of non-state law, and Chapter 7 considers international law.

by public coercive agents. This latter idea, which is less familiar, requires some elaboration.

3.1.1 Public Coercive Agents

Let us say that a *coercive agent* is any person or group that has the effective capacity to forcibly coerce other persons or groups. Coercive agents can be either public or private. In order for a coercive agent to be *public*, let us say that it must be generally known to specific persons or groups that the said coercive agent has the effective capacity to forcibly coerce them in an ongoing or sustainable manner. The expressions "generally known" and "ongoing or sustainable" here are admittedly vague, but they could be given a more precise specification if necessary, and for our immediate purposes they should be sufficient. Also note that our definition is strictly agnostic as to the purposes or aims – for good or for ill – toward which the agent's coercive activities are directed.

In practice, of course, public coercive agents will nearly always have to be group agents. This is for the obvious reason that, as Thomas Hobbes famously observed, "when all is reckoned together, the difference between man, and man, is not so considerable" since "the weakest has strength enough to kill the strongest, either by secret machination, or by confederacy with others."[6] Only through mutual coordination will a group of individuals be capable of effectively wielding coercive force over others for a sustained period of time. (The converse is not true, however: group coercive agents need not always be public: transient criminal gangs, for example, might coordinate for a time in the exercise of clandestine coercive force.) That public coercive agents must be group agents will have significant implications for our understanding of law, as we shall later see.

Some further observations will also be useful in the discussion that follows. First, when group agents coordinate in exercising coercive force, this will not usually mean that they all agree to perform the same actions at the same times. For instance, in deciding to coerce Bob, a group agent might designate Andrea as the specific person to use or threaten physical violence against him, the rest perhaps lending support to her efforts only if needed. Coordination in the relevant sense

[6] Hobbes 1651, I.13.1: p. 82.

rather entails only that the actions of the individuals constituting the group agent be so organized as to produce a coherent and consistent set of effects. Typically this will require solving two problems. On the one hand, the group must have some sort of internal decision proced-ure structured so as to avoid social choice dilemmas: the diverse preferences of the group's members concerning when, where, and how to exert coercive force must be successfully aggregated. This might be accomplished, for example, by having a group dictator, by requiring unanimity, or by some other method. On the other hand, once a decision has been made, the group must also have mechanisms in place to ensure that each of its members performs his or her part in generat-ing the desired outcome. Internal free riding, for example, must be held to an acceptable minimum. Public coercive agents are, per assumption, groups that have in some measure managed to overcome both sets of challenges.[7]

Second, not only is it possible, but indeed it is common for group coercive agents to coerce their own members. Often this is partly, though it cannot be entirely, how the group manages its own internal coordination. (Andrea might be induced to coerce Bob, for instance, by the possibility that she will be coerced in turn by the rest of her group if she does not.) In some cases, these are the *only* persons over whom the group agent exercises coercive force; in other cases, any number of non-group members might be coerced as well. Let us term the set of persons over whom a given coercive agent effectively wields coercive force its *effective range*. (Coercive agents might, of course, claim to wield coercive force over persons beyond this range as well: we might term this the agent's *purported range*.) For the purposes of discussion here, the set of persons or groups all falling under the effective range of a given public coercive agent will be referred to as its *subject community*.

Finally, it is entirely possible for specific persons or groups to fall within the effective range of more than one coercive agent (and thus be a member of multiple subject communities). These different coercive agents might compete with one another for effective jurisdiction, but of course they need not. They might tacitly or explicitly agree to limit their respective coercive activities to complementary situations,

---

[7] For further discussion of group agency in general, see the comprehensive treatment in List and Pettit 2011.

for example. The significance of this observation, like that of the previous ones, should become clear as the discussion proceeds.

3.1.2 Social Rules and Public Coercion

The previous remarks are hopefully sufficient to convey the basic idea of a public coercive agent and its (effective) range. Now in Chapter 2, we discussed several different types of social rules. Sometimes our reasons for observing a social rule are internal to that rule itself – our reason for driving on the right, for example, is simply the fact that others are driving on the right. Social rules like this we termed coordination conventions. In other instances, however, social rules additionally incorporate sanctioning mechanisms, such that failures to observe the base rule result in some sort of punishment. These sanctioning mechanisms are sometimes informal – public expressions of disapproval, for instance. Social rules maintained in part with the help of informal sanctions like these we termed social norms. Another possibility, however, is that failures to observe a social rule might be punished by a public coercive agent with the use or threat of violence or physical restraint. This third sort of social rule, I want to argue, is roughly what we mean by a law.[8] More precisely, a set of social rules has the character of law (i.e., will be experienced as law and not something else) for those persons within the effective range of some public coercive agent when it is common knowledge that the rules in that set are supported, directly or indirectly, by that public coercive agent.

The basic idea here can be represented as in Figure 3.1. There are many comments to make with respect to this figure. First, observe that by no means are all social rules law. To a considerable degree, every society relies on coordination conventions and informal social norms to manage expectations and motivate cooperation. The law is but one

---

[8] Note that the category of sanction-supported social rules might not be exhausted by social norms and laws: consider the official rules issued by the National Football League or the World Chess Federation, for instance, which appear to fall between those possibilities. Interestingly, by characterizing law as any system of coordinated enforcement regardless of whether it involves the use of coercive force, Hadfield and Weingast 2014, p. 32, would apparently have to count such rules as laws. Unfortunately, this topic falls outside the scope of discussion here.

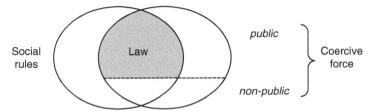

Figure 3.1. Social rules, coercive force, and law.

possible source of social order.[9] Second, note that by no means does every use of coercive force constitute law. For one thing, the use of coercive force by non-public agents is excluded from our definition. (When non-public agents employ coercive force in support of a social rule we term it *vigilantism*, and otherwise *crime*.) Moreover, not every use of coercive force by a public coercive agent necessarily constitutes law. When the United States government interned Japanese-Americans during the Second World War, it was not doing so in support of some social rule.[10] This last point will be important for our subsequent discussion of the value of the rule of law, in Chapter 4.

Since we have defined public coercive agents in a way that is agnostic with respect to their aims, our conception of law is not tethered to some particular view regarding its essential purpose or function – as for example, that the function of law is to maintain social order or settle disputes.[11] On the one hand, while it is true that the law often performs these services, it evidently performs many others as well: it facilitates collective projects, creates social institutions, expresses community values, and so forth. On the other hand, many diverse practices and institutions help maintain social order and settle disputes, either in tandem with or in place of law.

[9] This fact is emphasized in Tamanaha 1997, pp. 109–111.

[10] See *Korematsu v. United States*, 323 U.S. 214 (1944). Given that the government's action was endorsed by the Supreme Court, it might count as a legally valid command: not everything that is legally valid counts as a law, as we shall see later. Once these concepts are properly understood, this statement will not seem so paradoxical.

[11] Ehrlich 1913 and Malinowski 1926, for example, essentially identify law with whatever practices and institutions maintain social order; Hart and Sacks 1994 and Schauer 1991 associate law with whatever practices and institutions settle disputes. Many other examples of these and other functional theories could be cited.

Functional accounts of law thus cannot help us characterize what is *distinctive* about the law as a social phenomenon.[12]

Our conception of law is more congenial, however, with the accounts of either Max Weber or E. Adamson Hoebel, though with some possible differences. According to Weber, laws are those social rules enforced by "persons whose special task it is to hold themselves ready to apply specially provided means of coercion," such as "priests, judges, police, the military, etc."[13] This definition seems to exclude public coercive agents not employing specialized institutional offices. No doubt many do, as we observed earlier, but in my view it is not necessary that they do for a legal system to exist. Indeed, later we will imagine a basic legal community in which there are no designated legal officials. Hoebel defines a law as a social rule whose "neglect or infraction is regularly met, in threat or in fact, by the application of physical force by an individual or group possessing the socially recognized privilege of so acting."[14] This definition seems to exclude legal systems successfully imposed on persons or groups who reject the legitimacy of that system. No doubt legal systems are more effective when they are perceived as legitimate, other things equal, but that is neither here nor there. Imposed legal systems are still legal systems. Subsequent examples will clarify this point as well.[15]

At first pass, our conception of law as a system of social rules supported through public coercion may seem far too narrow to be correct, for are there not many unenforced laws? Here we should clarify that *active public enforcement* is not what makes a given social rule count as law, but rather the *availability* of that enforcement.[16] More formally, we might say that a given social rule R counts as a law whenever it is common knowledge that, provided a suitable request is made, the objective probability of enforcement by some public coercive agent is sufficiently high. The observed rate at which particular laws are actively enforced obviously depends on many different factors. Active enforcement might be rare if the level of voluntary compliance

---

[12] Tamanaha 1997, pp. 105–107, 127–128, similarly critiques functional accounts of law.

[13] Weber 1922, pp. 313, 326.   [14] Hoebel 1954, p. 28.

[15] The difference between my view and Kelsen's, which identifies law with coercive social order (1960, p. 33 and *passim*), will be discussed in Chapter 4.

[16] I am grateful to Brian Tamanaha and Greg Magarian for pressing me to clarify this point.

Table 3.1

		Bob	
		P	R
Andrea	P	2, 2	0, 3
	R	3, 0	1, 1

is relatively high (as perhaps with federal tax law in the United States), or if the occasions on which that enforcement is desired are relatively uncommon (as perhaps with laws against underage drinking).

Even so clarified, however, not everyone will agree that the availability of public coercive enforcement is a necessary feature of law. Objections to such a view will be considered shortly.

First, however, let us consider how our conception of law helps make sense of the imagined contract dispute between Andrea and Bob. Consider the base rule 'perform contracts made'. Many people, no doubt, feel it is only fair to keep their word, and thus they adopt something like this principle as a personal rule for themselves. But personal commitments of this sort are insufficiently robust to serve as the basis for a complex economic system: we simply cannot know enough about the internal psychology of each of the multitude of persons (strangers, mostly) with whom we will have commerce. What is required, clearly, is some sort of social rule. In such cases, however, a mere coordination convention will not do the trick (see Table 3.1). Imagine that Andrea and Bob have entered into a contract to exchange wine for bread. If Bob planned to perform his part of the agreement, then Andrea's best response would be to renege, absconding with his bread and keeping her wine; if Bob instead planned to renege, then Andrea's best response would be ... the same! – i.e., to renege herself before he has a chance to take advantage of her first. In other words, no matter what Bob does, Andrea's best response is to renege. The situation is exactly the same from Bob's point of view. It follows that 'perform contracts made' cannot by itself constitute a coordination convention. Bob's planning to perform *does not itself* give Andrea a reason to perform, and vice versa.

If the principle 'perform contracts made' is to become an effective social rule, it will thus require some sort of sanctioning mechanism.

One possibility is for there to be an informal sanction. If Andrea and Bob are both participants in a marketplace characterized by repeated public trading, a somewhat more complex rule might be sustainable as an equilibrium – something like 'perform contracts made with partners who performed their previous contract, renege on contracts made with partners who reneged on their previous contract'. In a famous paper it was shown that a rule like this might constitute, under the right conditions, what we have called a social norm.[17] In most modern societies, however, contracts are generally supported not only by personal rules and informal social norms, but also *in extremis* by some public coercive agent – usually, though not necessarily, the state. Of course, the actual application of public coercion will only rarely be required. In the hypothetical dispute we imagined, Bob ultimately paid damages to Andrea voluntarily, but had he resisted unto the bitter end, he could presumably have been forced to comply by the court (or more precisely, perhaps, by police acting on behalf of the court). His expectation that this was the case, we might suppose, prompted his voluntary compliance once the final judgment went against him.

More broadly, the general expectation that judicial decisions will go against those who renege on their contracts almost certainly helps maintain widespread voluntary performance: indeed, of the millions of contracts formed in modern societies, only a small fraction end up in court. To be sure, informal social norms, shared habits and personal rules, and the usual anticipated long-run benefits of performance also play their part. In small, less complex, and more tightly knit economic communities, it is possible that these latter factors alone would suffice. But it is unlikely that complex modern economies could do without the additional background expectation that public coercion is available as a last resort. If we forget about strategic anticipation and restrict our attention to those few cases that end up in court, we will significantly underestimate the overall impact of law and fundamentally misunderstand its character as a social phenomenon.[18]

---

[17] Milgrom et al. 1990. Note that, despite the name, the "Law Merchant" discussed in their paper was not law, insofar as the sanctions sustaining its various provisions were not implemented by a public coercive agent. The Law Merchant was rather a sophisticated system of social norms involving specialized roles for different market participants.

[18] Cf. here the influential work of Mnookin and Kornhauser 1979 on "bargaining in the shadow of the law." In the case of divorce law, which serves as their main

Thus the various social rules governing contracts count as law in most societies because it is common knowledge that some public coercive agent will ultimately support the base rule 'perform contracts made' when suitably called upon to do so. Many areas of law are similar to contract law in this respect: public coercion provides remedial support in the event of non-compliance with what, in the absence of that support, might have been an ineffective, or at any rate less effective, social rule. Laws prohibiting murder, assault, and so forth might be other examples. For obvious reasons, all societies have social rules regulating violent behavior: attaching public coercive sanctions to these rules may enhance their reliability.[19]

Other areas of law, however, are better described as the superimposition of public coercion on underlying coordination problems.[20] Large swaths of property law might be described in this way, for example: it is crucially important that we be clear what the rules of property are so everyone can plan and coordinate their various activities in pursuit of their particular aims. But while nearly any settled property system is better than none at all, different systems will clearly favor different groups. It follows that there will not be one obvious point of coordination: for better or worse, a choice will have to be made, and the law can help implement that choice for a particular society. The expectation of remedial public coercion ensures that everyone plays along despite disagreement.

Public coercion can also be employed to push a society from inferior social rules to superior ones, to prevent a society from sliding from good social rules into bad ones, or to create new social rules where none previously existed. In so doing, the law will sometimes revise or reform previously existing social institutions (such as the family), and sometimes make possible entirely novel social institutions (such as the limited liability corporation). These topics belong to a discussion of the dynamic aspect of law, however, addressed in Chapter 6.

In addition to the general sorts of rules we have discussed, there will also be rules addressed specifically to officials – judges, the police, and so forth – concerning the use of coercive force itself. For example, there might be a rule among officials to enforce rules of contract, but not a

example, they cite estimates that 10 percent or fewer of divorce cases end up in court.
[19] Cf. Hart 1994, pp. 197–198.
[20] Waldron 1999b, pp. 101–106, rightly emphasizes these situations.

similar rule to enforce the rule of waiting in line for service (more on this subsequently). Often the rules addressed to officials are themselves lent support by public coercion: recalcitrant judges and police officers can, if necessary, be compelled to comply with such rules. If so, then these social rules are also laws.[21]

The examples we have sketched should be sufficient to convey the main point: that at its core, a legal system is best understood as a system of social rules supported by some public coercive agent – supported, that is, in the sense that it is common knowledge the public coercive agent will enforce the rules of that system when suitably called upon to do so. We must caution that these are merely illustrations of how the law might operate in practice. They are not intended to suggest that the law should be defined functionally by its role in supporting social rules, for, as we have noted, many social rules do not need the support of law and many laws are introduced for reasons other than enhancing compliance.[22] Thus, for instance, while a law prohibiting murder *might* enhance compliance with an underlying social norm to that effect, it *need not*. It is possible that in some societies a social norm alone would have been just as effective at restraining would-be murderers, and that a law prohibiting murder has been added merely for symbolic or ideological reasons. Regardless of the actual functional role public coercion may or may not serve in practice or intention, the mere social fact that some public coercive agent will lend remedial support to a given social rule, together with common knowledge of this fact, is sufficient to constitute law.

3.1.3 Law Without Sanctions?

Sometimes, public coercive agents provide social rules relatively direct support. In such cases, the application of coercive force is near the surface, so to speak. Laws against resisting arrest might be an example: failures to comply with this rule are often met with immediate force. More commonly, however, the support provided is relatively indirect, insofar as many intermediate steps are required to get from a breach of law to the actual application of coercive force. In the

---

[21] For further discussion of the various levels of social convention in a complex legal system, see Postema 1982, pp. 182–194.

[22] See Green 1985, pp. 338–342, and 1999, pp. 47–49.

vast majority of cases, people voluntarily acquiesce in anticipation of this eventual outcome long before it arrives. It follows that relatively little overt public coercion may be observed in a reasonably well-functioning legal system. Nevertheless, I have argued, it is the ultimate availability of public coercion that transforms a mere system of social rules into law.

This brings us to an important and well-known objection, however. There are countless laws on the books in modern societies to which *no* penalties of any sort – not even indirect ones – seem to have been attached. For example, constitutions sometimes impose legal duties on high-level public officials without indicating sanctions for the specific failure to perform such duties.[23] The U.S. Constitution prohibits the Congress from passing an *ex post facto* law, but no punishment is indicated in the event that it attempts to do so. More interestingly, perhaps, a considerable part of the activity of modern national legislative assemblies consists in issuing broad directives to other government officials. A national assembly might issue a directive creating an agency for highway safety, for instance, and instruct that agency to reduce traffic accidents at a reasonable cost. Ordinarily, no explicit sanctions for non-compliance are attached to these directives.

The various complexities of administrative law will be discussed later, in Chapter 6. For the moment it will suffice to observe that sanctions are often not only *indirect*, but also *implied* rather than expressed. When the Congress directs the National Highway Traffic Safety Administration to pursue such-and-such a policy, the law expressing this directive may contain no explicit sanctions. But it would be a mistake to conclude that the law in question is not ultimately supported by the availability of public coercion. Suppose the agency failed to discharge its assigned task. Congress would then subject its directors to committee oversight. If those directors refuse to respond to the committee's summons, they would be served with a court order. If they refuse to comply with the court order, they would be held in contempt of court. And so on. Of course things never (or rarely) run to this extremity, because everyone anticipates what will happen at the end of the game tree. No doubt similar stories could be

---

[23] As noted by Raz 1999, p. 158, and Lamond 2001, p. 53.

told of recalcitrant, high-level public officials who can eventually be subject to impeachment for breach of their constitutional duties.[24]

There are however, more sophisticated versions of the objection. These start with the observation that people often guide their conduct by law for reasons that have little or nothing to do with a desire to avoid its sanctions. For example, if Congress decides that everyone should drive on the right, people may observe this rule simply because that decision provides a useful focal point for their coordination. If Congress decides to restrict smoking in public spaces, people may observe this rule because they take it as a signal that expert opinion has concluded smoking is bad for one's health. If Congress decides to punish sexual harassment in the workplace, people may observe this rule because it leads them to recognize for the first time that sexual harassment is inappropriate behavior.[25] Explicit sanctions may or may not be attached to such laws, but clearly those sanctions do not fully explain why many people choose to guide their behavior accordingly. This suggests that legal systems might have purposes more fundamental than lending remedial support to social rules. Among the most important of these more fundamental purposes, presumably, are clarifying expectations and motivating coordination. But then it seems sanctions cannot be a conceptually necessary part of law, for we can easily imagine an association of perfectly well-meaning and rational individuals who nevertheless need help coordinating their diverse activities. Contrary to Madison's famous dictum, even if men were angels, they would still need to decide which side of the road to drive on – it's just that sanctions would not be necessary to secure their compliance. Thus, while sanctions might be *practically* necessary for law, given the sort of imperfect creatures human beings generally are, they are not *conceptually* necessary, and thus are not a part of the correct definition of law.[26]

This more sophisticated version of the objection is correct to distinguish between what explains *compliance* with law and what *constitutes* law in the first place. Sometimes law depends heavily on public

---

[24] This last point does not apply, however, to those aspects of constitutional law describing a rule of recognition, as discussed subsequently.

[25] These sorts of "expressive" effects of law are explored in McAdams 2005.

[26] Versions of this argument, which can be traced to Aquinas, appear in Raz 1999, pp. 157–161; Finnis 1980, pp. 266–270; and Shapiro 2011, pp. 169–170. Cf. Hart 1994, pp. 198–200.

coercion to secure compliance, and other times hardly at all. In Chapter 2 we similarly noted that people observe social norms for a variety of reasons, and thus that the informal sanctions attached to such norms only in part explain the full extent of observed compliance. The same is true of laws, which people observe sometimes because they fear public coercion, sometimes because they fear informal social disapprobation, and sometimes because they have adopted certain rules of law as personal rules for themselves (i.e., they adopt an "internal point of view" toward such laws). Public coercion thus explains only some of the observed level of compliance.

But explaining the observed level of compliance is not, of course, our present aim. Our aim is rather to understand what constitutes law – what makes some particular social phenomena count as law and not something else. Unfortunately, the sophisticated objection proves too much. There is no question that even an association of perfectly well-meaning and rational individuals need to coordinate their diverse activities somehow or other. But to reiterate an earlier point, we should not confuse law with the functions it might contingently serve: surely not every possible means by which people might coordinate their activities must count as law. For example, people might coordinate by deferring, in every instance of uncertainty, to the arbitrary will of a respected community elder. Whether this is the *best* way to coordinate their activities or not, it is certainly a *possible* way. It is not, however, an example of what we would characteristically regard as law. Even if we exclude such examples on the grounds that, at the very least, a system of law must be a system of rules, we would still presumably want to distinguish among the various rule-based methods of coordination.[27] The social norm of waiting in line for service is a way of coordinating actions through the instrument of a rule, but surely it does not count, by that fact alone, as a law. What picks out those particular social rules as having the distinct experiential character of law, in my view, is the fact that they are lent remedial support by some public coercive agent through the use or threat of violence or physical restraint.[28]

---

[27] Many classic sociological and anthropological studies, such as Malinowski 1926 or Ehrlich 1913, failed to do this. For a parallel discussion, see Schauer 2010, pp. 14–17, who suggests that coercion may be what distinguishes a system of law from a system of morality.

[28] Note that the argument here should be distinguished from the claim that coercion is a necessary part of law because coercion is necessary for legal systems

Of course, it cannot be denied that there are often public pronouncements having the form of law which are not, and are never
intended to be, enforced. For example, there might be a "law"
describing the proper method for folding an American flag; there
might be a "law" stating that daylight savings time begins on such-
and-such a date each year; there might be a "law" stating that the
bald eagle is an official symbol of the United States; and so forth.
Despite having the form of law, no sanctions are attached to such
public pronouncements, nor is there any intention of punishing persons who refuse to comply with their terms. These pronouncements
certainly can have behavioral effect, but for something to have behavioral effect is not for that thing to count as a law in the strict sense.
Suppose that Congress failed to issue a pronouncement as to the start
of daylight savings time, but some minor private association of
farmers did. While people might start to take that association's pronouncement as a focal point for their coordination, it does not follow
that the pronouncement counts as law.

In the strict sense, then, what makes one particular social rule
and not another law is the common knowledge expectation that some
public coercive agent will ultimately lend remedial support to the
former and not the latter. While certainly not decisive, conventional
usage supports this view. One would not ordinarily accuse a
person of "breaking the law" if she folded an American flag incor-
rectly, or refused to reset her watch for daylight savings. By contrast,
consider a situation in which some law-making authority introduces a
new tax on large gifts, but delegates to an administrative agency
the task of assigning the corresponding sanctions. Even before the
latter does so, one might plausibly accuse a person of "breaking
the law" if she failed to report a large gift, but this is precisely because
we expect the new law to eventually be enforced. When this expectation is absent or unwarranted, there may be the form of law, but not
its real substance.[29]

---

to be practically effective. Lamond 2001, pp. 45–50, rightly points out that this
claim, even if correct, would establish only an empirical prerequisite of law,
not an aspect of its nature. Some important prerequisites of law are discussed in
the following section.

[29] Included in this view is the thought that old rules of law falling into disuse and
no longer enforced are not, properly speaking, laws; neither are rules announced by
a public coercive agent which that agent is known to be unable to enforce.

3.2 The Possibility of Law

At this juncture, two questions might have occurred to the reader. First, how are the boundaries of law determined as a matter of practice in actual communities? In other words, how do communities settle which social rules in particular will receive remedial support from a public coercive agent, and which will not? Second, do all human associations (or at least all of any size and complexity) have legal systems, or must some additional conditions or prerequisites be satisfied? Must the association, for example, be governed by a state?

Interestingly, it turns out that these two questions are very much related to one another. In order to answer them, I begin by sketching a "basic legal community" – an imagined human association that meets the minimal criteria for having a legal system. The point of this exercise is not to engage in speculative anthropology, nor is it to make any empirical claims about the historical origins of law. Although the examples discussed in this section are loosely based on the research of legal anthropologists and historians, they are strictly hypothetical.[30] The point is rather to better understand the distinctive character of those legal systems with which we are already familiar by clearing away some of their unnecessary or historically contingent features. Reflection on the basic legal community, it turns out, will help us understand how the boundary between law and ordinary social rules is determined in practice. Having thus answered our two questions, I will then discuss more elaborate legal systems by way of accounting for some of the peculiarities we observed in the introduction to this chapter.

3.2.1 The Basic Legal Community

Imagine a small community with no formal political or legal institutions or offices whatsoever. Whenever necessary, decisions affecting the group are made through a process of consensus-oriented deliberation in which the entire community has the opportunity to take more or less equal part. The day-to-day interactions of community members are governed by informal social rules, which include not only various

---

[30] I have been especially influenced by the work of Hoebel 1954, Berman 1983, and Watson 2001, among others.

coordination conventions, but also the usual sorts of social norms about respecting the integrity of persons and property, distributing benefits and burdens fairly, and so forth. None of these rules is written down anywhere, and for the most part they are sustained as equilibria through some combination of informal sanctioning and the adoption of personal rules. Suppose, however, that at least a few rules are regarded as so important (materially or symbolically) that their breach will be met with an organized coercive response from the community as a whole. For example, perhaps there is a rule prohibiting murder, the punishment for which is exile.[31] When there has been a killing, the community first discusses whether the killing amounts to murder (it was not an accident, say), and if it is determined that it does, the guilty party is then banished. Since there are no police to coercively enforce this judgment, it is merely implicit that the whole community will do so if necessary, though probably it will not be: the banished individual can hardly expect to prevail over the group as a whole if it comes to force.

On my analysis, this hypothetical community has at least one law – a law against murder – and ergo it has a legal system. (If it seems odd to describe a single law as a system, we will see shortly that a second social rule is already implicit in that system.) The community as a whole operates as a public coercive agent prepared to support the rule against murder with the use or threat of violence or physical restraint against any one of its members individually. Note that our hypothetical community does not have lawyers, police, judges, or indeed any other formal political or legal institutions or offices. Its laws are not written down in any books or documents. Most interesting, perhaps, it does not have a state as that concept is now usually understood: there is no formal political organization claiming a monopoly on the legitimate use of coercive force over a defined territory (if indeed the community has a defined territory).[32] It is perfectly consistent with

---

[31] Though every community has some social proscription against murder, not all legally prohibit every murder. The Eskimo discussed by Hoebel, for instance, permit occasional murders and revenge killings, drawing the line only when a single individual commits murder more than once. The punishment in the latter case is death. The Cheyenne, by contrast, punish any murder of a fellow Cheyenne with exile. See Hoebel 1954, pp. 88–89 and 157–160.

[32] In earlier work I assumed that the public coercive agent would be a state (see Lovett 2002, p. 52). The account presented here is better and more general.

our story to imagine that the private use of violence apart from murder is governed by informal social norms alone, and it is also possible that some or all of the members of our basic legal community simultaneously fall under the effective range of other, competing, public coercive agents.[33] Thus, contrary to some claims, neither having a state nor indeed any specialization in coercive labor is necessary to have a legal system.[34]

Now it may be objected that from an outside observer's point of view, it will be difficult to determine the precise line between those uses of coercive force that are public and those that are not. This is indeed true. It may sometimes also be difficult to determine, from the outside, the precise line between those social rules whose breach might be met with public coercive force and those that will not. It follows that, as outside observers, we may not always be able to state with precision where the boundaries of law lie. For reasons that will become clear in Chapter 4, these are not serious problems for my argument. (To anticipate, the relevant normative issue will not be whether a given social rule counts as a law, but rather whether a given application of public coercive force tracks a social rule or not.) But regardless, difficulties in defining precisely the boundaries of social phenomena in no way entail that those phenomena do not exist. It would be preposterous to suggest there was no French Revolution merely because we could not agree when it started or when it ended.

From an internal participant's point of view, however, these are a very serious issues indeed. Communities will often be faced with the question, "Does the breach of this particular rule warrant public sanction?" This is essentially equivalent to the question of what should count as law for that community, and there is no unique or universal answer to that question. It can only be answered pragmatically from within each community, and all communities having a legal system must necessarily have an implicit or explicit procedure or mechanism for effectively answering it. Despite the diversity thus entailed, can we

---

[33] In many of the primitive communities studied by Hoebel 1954, a certain range of private violence was permitted, or at any rate constrained only by informal social disapprobation. Competing public coercive agents will be discussed in the following section.

[34] Hadfield and Weingast 2014, pp. 32–33, are thus correct to argue that law does not require a centralized enforcement apparatus.

say anything theoretically interesting about the nature of that mechanism? Indeed we can.

Recall from earlier discussion that, in practice, every public coercive agent will have to be a group agent. In order to constitute a group agent, a set of individuals must solve two sorts of problems.[35] The first is the problem of coherently aggregating some of their diverse preferences – specifically, their preferences with respect to when the group should exercise coercive force and when it should not. Suppose some members of the group believe that every murder should be punished, but others only the murder of another group member; again, some members believe the appropriate punishment for murder should be exile, but others immediate execution; and so forth. If each operates under his or her own beliefs independently, their coercive efforts will be ineffectual. Only if they manage to reconcile their discordant beliefs in such a way as to produce a determinate group decision can they coordinate their coercive efforts *as a group*. This preference aggregation mechanism, whatever form it takes, is precisely the set of procedures for determining what is law in the subject community corresponding to the effective range of the relevant public coercive agent. In our hypothetical basic legal community, for example, the procedure is roughly consensus-oriented deliberation. But many other mechanisms can easily be imagined. In authoritarian political systems, the procedure might simply be to consult the will of a dictator; in theocratic states, it might be to reference some set of scriptural texts; and in modern democracies, it might involve undertaking a complex political process explicitly specified in constitutional documents.[36]

While there are a myriad of logically possible preference aggregation mechanisms, only a subset of these will be viable in practice. Here we run up against the second problem any set of individuals must solve in order to constitute a group agent: namely, internal free riding and other collective actions problems must be overcome so as to ensure that each of its members performs his or her part in carrying out the

[35] The following two problems are discussed in further detail by List and Pettit 2011 in chs. 2 and 5, respectively.

[36] Hadfield and Weingast 2014, p. 32, term this mechanism a "classification institution," which they say can be either "a person or an organization." This is not strictly correct: the mechanism is the *conventional social rule* to respect the determinations of some specific person or organization – or, for that matter, the rules set out in a foundational document.

group decision, whatever that happens to be. Put another way, the preference aggregation mechanism must be *incentive compatible*: expressed in game theory language, implementing the group's decision must constitute a sub-game perfect Nash equilibrium strategy for each of the relevant members of the public coercive agent.[37] In our hypothetical community, we might imagine that social approbation and disapprobation are sufficient to ensure that each member of the community does his or her part to enforce the law against murder. The public coercive agent in complex modern societies, by contrast, is typically a hierarchically ordered state apparatus in which lower-level officials can be internally coerced to perform their respective duties by higher-level officials. It is important to observe, however, that no group agent can rely *exclusively* on internal coercion to get the job done: at some level or other, the lines of authority must always devolve onto social rules. The inner core of a dictator's henchmen, at least, must observe a convention of following their dictator's commands.

Here indeed we arrive at an interesting result, for we have established as an existence condition for legal systems that there be a group agent whose members have as a social rule among themselves some incentive-compatible preference aggregation mechanism for coordinating their diverse coercive efforts over a subject community. Coincidentally, legal theorists and philosophers already have a name for this very special sort of social rule: it is called a *rule of recognition*.[38] In that literature, however, the rule of recognition is usually characterized somewhat differently, as a rule for conferring legal validity. For our purposes, let us say that a given rule or command is *legally valid* whenever it is common knowledge that a public coercive agent has an effective intention to support that rule or command. (Note that legal validity can extend to commands as well as rules, a point relevant for our discussion of the value of the rule of law in Chapter 4.[39]) Insofar as a rule of recognition describes the mechanism

---

[37] Here I use the expression "incentive compatible" in its broader sense, rather than in the narrower sense used by some economists and others. In the narrower sense, incentive compatibility requires that the equilibrium strategy of each participant involves truthfully revealing relevant private information, which is one aspect of incentive compatibility in the broader sense.

[38] Following Hart 1994, p. 94 and *passim*.

[39] In the United States the rule of recognition confers on the U.S. Supreme Court veto power over certain public coercive plans, in effect denying legal validity to

or procedure by which some public coercive agent actually manages to coordinate its coercive efforts, we can thus say that it operates, in effect, as a rule for conferring legal validity so defined.

Public coercive agents can, with a suitable communication of their intentions, easily generate common-knowledge expectations that they will support given rules or commands well in advance of any actual enforcement activity. In this sense, legal validity normally precedes the sanction. Given that we have defined laws as social rules supported by public coercion, this observation has the interesting further consequence that there can sometimes be a significant overhang, so to speak, in legal validity. Especially in the event of contested legal change, the enforcement activities of public coercive agents may for some time run well ahead of corresponding changes in the underlying pattern of observed social rules. In such cases, certain legally valid prescriptive rules will apparently not count as laws. Chapter 6 addresses this issue in more detail.

To conclude our exercise, let us summarize its results. We have found that law is not possible without a (formal or informal) rule of recognition. There need not be a state. There need not be judges, police, or lawyers. There need not be written or published law, nor indeed much else – provided there is an effective social rule that coordinates the activities of those individuals constituting the public coercive agent.[40] This claim is sometimes confused with the functionalist view that the point of law is to solve coordination problems. On the contrary, the rule of recognition is the solution to a coordination problem that must be solved if law is to exist in the first place. Law is the outcome, not the solution.[41] Furthermore, since the rule of recognition determines when and where public coercion will

those plans. Its failure to do so in *Korematsu* (see n. 10 above) thus confirmed the legal validity of the internment command.

[40] Note that it is unlikely the rule of recognition will be a pure and symmetric coordination convention as defined in Chapter 2. Postema 1982, building on Lewis 1969, inadvertently implied otherwise, thus generating much misdirected criticism such as Green 1999, pp. 41–43; Coleman 2001, pp. 94–98; Marmor 2001, pp. 7–10; and Shapiro 2011, pp. 105–110. Once Lewis-style conventions are understood to be only a special case, we can dispense with the various alternative devices to which these authors have resorted ("constitutive conventions," "shared cooperative activities," and so on) in properly characterizing the rule of recognition.

[41] Coleman 2001, pp. 92–94, also makes this point.

be brought to bear, and thus cannot itself ultimately be supported by public coercion, it is not itself a law on our definition. Modern societies often attempt to describe their rule of recognition explicitly, usually as part of a written constitution. While perhaps having the form of law, such provisions cannot be understood as law in the strict sense. This is not to say there are no important advantages to explicitly publishing the rule of recognition in the form of law, however, as we shall see.

3.2.2 Varieties of Legal Systems

The legal system of our hypothetical basic legal community described earlier had at least two parts: first, a rule of recognition, and second, a law against murder. Legal systems are thus not merely unordered sets of social rules, but specifically *hierarchically ordered networks* of social rules. Having a rule of recognition is a necessary condition for having a legal system; having a rule of recognition plus at least one legally valid prescriptive rule are together sufficient. This is why Hart famously described legal systems as consisting in the "union of primary and secondary rules."[42] The rule prohibiting murder is a primary rule, in that it governs human conduct directly, whereas the rule of recognition is a secondary rule about rules: in our terms, it is a social rule governing when and under what conditions some public coercive agent will lend remedial support to other rules.

Naturally, however, many advantages come with our having a system of law more elaborately developed than the basic one we have imagined. For example, it will often be beneficial for the rule of recognition to be explicitly published in the form of a written constitution.[43] This can have the advantage both of facilitating the coordination of those individuals constituting the public coercive agent, and also of clarifying the expectations of those individuals falling under its effective range. Likewise, legal systems will often benefit from a specialization of labor: hence we might have police, whose job it is to enforce rules of law; judges, whose job it is to resolve disputes concerning legal interpretation; legislative assemblies, whose job it is to

---

[42] Hart 1994, p. 79.
[43] Cf. Kelsen 1960, pp. 221–224, discussing the relationship between "formal" and "material" constitutions.

initiate and direct legal change; administrative agencies, whose job it is to implement the details of legislation; and so forth.

These two sorts of elaboration complement one another in modern constitutional democracies. In societies of any size and complexity it will not be feasible for everyone to exercise public coercion directly, and thus responsibilities for enforcing, interpreting, and changing the laws are delegated to specific legal and political institutions. Explicitly articulating the terms of that delegation in a written constitution helps ensure that those institutions are responsive to the aims of their designers by clarifying expectations and thus facilitating a coordinated response in the event that anyone deviate from the overall plan.[44] Of course, to say that political institutions and written constitutions have these benefits is not to *explain* either their existence or the particular character they assume in any given community. Some written constitutions might exist *because* people foresaw these benefits and deliberately introduced a written constitution to secure them, for example, but more convoluted historical paths are certainly possible, in which case these benefits are merely unintended but fortuitous outcomes. Regardless, it is beyond the scope of this study to explore the historical origins either of particular legal systems, or of legal systems in general. These remarks are intended only to suggest the possible effects of such devices, and thus possible reasons for wanting to have them.

As we have seen, however, legal systems can exist without written constitutions. They can also exist without organized police, judges, or legislatures. Historically speaking, many communities have relied on private individuals or the group as a whole to enforce legal rules. Among the Eskimo, for example, the punishment for repeated murder was death, but the job of carrying out this sentence was, if possible, delegated to a kinsman of the murderer.[45] Likewise, judicial functions might be exercised by the community as a whole, by official judges, or – as in the Roman system of private law – by private arbitrators.[46] Even formal legislative procedures can be done without, as for example in ancient Sparta where legal change was officially proscribed. Rules of

---

[44] See Weingast 1997 for a model of constitutional democracy along these lines.

[45] Hoebel 1954, p. 89. The rationale for this procedure was to remove any grounds for kinship revenge in response to the execution.

[46] Nicholas 1962, p. 27.

recognition need not specify procedures for legal change, though they often do (especially in modern societies).[47]

Once it is fully appreciated that these familiar features of modern legal systems are not in fact essential, but rather auxiliary additions, the puzzles with which we opened this chapter can more easily be explained. Suppose, for example, there is a society in which 'perform contracts made' is a social rule supported by public coercion. This fact alone means that the rule 'perform contracts made' counts as a law in that society, even if it is not written down in any official book of statute or code, and even if it was not formally adopted by any official legislative body. In time, however, some members of the community might desire greater clarification on the legal rules of contract. (Persons engaged in commerce might especially have such desires.) Responding to this demand, perhaps, some legislating authority in that community implements a series of statutes defining the formal elements of contract. These statutes might declare that a valid contract consists of offer, acceptance, and consideration, without saying more. Confusion about appropriate remedies then prompts a second bout of statutes clarifying when specific performance is required, what damages can be claimed, and so forth. It is easy to see how this process could produce something very much like the haphazard published statutes as we find them in the United States. It is entirely possible that this patchwork could become extremely detailed without there ever being an explicit statement of the underlying rule 'perform contracts made'.[48] Of course, other communities might take a different approach, attempting to spell out their entire legal system in a single comprehensive code. The result would be much like what we commonly refer to as civil law systems.

---

[47] In contrast with ancient Sparta, whose rule of recognition was embedded in an immutable set of fundamental social norms, the rule of recognition in modern Britain is roughly that acts of Parliament count as law. The United States, perhaps, falls between these examples: its rule of recognition might be seen as the amendment clause of the Constitution, plus the provision guaranteeing each state two senators. Schwartzberg 2009 argues against having immutable constitutional provisions.

[48] Interestingly, though Bentham's account of law as command of the sovereign differs from the one presented here, his strategy for analyzing published statutes and codes as fragments of complete laws is essentially the similar: see Bentham 1970, esp. ch. 14. Hart's 1994, pp. 27–42, objection that this strategy involves distortion seems to me unpersuasive.

Similar stories might be told about other confusing areas of law, such as family law, the law of corporations, or the law of slavery. Suppose that in some community there is a social rule dictating that third parties not interfere when a master beats his slave, and another dictating that slaves not leave the property of their master without explicit permission. Either or both of these social rules may come to be supported by public coercion, in which case they would count as laws. What gets articulated in the official statutes of the community, however, might largely be a detailed patchwork of clarifications and definitions, especially governing who counts as a slave, the conditions by which persons might enter or exit the condition of slavery, and so forth. The official statutes relating to families and corporations might bear an analogously indirect relationship to a variety of underlying social rules such as 'educate your children', 'respect the property of others', 'repay your debts', and so forth.

Thus in order to fully understand the nature of legal systems, it is essential to appreciate the often complex relationship between published legal texts, on the one hand, and the underlying social rules supported by public coercion, on the other. As a useful approximation, we might think of published legal texts as an "equilibrium manual."[49] Thus, while they can certainly *affect* what the law is – for instance, by creating or changing expectations regarding the incidence of public coercion – in an important sense those texts are not *themselves* the law. Properly speaking, the law is the underlying system of social rules.[50] To further test this conception of legal systems, let us examine some challenging examples.

(a) *Medieval law.* Earlier we noted that persons or groups might easily fall within the effective range of more than one public coercive agent. This was commonly the situation during the middle ages. There were few effective states in the medieval period, in the sense of a centralized organization monopolizing the use of violence within a defined geographic territory. Instead there were multiple public coercive agents with overlapping effective ranges. Each of these was capable of constituting its own legal system, and to some

---

[49] Maravall and Przeworski 2003, p. 5.

[50] Thus my view does not include what Greenberg 2014, p. 1296 and *passim*, calls the "standard picture" of law, according to which law's content is constituted by authoritative legal texts. In his language, roughly speaking, my account holds that law's content is constituted by the social (not moral) effects produced by the actions of legal institutions.

extent many did. Hence the confusing array of church law, feudal law, urban law, and so forth. Someone living in a free city of Northern Italy, say, might find herself sometimes subject to Imperial Law, sometimes to Canon Law, sometimes to the municipal law of her city, and sometimes to two or more of these simultaneously. Unified state law might be the paradigmatic form of law in the modern western experience, but it is by no means the only form of law, and indeed it may not be the best model for law in the future, if regional and international forms of law continue to develop as they recently have.[51]

(b) *Organized crime*. Transient criminal gangs do not challenge my conception, since by definition they do not constitute public coercive agents. But more fully organized crime syndicates, such as the American Mafia or the Japanese Yakuza, might seem more difficult. Certainly it can be common knowledge (at least within certain populations) that such syndicates have the effective capacity to exercise coercive force over others in an ongoing or sustainable manner. Of course, many if not most of their coercive activities will have neither the intention nor the effect of lending support to social rules. Suppose, however, there exists a clear social rule – 'never offend members of the syndicate', say – which the syndicate actively enforces with the use and threat of violence. On my theory, this social rule apparently counts as a law for those persons and groups falling within the syndicate's effective range. This may seem counter-intuitive, but it should not. Suppose the official government suddenly collapsed, leaving the syndicate unscathed. In this scenario, I think we should have no difficulty in recognizing any social rules enforced by the syndicate as, in effect, a system of law for the community of persons or groups it now governs: hence Kelsen's observation that a legal order is really just the order imposed by the most effective robber band in a given territory.[52] Our hesitation is probably due to our adverse moral judgments

---

[51] For a discussion of pre-modern medieval law, see Berman 1983; for a discussion of recent developments away from the model of unified state law, see Twining 2009. With respect to international law, see Chapter 7.

[52] Kelsen 1960, pp. 44–50. With important caveats to be discussed in Chapter 4, he is essentially correct. Note that any reference to the fact that social rules enforced by crime syndicates do not emanate from self-purportedly "legal" institutions is obviously circular.

regarding the rules enforced by such criminal organizations, on the one hand, and the usual asymmetry in long-run effectiveness between modern states and organized crime syndicates, on the other.

(c) *Customary law*. On one well-known traditional view, informal social rules or customs may become law when they are widely practiced in the *belief* that they have legal validity (the so-called *opinio necessitatis*), whether or not that belief is accurate. This view is not consistent with the conception of law developed here.[53] Legal validity on our earlier definition requires that some public coercive agent actually have the effective intention to support a given prescriptive rule. Since public coercive agents are necessarily group agents, such an intention can be generated only through the operation of an incentive-compatible preference aggregation mechanism (i.e., the rule of recognition). In its absence, there is no law, regardless of what people may or may not believe. Of course, an *opinio necessitatis* may lead people to informally sanction failures to observe a rule with special enthusiasm, in which case it might become a particularly robust social norm. But whatever the beliefs of the participants, so long as no public coercive agent will in fact lend support to a given prescriptive rule, it does not count as law in the strict sense. There are many cases historically, of course, in which public coercive agents have decided to begin enforcing preexisting social rules – sometimes in part because there is indeed an *opinio necessitatis* in the community – without explicit legislation. When this happens, we might speak of custom as having been a *source* of law, though not itself *being* law.[54]

3.3 Law and Authority

According to the classical positivists such as Hobbes, Bentham, and Austin, the law is constituted by patterns of habitual obedience in a population to the commands of a sovereign. Hardly anyone accepts

---

[53] I am grateful to Chad Flanders for helping me clarify this point. Note that here I am not discussing the rule of recognition itself, which may be customary in the sense of its being an unwritten rule.

[54] See Watson 2001, ch. 4, for an excellent discussion. Cf. Kelsen 1960, pp. 224–229.

this view today. Among many other difficulties, the command theory cannot explain the existence in many communities of effective formal and informal limits on the exercise of sovereign power, nor can it explain the continuity and persistence of legal systems when sovereign power passes from one person or group to the next. These two important criticisms were canonically presented by Hart, and they are together decisive against the classical view.[55] Modern legal positivism solves these problems by recognizing that legal systems are built on rules, not commands.[56] Consider, for instance, a rule designating Rex and his lineal descendants as the official legislator, subject to the constraint that he respects certain basic liberties. Using this rule as a coordination mechanism among themselves, a group of persons might constitute a public coercive agent over some population, enforcing only those laws issued by Rex and his descendants, and only to the extent that they are suitably liberty respecting. Such a rule of recognition will be effective provided it constitutes a (sub-game perfect) Nash equilibrium – provided, that is, no one of the individuals constituting the public coercive agent can do better deviating from the rule, given that the others are following it.

There was another difficulty Hart raised with the classical command theory, however, namely, that it cannot explain the normativity or authority of law. Hart expressed this problem as the difference between being *having an obligation* to do something, on the one hand, and merely *being obliged* to do something, on the other.[57] When the armed highwayman demands "your money or your life," you are naturally obliged to hand over your money, in the sense that you are compelled by his threat to do so, but we would not ordinarily say that you have an obligation to hand over your money, in the sense that you would be doing something blameworthy if bravely (albeit, perhaps, foolishly) you refused. Characteristically, we believe the law can have an authority the highwayman lacks – we believe, in other words, that the law can create genuine obligations. The extent to which any

---

[55] See Hart 1958, pp. 603–604; 1994, pp. 42–44, 51–71.

[56] In Lovett 2012, I argue that underlying the classical conception was a particular view about the nature of political order, and that in his critique of Hobbes, James Harrington to some extent anticipated Hart's move toward conventional social rules.

[57] Hart 1994, esp. pp. 82–91. For a critique of the distinction, see Schauer 2010, pp. 12–13.

particular legal system actually does have authority, of course, is a question properly addressed to normative political theory or philosophy, and is thus besides the point here. Nevertheless, it is an undeniable aspect of the descriptive phenomenology of law that people *experience* it as imposing obligations, and so it appropriately falls under the purview of any jurisprudential theory to provide an account of that experience.[58] While it is easy to see how the law can *oblige* its subjects on the classical positivist view of law as the coercive commands of a sovereign, it is not at all clear how it can ever *obligate* them on that theory.

Hart thought that replacing commands with social rules solved this third problem as well the first two. Social rules, he believed, can generate obligations in a way that mere commands cannot. Specifically, he observed that with some social rules, "the general demand for conformity is insistent and the social pressure brought to bear on those who deviate or threaten to deviate is great." This will be the case typically when a social rule is "believed necessary to the maintenance of social life" but also involves "sacrifice or renunciation" on the part of those individuals expected to comply with it. Obligation or duty, he argued, is thus properly understood as the emphatic demand to comply with an especially important social rule.[59] Since the social rules underwriting legal systems generally meet these conditions, the law accordingly generates obligations.

Hart subsequently hedged his argument in two ways.[60] First, he clarified that he only meant to give an account of some obligations, not an account of obligations in general. Only some types of obligations are generated by social rules. This correction was obviously necessary in light of the fact that we can clearly have moral, ethical, religious, or other obligations in the absence of any social rule: we probably have an obligation to give money to charity, for instance, even if hardly anyone does so. Second, Hart clarified that by social rules he did not mean what we have termed mere custom, but rather coordination conventions. Hart believed this second move necessary because, not having a more sophisticated version of the practice theory

---

[58] In order to do so, however, Hershovitz 2015 is quite correct that we need not posit the existence of some special domain of "legal obligations" distinct in any deep sense from ordinary obligations of the moral or prudential sort.

[59] Hart 1994, pp. 86–87.   [60] See esp. Hart's postscript, ibid., pp. 255–259.

of rules, it was not apparent to him how conventional practices other than coordination conventions could supply independent practical reasons (the mere fact that other football teams regularly punt on fourth down does not itself give any given team a reason to do so, etc.). This obstacle was removed in Chapter 2 with the addition of social norms to our conceptual repertoire.

Even with these clarifications, however, many regard Hart's attempt to explain the authority of law a failure.[61] Roughly speaking, the problem is as follows. For the sake of argument, let us grant that the emphatic demand to comply with an especially important social rule is sufficient to generate an obligation. Now according to the practice theory, social rules are constituted by the conventional practices of human behavior. It would seem to follow that conventional practices must, at least under certain conditions, be sufficient to generate obligations. But this is false. Consider a judge who is asked why she applies (from our earlier example) the liberty-respecting rules issued by Rex. She might reply, "Because it is my legal obligation as a judge in this community to apply the liberty-respecting rules issued by Rex." Or she might reply, "Because around here judges tend to apply the liberty-respecting rules issued by Rex, and I can do no better for my own part deviating from that convention." On Hart's view, the two statements can apparently be regarded as equivalent. Analogously, consider a citizen who is asked why he obeys the rules implemented by judges. He might reply, "Because it is my duty to obey the law." Or he might reply, "Because disobeying the rules generally implemented by judges will be worse for me." Again, the two statements can apparently be regarded as equivalent. Neither alleged equivalency rings true, however. When judges say they have an obligation to apply the law, and citizens a duty to obey it, they do not (usually) mean to say only that doing so is the general practice.

Hart's failure to explain the experience of legal authority is commonly thought to rest on his commitment to the practice theory of social rules.[62] Conventional practices of human behavior cannot generate obligations, so it is thought, and thus the practice theory cannot

---

[61] Versions of the following argument can be found in Dworkin 1977, pp. 50–54; 1986, pp. 135–139; Raz 1999, pp. 56–58; and Green 1999, pp. 43–52.

[62] Thus here we address the third objection to the practice theory postponed in Chapter 2. The discussion that follows, hopefully, improves on my earlier inadequate attempt to address the objection in Lovett 2002, pp. 50–51. It

account for the authority of law. This objection to the practice theory, however, is misguided. The problem lies not in the practice theory, but rather in Hart's peculiar phenomenology of obligation.

Considered descriptively, the social phenomenon of law has many different aspects, and a complete theory of the law (positivist or other) would presumably want to explain each of them, both separately and as a coherent whole. It need not follow, however, that the same explanation must be offered for every aspect, at least not provided the various explanations ultimately cohere. One interesting aspect of the law concerns its existence conditions: what must be true for a genuine legal system to exist? Another interesting aspect of the law concerns its authority: what accounts for the fact that we often experience law as imposing obligations? The practice theory, suitably revised, can explain the existence of law very well, I have argued. Legal systems exist, as we have seen, whenever the members of a group agent manage to coordinate their efforts in lending public coercive support to at least a few social rules. For these conditions to obtain – and, thus, for law to exist – it is sufficient that some rule of recognition form a sub-game perfect Nash equilibrium in the relevant group. Each of the members of this group is obliged to observe the rule insofar as none can do better for her own part deviating unilaterally. Having established the existence conditions of law, the practice theory of rules has served an important purpose, and we need not assume it must do more. As it happens, on my view, when it comes to explaining the authority of law, the practice theory serves in no more than an auxiliary role, as we shall see.

Let us return to our judge, who reports that she applies the law because she regards this as her obligation. When people say they have an obligation or duty to ϕ, they normally do not mean to say only that ϕ-ing is the general practice (and indeed, they cannot mean this in the case of unobserved moral rules). Put another way, when pressed on the source of their obligation, they normally refer to the reasons that in their view justify ϕ-ing, not to general practice of ϕ-ing (if there is one). In the language of this study, to experience obligation is to have adopted some prescriptive rule as personal rule for oneself.[63]

---

parallels, in some respects, the discussions in Marmor 2001, pp. 25–34, and Kutz 2001, pp. 452–453.

[63] Perhaps, as Hart suggested, a prescriptive rule one regards as especially important. It is not necessary for the argument here that we characterize "importance" in the relevant sense.

As noted in Chapter 2, there are many reasons for adopting personal rules. When it comes to legal obligation specifically, a number of plausible theories have been suggested. Among legal theorists and philosophers, one popular view is Raz's service account: we have good reasons to adopt rules of law as personal rules, he argues, to the extent that in obeying the law, we will tend to better discharge our various obligations as a whole than we would if we attempted to do so without its guidance.[64] Many other theories have also been proposed, however. Apart from traditional contractualist and utilitarian accounts, two other approaches have recently been much discussed: first, according to so-called fairness theories, we might have reasons to obey the law insofar as we have voluntarily accepted the benefits living under a system of law provides; second, according to various democratic theories, we might have reasons to obey the law insofar as we ought to respect the upshot of a democratic legislative process.[65] It is beyond the scope of discussion here to review the strength and weakness of these various theories. The main point is that when our judge reports she has "an obligation to apply the law," we should understand her as reporting that she has adopted the rule of recognition as a personal rule for herself, presumably on normative grounds such as the ones commonly discussed by legal and political philosophers.[66]

This explanation of the phenomenology of obligation is perfectly consistent with the practice theory of rules we have developed. Further, while not itself explaining the experience of obligation, the practice theory does have an important auxiliary role to play in that explanation. This is because some obligations arguably have the feature that they do not bind us *except* in the case where we have some assurance that others will observe them. Thomas Hobbes apparently believed this was a general feature of obligation:

---

[64] See Raz 1979, chs. 1–2; 1986, chs. 2–4; and 2009, ch. 5.

[65] The fairness theory was proposed by Hart 1955, pp. 185–186, and developed by Rawls 1971, pp. 111–114, 342–350; different versions of the democratic theory have been advanced by Waldron 1999b, chs. 5–6, and Estlund 2008, chs. 7–8. Note that, while obviously related, one's obligation to obey a law is not necessarily reducible to that law's substantive moral justification.

[66] Perry's 1995 critique of positivism on the grounds that it does not provide an answer to this question – whether we should adopt an internal point of view toward the law – thus seems to me besides the point.

The laws of nature oblige *in foro interno*; that is to say, they bind in a desire they should take place: but *in foro externo*; that is, to the putting them in act, not always. For he that should be modest, and tractable, and perform all he promises, in such time, and place, where no man else should do so, should but make himself a prey to others, and procure his own certain ruin, contrary to the ground of all laws of nature, which tend to nature's preservation.[67]

In this respect he was certainly wrong: it is hardly plausible to say we would have no obligation not to murder defenseless children for sport in the event that we did not expect others to observe such a rule. Nevertheless, it does seem likely that at least *some* obligations have this feature. In particular, certain types of legal obligation might.[68] The duty of a judge to observe the rule of recognition R plausibly derives from a conjunction of the fact that other judges can be expected to observe R, together with the best normative reasons for observing R, whatever these happen to be.[69] If so, then the practice theory helps us understand how one necessary condition for the authority of law can be met, even if it does not supply sufficient conditions for that authority.

3.4 Conclusion

Legal systems are hierarchically ordered networks of social rules. Individual laws within that system are social rules supported by a public coercive agent through the use or threat of violence or physical restraint. The existence and content of law, on this view, is strictly a matter of social fact – specifically, facts about the participation of persons and groups in certain conventional practices.

In the previous section, we observed that for various reasons, people might further elect to adopt rules of law as personal rules for themselves, in which case they will regard themselves as having legal obligations. Many Americans, for example, no doubt regard themselves as morally or ethically committed to the constitutional essentials underwriting the American legal system, and thus obligated to respect the laws of the United States. In our terms, these citizens have adopted an

---

[67] Hobbes 1651, I.14.36: p. 105.

[68] The discussion here might be productively compared with the detailed analysis in Greenberg 2014, pp. 1310–1319, of the many different ways in which the actions of legal officials can change our moral obligations.

[69] Cf. Kelsen 1960, pp. 211–214, arguing that effectiveness is a condition of legal validity.

internal point of view with respect to the law. This observation invites a question, however: does the viability of legal systems in general hinge on whether people do this or not? Must at least some high-level public officials, say, adopt the rule of recognition as a personal rule for themselves? If so, it would seem that the normative content of the rule of recognition might matter. It cannot just be any arbitrarily settled-on incentive compatible preference aggregation mechanism, for it must at least appear to have moral or ethical merits that resonate with those who would accept it.[70] Hart apparently believed that legal systems do indeed require at least some core public officials to adopt an internal point of view toward the law, though there is some confusion in his discussion.[71] But in fact they do not. It is important to reiterate, of course, that the rule of recognition cannot *itself* rely on the support of a public coercive agent, insofar as it is precisely the mechanism constituting that group agent. Nevertheless, it does not follow that the rule of recognition depends for its effectiveness on its being adopted as a personal rule by those observing it, any more than the rule of driving on the right does. This can be seen with the help of two illustrations.

Imagine a group of cynical officials who successfully impose a deeply unjust legal order on a population.[72] Let us consider this situation from the point of view of one of those officials. So long as she continues to observe the rule of recognition and thus participates in the unjust regime, she reaps many benefits of elite privilege. It is entirely possible to imagine that she, and indeed all the others as well, continue to observe the rule without believing it represents a just or legitimate legal order. They do not adopt the rule as a personal rule for themselves – as a rule they believe they have moral or ethical reasons for observing. Rather, they observe it simply in order to continue receiving the various advantages doing so will bestow. When they fail to respect the rule by accident, say, they might privately criticize themselves as having acted imprudently, but not as having acted wrongly.

---

[70] Versions of this thought can be found in Fuller 1958, pp. 638–643; Green 1999, pp. 40–41; Marmor 2001, p. 9; Coleman 2001, pp. 94–95; and Shapiro 2011, pp. 109–110.

[71] See Hart 1994, pp. 57–66. The confusion arises because he muddles the internal point of view with the practice conditions for social rules: he saw clearly that legal systems are not possible without social rules, but perhaps not that social rules are possible without the internal point of view.

[72] Cf. the discussion in Tamanaha 1997, pp. 134–135.

Table 3.2

		Henchman II	
		R	O
Henchman I	R	5, 5	– 10, 1
	O	1, – 10	1, 1

This first illustration may be complicated, however, by two factors. First, it is perhaps human nature that people tend to experience cognitive dissonance in such situations, and thus can be expected to develop ideologies purporting to justify the legal system from which they personally benefit. Once such an ideology is available, nothing prevents the formerly cynical officials from adopting an internal point of view toward the unjust legal order. No doubt their *believing* the legal order just, even if they are wrong about this, will lend greater stability or robustness to the system. Second, whether such ideologies develop or not, we might nevertheless regard the group of cynical officials as having a joint intention that they oppress the population for their own benefit. On a broader construal of the internal point of view, this might be seen to count as their each having adopted the rule as a personal rule for him- or herself: each takes the "point of view of the rule," so to speak, even if none of them regards the rule as having moral or ethical merit. Thus a second illustration might help.

Imagine a ruthless dictator and his cadre of henchmen. Each of these henchmen secretly hates the dictator, but does not know that the others hate him as well, and thus fears acting unilaterally against him. In game theory language, this scenario is often described as an assurance game (see Table 3.2). What each henchman fears most is precipitating an unsuccessful rebellion. Absent assurance that the other henchmen will support a rebellion, each adopts the less risky strategy of obedience.[73] Now suppose the dictator and his henchmen successfully impose a legal system on some subject community. In this situation, notice that the henchmen do not accept the rule of recognition ('obey the will of the dictator') as a personal rule for themselves. Further, it is

---

[73] This dilemma facing would-be conspirators against an unpopular ruler is cleverly analyzed by Machiavelli 1532, p. 73.

entirely possible that none of them intends the outcome of their joint activity: indeed, each may secretly abhor that outcome as not only unjust, but also as contrary to their own personal interest. Alas, fear holds everyone in line, inducing the henchmen to act together as a public coercive agent.

How robust or stable these sorts of arrangements are likely to be is an empirical question. One might suppose (though there is plenty of grim historical evidence to suggest otherwise) that legal systems in practice are more effective and durable when many people – both officials and citizens – regard the system as just and legitimate. Nevertheless, we must admit that a legal system need not rely on the moral or ethical commitments of its participants. It follows not only that unjust legal systems are possible, but indeed that legal systems *widely believed to be* unjust are possible. It is precisely an advantage of legal positivism that it helps us see this clearly. What is more, as we shall see, recognizing this fact is the essential starting point for building a viable defense of the rule of law. While this may seem counter-intuitive, it will I hope make sense after the discussion in Chapter 4.

4 | *The Rule of Law and Its Value*

In Chapter 3, I proposed that we think of legal systems as hierarchically ordered networks of social rules governing the use of coercive force. That discussion was simplified in several respects. For one thing, it offered no more than a vague account of legislation and legal process; even worse, it offered no account at all of legal uncertainty or disagreement. The image presented was of a perfectly serene equilibrium in which the laws never change, and their meaning is always clear. Obviously, legal systems in the real world are very different from this, and it is often precisely with respect to these differences that the plausibility of the rule of law as a normative ideal has been most strongly challenged.

Nevertheless, my strategy in what follows is to divide the argument for the rule of law into two parts or steps. First, in this chapter, I present the basic normative case for the rule of law, relying on the simplified image of a reasonably static and generally clear legal system presented in Chapter 3. Doing so will, I hope, illustrate as simply and forcefully as possible the important value of the rule of law. Then, in Part II, I turn to the challenges raised by legal dynamics, and try to show that our understanding of legal systems can be deepened and refined so as to address such challenges without detracting from the basic normative argument for the rule of law presented here. In Part II, I address such complex issues as legal disagreement and interpretation, legislation and legal change, administrative law, discretionary authority, and so forth.

4.1 Defining the Rule of Law

In order to consider whether and to what extent the rule of law has value, we must first of course know what the rule of law is – we must be able to identify it when we see it. As observed in Chapter 1, this is precisely why it is essential to adopt a positivist approach to the study of law. Defining the rule of law, however, is not so simple as perhaps one might expect. Consider, for example, the classic statement of A. V. Dicey. On his view, the rule of law exists where:

... no man is punishable or can be made to suffer in body or goods except for a distinct breach of law established in the ordinary legal manner before the ordinary courts of the land.[1]

This cannot be exactly right, however: people are "made to suffer in body or goods" all the time in modern societies. For example, whenever the tax code is modified, some people are advantaged and others disadvantaged; whenever workplace regulations are introduced or recast, costs and benefits among workers, employers, and consumers are redistributed; whenever the central bank raises or lowers interest rates, some investors gain and others lose; and so forth. In none of these examples do the burdens generated follow any "distinct breach of law" on the part of those specific individuals who must bear them. Surely these sorts of common government activities cannot thereby count as violations of the rule of law, however, or at any rate not of any conception of the rule of law that is going to be practically useful under modern political conditions.[2] But Dicey's expression is close to what I have in mind, as I will try to explain in what follows.

4.1.1 Methods of Coordination

It is obvious that there are enormous benefits to be gained from association with others – benefits from mutual assistance, from the division of labor, from exploiting diverse talents or abilities, and so forth. These benefits can only be secured, however, when people manage to coordinate their various efforts, and the mere promise of

---

[1] Dicey 1915, p. 110. In truth this is the first of three criteria indicated by Dicey, but the other two can be seen in retrospect to have described idiosyncratic features of English law in the late nineteenth century. For discussion, see Waldron 1989, pp. 79–81, or Craig 1997, pp. 470–474.

[2] Of course, if one wishes to condemn these commonplaces of modern political organization, as Hayek and others did, one can always define the rule of law so as to preclude them (see Tamanaha 2004, pp. 65–71). Since there is no truth in definition, we cannot say such critics are strictly speaking wrong to define the rule of law as they do, though we can question the pragmatic value of their having done so. These issues will be discussed further in Chapter 6.

benefit is not itself always sufficient to ensure that they will do so.[3] Successful coordination is not automatic. It requires, first, that each individual have reasonably clear expectations about what everyone is supposed to do; and second, that each individual be sufficiently motivated to perform his or her part in particular. Coordination can fail, therefore, through either a failure to clarify expectations, or a failure to sufficiently motivate cooperation, or both.[4] There are many reasons these failures might arise despite the promise of mutual benefit. Three in particular stand out.

The first is lack of information. Individuals might not be aware there are benefits to be had from coordination, or how those benefits might be obtained. Especially when it comes to economic planning, for example, the relevant information might simply be too vast and dispersed to be collected and properly understood by all the relevant actors.[5] Even in much simpler situations, however, merely not knowing one another's preferences can obstruct coordination. Recall the dilemma posed at the end of Chapter 3: a group of henchmen who all detest the dictator, but each without knowing that the others do. Even if it would be easy for them to depose the dictator working together, they might not succeed simply for want of confidence that the others will go along.

The second is disagreement. Even when individuals know each other's preferences, and know how benefits can be obtained through mutual cooperation, they might disagree about how that cooperation should be organized. Sometimes this will be because they have different goals or aims. A group of environmentalists might only succeed in influencing Congress, for example, provided they coordinate their lobbying efforts. Unfortunately, some believe they should all focus on wilderness preservation and others on preventing global climate change; alternatively, they agree to focus on wilderness preservation, but disagree on who should do the fund raising and who should write

---

[3] The functionalist fallacy discussed by Elster 1982 consists in assuming that establishing the benefits of coordination is sufficient to explain successful coordination. Valid functionalist explanations are possible, of course, but only with the addition of a selection mechanism.

[4] See Elster 1989, esp. pp. 1–15 and *passim*. Note that the conditions for securing associational benefits are weaker than the conditions of group agency (discussed in Chapter 3). This is because coordination as such does not always require preference aggregation.

[5] This was famously argued in Hayek 1960, esp. ch. 2.

the policy recommendations. Disagreements can also arise concerning how to divide the benefits of cooperation. Even supposing the dictator's henchmen manage to communicate their mutual preferences to one another, they might fail to organize a coup because they cannot agree who among them should become the new ruler.

The third is incentive failure. Sometimes, even when we know about the mutual benefits of coordination, and agree how that coordination should be organized, we fail through the lack of sufficient incentive. This problem commonly arises when there are externalities to the actions of individuals. Imagine a group of workers who can secure better terms of employment if they present a united front to their employer. Unfortunately, so long as the other workers remain on strike, it is in the interest of each individual worker to go back to work, since the benefit of doing so accrues entirely to the lone defector, whereas the cost is shared by all. Likewise, even if we all know that reducing pollution is necessary, and even if we all agree how to distribute the cost of that reduction, there still remains the problem of ensuring that each does his or her particular part.

In order to secure the benefits of association, then, these and perhaps other challenges must be overcome: mutual expectations must be clarified, and cooperation sufficiently motivated. Fortunately, many methods are available for this purpose. Here we might consider four in particular.

(1) *Method of authority.* Designate one individual as chief, or settle on a comprehensive hierarchical ranking among the members of the group. Whenever there is disagreement as to what should be done, the will of the more authoritative person governs. If two parties to a dispute have the same rank, their dispute is settled by some mutual superior.

(2) *Method of deliberation.* Regard members of the group as equals. Whenever there is disagreement as to what should be done, everyone gathers together and debates the merits of the different points of view. After deliberation has run its course, consensus (if reached) or the will of the majority governs.

(3) *Method of bargaining.* Suppose that property rights are initially settled. Whenever there are some questions as to what should be done, the interested parties engage in bargaining, each having veto power over the outcome. Generally, the preference of the party

willing to pay most determines the outcome, though often with side-payment to the others.

(4) *Method of convention.* Regarding certain recurring scenarios of possible coordination, set out a schedule of rules in advance. Whenever there is disagreement, the outcome is determined with reference to the expectations most naturally implied by those rules.

Now it is important to observe here that, at their base, each of these methods must depend ultimately on conventional social rules. Consider the method of authority, for instance. Given that even the strongest human being could not indefinitely impose his will on many others through physical force alone, institutionalized authority depends on the observance of a convention: a group of henchmen must agree to regard the will of their designated leader as authoritative. The methods of deliberation and bargaining similarly rest on underlying conventions concerning deliberative procedures and property rights, respectively. What distinguishes the methods from one another is thus the *character* of their respective underlying conventions. Coordination will be organized differently – and thus will be experienced differently by the coordinating parties – under the auspices of a convention of authority then under a convention of bargaining, and so forth.

Which method is best? It should be obvious that there is no general answer to this question. Some methods are better for some sorts of problems and situations, others are better for other sorts of problems and situations. Often, they work best in combination, and thus it is not surprising that many examples of each can be found in various domains of all reasonably complex societies. In coordinating our various economic activities, for example, experience suggests that the method of bargaining often performs better than the alternatives: decentralized bargaining efficiently aggregates dispersed economic information and reconciles disparate individual incentives. Bargaining is less reliable, however, when it comes to supplying public goods or resolving distributive disagreements fairly. The method of convention is ideal for establishing clear and stable expectations, such as which side of the road to drive on. Relying on this method exclusively, however, would inhibit change in response to new circumstances or ideas. Feudal social norms, for instance, retained their hold long after they ceased to be pragmatically or normatively justifiable. Which method is best clearly depends on the circumstances.

4.1.2 Coordination and Coercion

Among the more important issues facing any association of human beings must be how to govern the use of coercive force – specifically, who may employ it, to what extent, and on which occasions. In the absence of clear expectations concerning when we are likely to experience the use or threat of violence or physical restraint, hardly any of the other benefits of human association are possible. When people "live without other security, than what their own strength, and their own invention shall furnish," Hobbes famously observed,

> ... there is no place for industry; because the fruit thereof is uncertain: and consequently no culture of the earth; no navigation, nor use of the commodities that may be imported by sea; no commodious building; no instruments of moving, and removing such things as require much force; no knowledge of the face of the earth; no account of time; no arts; no letters; no society; and which is worst of all, continual fear, and danger of violent death. ... [6]

It is thus crucially important that we establish guidelines concerning the use of coercive force, and sufficiently motivate the relevant individuals to respect those guidelines. Any of the methods suggested above, either singly or in combination, might be pressed into service for this purpose.

In totalitarian political systems, for example, coercive force is largely governed by the method of authority – an unfortunate scenario all too familiar from historical experience. (Hobbes erroneously believed this was, fundamentally, the *only* possible way to govern the use of coercive force.) The method of deliberation and the method of bargaining are, by comparison, less often used for this purpose. In its pure form, the former would look like this: whenever there is a question as to whether the application of coercive force is warranted, the people assemble, deliberate, and vote. The citizen juries of ancient Athens look something like this – though not exactly, since what they took themselves to be doing was applying prior laws or norms: the issue was always whether this particular individual had violated the rules, and if so, what coercive punishment was appropriate. If their debates were not like this, but rather a series of case-by-case decisions unconstrained by any prior rules, we would have a pure form of the method of

---

[6] Hobbes 1651, I.13.9: p. 85.

deliberation. Following the method of bargaining, coercive services would be available on a pay-as-you go basis. This method, to my knowledge, has never been tried, even in approximation (except, perhaps, to some extent in the world of organized crime).[7]

So what is the rule of law? Roughly speaking, it is the successful restriction or limitation of the use of coercive force by all persons, groups, or organizations in society to the method of convention. This rough idea must be given greater precision, however. Recall from Chapter 3 that laws should be understood as social rules provided direct or indirect support by a public coercive agent, and legal validity as the common knowledge expectation that some public coercive agent will indeed support a given rule or command. We may thus more precisely define the rule of law in a given society as the extent or degree to which no individual in that society will be exposed to coercive force (at the hand of any other person, group, or organization) except as the consequence of her having failed to observe some legally valid prescriptive rule. Notice that what counts on this definition is the actual felt experience of individuals potentially exposed to the use or threat of violence or physical restraint.

It should be apparent that achieving the rule of law, so defined, will typically have two important dimensions. The first involves successfully restricting the use of coercive force – whether justified or not – to public coercive agents alone. Historically, the various challenges societies face in accomplishing this feat have been discussed as the *problem of social order*. For better or worse, the solution generally settled on in the modern era has been the creation of territorial states with internal monopolies on the legitimate use of violence.[8] Alternative arrangements might be consistent with the rule of law, however. Legal pluralism, for instance – the coexistence in a given population of multiple legal systems, underwritten by distinct public coercive agents – poses

---

[7] Similarly, in societies with rampant corruption, people may be able to evade public coercion – and perhaps sometimes direct it toward others – through bribery.

[8] Anarchists, of course, contend that this is a bad solution. They disagree, however, on how the use of coercive force by individuals should instead be governed: moderate anarchists might permit the instrument of law, so long as it is not state law, while radical anarchists might insist that there be no public coercive agents at all. In my terms, the latter would entail relying on vigilantism (as defined in Chapter 3) to govern the use of coercive force.

no theoretical challenge to the rule of law as here defined, though of course it may pose any number of practical difficulties.

The second dimension involves successfully limiting the coercive activities of public coercive agents to the enforcement of rules. Presumably, some of these rules will be themselves designed to solve the problem of social order (rules such as 'don't commit assault', for instance), while others will not (rules such as 'perform contracts made', for instance). The various challenges societies face in accomplishing this second feat might be loosely termed the *problem of constitutionalism*, where this expression is understood in its traditional sense of imposing legal limits on government authority. Of course, states and other public coercive agents often engage in a variety of non-coercive activities as well: they establish national currencies, conduct scientific and medical research, manage public properties, and so on. Whether and how our conception of the rule of law should extend to cover these latter sorts of activities is an interesting issue, addressed in Chapter 6. For the present, however, we can safely say that the rule of law should *at least* cover all potential uses of coercive force.

Remarkably, many contemporary authors ignore the first aspect of the rule of law. The most explicit in doing so is Raz, who states that "the rule of law is designed to minimize the danger created by the law itself," but it is equally true of many other accounts as well.[9] When we ignore the first aspect of the rule of law, however, we significantly underestimate its full value, as will be clear subsequently. Only societies that have solved, in some reasonable measure, both the problem of social order and the problem of constitutionalism enjoy, to that extent, the rule of law. We need not define some specific threshold of success here, provided we plausibly establish that having the rule of law in some degree is itself a good and that, other things being equal, having more of it is better than having less.[10] Other things are not always equal, of course, as we shall later see.

A legal system, we have said, is a hierarchically ordered network of social rules. As such, it is a complex bundle of public practices for clarifying expectations and motivating cooperation largely through what was above described as the method of convention. This fact lends

---

[9] Raz 1979, p. 224. Others who focus exclusively on controlling public coercion include Fuller 1969 and Dworkin 1985, ch. 1. Gowder 2013, pp. 569–570, at least attempts to defend this focus.

[10] For a discussion of how the rule of law might be measured, see Appendix B.

the social phenomenon of law a particular character distinct from, say, the practices of market exchange, or the practices of democratic politics, which rely more heavily on other methods. Traditionally, the rule *of* law was thought mean the rule *by* law and not by other means – or in Harrington's words, an "empire of laws and not of men."[11] To be sure, these traditional expressions can be interpreted (unhelpfully) as the mere formal requirement that every use of coercive force be given official legal authorization – a stamp of legal approval, so to speak. This view will be discussed in the following section. Here I will observe only that such an interpretation largely misses the main intuition the traditional authors were trying to express: read more charitably, in my view, they were trying to describe a society in which the use of coercive force is successfully governed by the method of convention.[12]

The rule of law can also be expressed as a normative ideal. From this point of view, it is simply the claim that it is *best* for the use of coercive force to be, in most cases, governed by the method of convention. To restate the spirit of Dicey's expression quoted earlier, no person should ever be exposed to the use or threat of violence or physical restraint on the part of other persons, groups, or organizations, except as a consequence of her having failed to observe some legally valid prescriptive rule. This central normative claim, which I aim to defend in this chapter, should not be confused with two other, rather different claims. First, the claim that *all* human coordination should be organized according to the method of convention. This is neither desirable nor feasible. Second, the claim that all social rules should be given the force of law (or, more weakly, that every social rule should *either* be given the force of law or else abandoned). These latter claims are also implausible, and I make no attempt to defend either.

4.1.3 *Competing Conceptions of the Rule of Law*

Whatever else might be said for or against it, a conception of the rule of law should be useful: it should at least be capable of making a practical difference. In Chapter 1, I suggested a number of ways conceptions might fail in this regard. Here it is perhaps worth briefly scoring the

[11] Harrington 1656, p. 161.
[12] With respect to Harrington, at any rate, I defend this reading in Lovett 2012.

definition offered above as against some alternatives, with respect to this pragmatic criterion.

Recall that one way a theory of the rule of law might fail is if it sets goals or aims that are impossible to achieve. Many doubts regarding the feasibility of a genuine rule of law arise when *the law* is confused with *published legal texts*, a confusion addressed in Chapter 3.[13] Having there defined law as merely a special sort of social rule, it should be clear that the feasibility of a genuine rule of law is no more or less mysterious than the feasibility of social rules generally. It would be naïve to assume that all such doubts have thus been settled, however, particularly when it comes to the existence of legal disagreement and the need for interpretation. The final resolution of such doubts, therefore, must wait on the discussion of legal dynamics in Part II.

But two other possible pragmatic failures can be addressed here. First, a conception of the rule of law will fail to make a difference if it is *too easily* achieved – in other words, if we cannot help but achieve the rule of law no matter what we do. Surprisingly, some well-known conceptions fail in precisely this way, most notably that of Hans Kelsen. Since his understanding of law is in other respects similar to mine, it will be especially instructive to compare our views. In order to do so, however, we must first carefully distinguish three different senses in which one might describe the use of coercive force as being "governed by law."

In the broadest sense, we might say the use of coercive force is governed by law just in case it has been *legally authorized*: in other words, whether exercised by a public coercive agent or a private citizen, it has been granted a stamp of legal approval. Imagine a community, for instance, in which the law explicitly permits blood revenge, provided that it is not excessive, and punishes individuals only when they commit murder repeatedly.[14] In this community, since revenge killings and isolated acts of murder are legally authorized, they might in a very broad sense be described as law-governed uses of coercive force. By contrast, we might instead say the use of coercive force is governed by law just in case it is *legally valid*. Imagine a

---

[13] Such a confusion is evident in the skeptical remarks of Maravall and Przeworski 2003, pp. 1–4, for instance. Note that here I am remarking only on feasibility of maintaining the rule of law once introduced, not on the likelihood of its being introduced. The latter will be discussed subsequently.

[14] This is roughly the situation in the Eskimo communities discussed by Hoebel 1954, pp. 88–89.

community in which the government commands that the members of some ethnic group be interned, as happened with Japanese-Americans during the Second World War. Especially once the Supreme Court acceded to this policy, it was common knowledge that the internment command would be enforced by a public coercive agent (the United States government).[15] Since the internment command was legally valid as defined in Chapter 3, we might describe it in a somewhat narrower sense as a law-governed use of coercive force. While all legally valid uses of coercive force are legally authorized, not all legally authorized uses of coercion are legally valid: only rules and commands supported by a public coercive agent can be legally valid, whereas any use of coercive force by any person or group can in principle be legally authorized. Finally, in a narrower sense still, we might say coercive force is governed by law just in case its use is strictly limited to the enforcement of laws – where "laws" are understood specifically as those social rules known to be supported, directly or indirectly, by a public coercive agent. So defined, *law-governed* uses of coercive force will always be legally valid (and legally authorized), but not all legally valid (or legally authorized) uses of coercive force will be law-governed.

Now in the light of these distinctions, what is the best way to understand the rule of law? On my view, as described in the previous section, we should define the rule of law as requiring that any use of coercive force be strictly law-governed, and not merely legally valid or legally authorized. What matters on my view is the actual felt experience of those persons potentially exposed to the use or threat of violence or physical restraint: for the rule of law to be satisfied in any given context, public or private, there must be some law the observance of which would permit individuals to reliably avoid being subject to violence or physical restraint. However, there is no truth in definitions per se. Nothing logically or conceptually prevents us from defining the rule of law in terms of either legal validity or legal authorization. In selecting among these possibilities, the relevant considerations are thus pragmatic: first, we do not want to stray too far from common language and understanding, and second, we want our conception of the rule of law to be useful. Let us consider, therefore, whether there is anything to be said in favor of the two alternatives to my view.

[15] *Korematsu v. United States*, 323 U.S. 214 (1944).

Obviously, there is little advantage to characterizing the rule of law in terms of mere legal authorization. This is not to say the concept of legal authorization as such is entirely worthless: presumably, there is some utility in our being able to distinguish those uses of coercive force which are authorized by law from those which are not (violent crime, for instance). But if we define the rule of law as requiring only that every use of coercive force by any person, group, or organization be legally authorized, it will be trivially easy to achieve. To meet this standard, one need only extend legal authorization to every sort of coercion one is unable, or else one does not wish, to regulate. Consider the violence and physical restraint exercised by masters over their slaves or husbands over their wives and children. In many societies such uses of coercive force were indeed legally authorized: not only did the law explicitly permit masters and husbands to employ a considerable degree of coercive force at their personal discretion, in some cases it specifically prohibited others from interfering with that discretion. But it is difficult to see how this should matter very much, normatively speaking. Certainly, in terms of the actual felt experience of the slaves, wives, and children thus exposed to the use or threat of violence or physical restraint, it mattered very little indeed.

What about characterizing the rule of law in terms of legal validity? Interestingly, this turns out to be the view of Kelsen. Roughly speaking, he defines a legal system as the coercive social order imposed by the most powerful organization in a given territory – i.e., in most contemporary instances, the state. By social order he means roughly the network of social rules and commands regulating human behavior through the instrument of formal and informal sanctions.[16] On its face, this understanding of law is similar to the one offered in Chapter 3. But Kelsen draws from it a very different conception of the rule of law. He observes that any use of coercive force by a public official counts as an act of the state only insofar as it is officially sanctioned by the law of that state. For example, the police in our society are authorized to arrest individuals when they are suspected of crime, but not simply when they are members of a minority ethnic group. Thus if Andrea attempts to arrest Bob without due cause, he will soon be released, and Andrea's action will not officially be attributed to the state. It follows, Kelsen argues, that:

---

[16] See Kelsen 1960, pp. 22–58.

A state not governed by law is unthinkable; for the state only exists in acts of state, and these are acts performed by individuals and attributed to the state as a juristic person. Such attribution is possible only on the basis of legal norms which specifically determine these acts.

In other words, the state cannot violate the rule of law, for whatever activities it decides to undertake will necessarily count thereby as legally valid: since "the state is comprehended as a legal order," it follows that "every state is a state governed by law." If the police start arresting the members of some ethnic group as a matter of state-sanctioned policy, these activities will count as legally valid, and thus conform to the rule of law. On this view, the rule of law is indeed, as Kelsen says, "a pleonasm."[17]

Needless to say, my view is rather different: insofar as the members of the ethnic group are exposed to coercive force for something other than their failure to observe a public rule, the actions of the police represent a violation of the rule of law on the conception described in the previous section.[18] Which view is better? Again, there is presumably some utility in our being able to distinguish between those uses of coercive force which are legally valid from those which are not – in knowing when commands, for instance, will be enforced by the state and when not.[19] But consider the Reichstag's Enabling Act of 1933, which granted the Nazi government legal authority to rule by decree, even in violation of the German Constitution: since every subsequent act of that regime was thereby granted formal legal validity, it would seem on Kelsen's view that the Nazi regime conformed to the rule of law. Simply in terms of common language, this is surely rather distant from our usual understanding of the rule of law! Such a view was emphatically rejected by Lon Fuller, for instance, among many others.[20] More importantly, any conception that characterizes the rule

[17] Ibid., pp. 312–313.

[18] From the perspective of the police, of course, there may not be a rule of law violation on my view: suppose, for example, they are expected to conform to the rule 'arrest all individuals in ethnic group *G*', and they know they will be subject to coercive sanction if they do not. This counts as a law *for them*, but not for those individuals subject to arrest.

[19] Vinx 2007 attempts to further explain Kelsen's reasons for characterizing the rule of law as he did: roughly, he believed that narrower conceptions (like mine) obscure the moral dilemma citizens must face in deciding whether to accept the legitimacy of their legal system.

[20] See esp. Fuller 1958, pp. 644–661; 1969, pp. 40–41, 54–55, 153–159.

of law in terms of mere legal validity would be far too easy to achieve, and would thus fail to make a practical difference. There is little point in our arguing for the rule of law if, for all practical purposes, states cannot help but respect it.[21]

The second possible pragmatic failure we can address at this juncture is more subtle than the first. In Chapter 1, I discussed how many contemporary conceptions of the rule of law describe it as a cluster of "principles of legality" which legal systems can exhibit to greater or lesser degrees. As we observed in that earlier discussion, there is little agreement on the precise list, though usually it is assumed to include such things as generality, prospectivity, internal coherence, and so forth. The difficulty with such list-based conceptions is that the principles of legality seem limited in value when interpreted formally, and redundant when interpreted substantively. Either way, an argument that the rule of law is a good thing would turn out not to make much a practical difference.

By now it should be clear that our theory of the rule of law charts a very different course. Principles of legality will serve as the conclusion to our argument, rather than its starting point. The rule *of* law is here understood as the rule *by* law, whether that law be good, bad, or indifferent. On the one hand, since all uses of coercive force by public or private agents can potentially be controlled or regulated by law in the relevant sense, the scope of our theory is not limited in the manner of the formal list-based conceptions. This has been shown in the discussion up to this point. On the other hand, since we have developed our conception of law within a legal positivist framework, our theory is not simply a view about social justice in disguise in the manner of substantive list-based conceptions. On the positivist view, laws do not necessarily possess any normative merits. It thus most emphatically remains to be shown where the value of being ruled by law lies, and that is precisely what we discuss next.

4.2 Value of the Rule of Law

Imagine that for various historical, economic, and cultural reasons, one group in some society manages to acquire a preponderance of

---

[21] Remarkably, the Nazi regime failed to respect even its own Enabling Act on a number of occasions, but this does not detract from the main point.

social power, which it wields over the members of other groups in that society directly and without constraint, much to its own benefit. Since the subordinate groups are in no position to challenge the preeminence of the powerful group, they humbly ask only that the various rights and privileges of the latter be written down, codified, and impartially enforced by independent judges. In short, without challenging the right of the powerful group to rule, they ask only that it rule *by law*. Though not in any way obliged to do so, let us suppose that in time the powerful group accedes to the request, perhaps on the view that since the laws can be designed to benefit them after all, the change will bring no significant costs, and indeed some practical advantages.[22] Now let us ask, is this an improvement for the members of the subordinate groups?

From one point of view, it seems obvious that it is not. The new laws unfairly advantage the powerful group, having been designed by them precisely toward that end. Even assuming that members of the powerful group strictly adhere to the laws they introduce, we are still very far from imagining a fully just society, or even a merely legitimate one. Nevertheless, the situation has changed in one very important respect: to the extent that the new laws *are* respected, members of the subordinate groups now at least know exactly where they stand. They can develop plans for their lives based on reliable expectations. Provided they respect the law, they need not go out of their way to curry favor with members of the powerful group. In a helpful metaphor promoted by Jeffrey Kahn, the "law is a causeway upon which, so long as he keeps to it, a citizen may walk safely."[23] These are genuine experiential differences, in my view. Intuitively, it seems they should matter. In this section, my aim is to explain why in fact they do.

4.2.1 Domination and the Rule of Law

One way to express the experiential difference in our imagined society after the introduction of law is to say that the members of the subordinate groups now enjoy some greater degree of *freedom from domination*. Let us say, roughly speaking, that persons or groups experience

[22] Some argue there will be significant costs, in the sense that the rule of law tends to undermine oppressive regimes in the long run. This possibility is discussed subsequently.

[23] Kahn 2006, p. 354 (quoting a passage in Robert Bolt's *A Man for All Seasons*).

domination to the extent that they are dependent on other persons or groups who wield uncontrolled or arbitrary power over them.[24] Though not without puzzles and complexities of their own, I will here take it as reasonably clear what it means for one person or group to be dependent on another, and also what it means for one person or group to wield power over another, so as to concentrate on the specific issue of arbitrariness.[25] Let us say that power is uncontrolled or *arbitrary* to the extent that its exercise is not subject to effective and reliable constraints that are common knowledge to all persons or groups concerned. Roughly speaking, in other words, the more the use of power is constrained, the less arbitrary it is, and vice versa. Several aspects of this definition will no doubt benefit from further elaboration.

First, we should understand *constraints* in the relevant sense rather broadly so as to include not only rules of the familiar bright-line sort (such as, 'take two pills each day'), but also looser standards ('take pills as needed') or even procedures ('consult a doctor before taking pills') under the right conditions. Provided people have or could develop a shared understanding of which paths of action count as conforming to the constraint and which paths of action do not, any sort of constraint will do for the purpose of reducing arbitrariness.[26]

Second, however, whatever particular form a given constraint on power happens to take, it must be *effective* – meaning that it must actually constrain how that power is used in practice. Formally, we might say that a constraint ϕ is effective with respect to some power A holds over B if the probability p that A will in fact wield that power over B according to ϕ is relatively high. Merely aspirational or ideological principles are thus not effective, unless of course we have good reason to believe that they will be respected with a high degree of probability.

Third and finally, a given constraint will not actually reduce arbitrariness unless or until it is *reliable*, as well as merely effective. Suppose a slave master chooses not to exercise the full measure of power granted him under the institution of slavery – perhaps out of a sense of paternalistic obligation, or merely because he happens to be a

---

[24] This definition is similar in spirit to the definitions found in Pettit 1997, pp. 52–58 and 2012, pp. 49–69; Viroli 2002, pp. 35–37; Maynor 2003, pp. 37–39; and others. Lovett 2010, esp. chs. 2–4, aims to develop the definition in detail.

[25] But see Lovett 2010, pp. 38–40 and 74–78, respectively, for analysis.

[26] Chapter 6 discusses bright-line rules, standards, and procedures in greater detail.

nice person. Given his contingent preferences and dispositions, it might be highly probable (i.e., the value of p will approach 1) that he will wield his powers within certain bounds. Nevertheless, those psychological constraints are not *reliable* so long as they remain wholly dependent on his contingent preferences and dispositions remaining as they presently are. Formally, we might say that some constraint ϕ is reliable only if the probability p that it will be respected remains high across a suitably wide range of nearby possible worlds.[27] This is evidently not the case with our kindly slave master: he might attend a meeting in which the humanity of slaves is denied by persuasive speakers; or his slave's familiarity might rub him the wrong way one morning; and so forth. Such events could easily alter his preferences and dispositions in such a way that his self-restraint evaporates.

It is terribly wrong for persons or groups to be subject to arbitrary power or domination when this can be avoided. Indeed, we might say that social justice requires organizing the basic structure of society so as to minimize domination, so far as this is feasible. Without rehearsing arguments that can be found elsewhere, I would suggest that this is because possessing some degree of freedom from domination is an important condition of human flourishing: when subject to domination, people are materially exploited, hindered by uncertainty from developing life plans, and deprived of self-respect.[28] Each of these claims certainly deserves further elaboration and defense, but for present purposes we may set such a task aside so long as we agree that freedom from domination is an important human good worthy of public promotion.[29]

Domination can take many forms, but one that is particularly worrisome arises when some persons or groups possess the uncontrolled ability to wield coercive force over others. It is precisely this sort of domination that is reduced to the extent that a society enjoys the rule

---

[27] This formal characterization of the distinction between effectiveness and reliability was inspired by the discussions in List 2006, pp. 209–212, and Pettit 2008, pp. 216–220.

[28] For further discussion, however, see Pettit 1997, pp. 85–89; Laborde 2009, pp. 152–156; or Lovett 2010, pp. 130–134.

[29] The importance of freedom from domination has been urged by many contemporary civic republican authors such as Pettit 1997, Skinner 1998, Viroli 2002, and Maynor 2003. However, with the more recent partial exception of Pettit 2012, ch. 2, these authors do not generally express this thought by linking freedom from domination to social justice explicitly as I do: see Lovett 2010, esp. pp. 159–179, 187–189.

of law as we have defined it.[30] To see this, imagine that Andrea is considerably stronger than Bob, and that they live in a world ungoverned by law. The probability p that Andrea will actually refrain from arbitrarily coercing Bob depends entirely on her subjective preferences and dispositions: if she is in the habit of respecting the personal integrity of others, the value of p might be reasonably high; if she has adopted 'respect the personal integrity of others' as a personal rule for herself, p might even approach 1. The difficulty is that, without having special insight into her private psychology, Bob cannot judge the reliability of her self-restraint. He is thus subject to domination.

The situation is transformed, however, once laws governing the use of coercive force are introduced. The constraints imposed by law supply publicly accessible reasons we can be confident will motivate across a wide range of contingent circumstances and psychologies, thus ensuring that the value of p will be reasonably high across a wide range of possible worlds. Notice here that the benefits of law are not reducible to predictability, which might be enhanced by raising the value of p alone: importantly, they involve broadening the robustness, so to speak, of that predictability.[31] Of course, we cannot expect p to equal 1 in all possible worlds. There may be, for instance, a possible world in which it turns out that Andrea is an especially determined thug who cannot be deterred even by law. This only goes to show that we cannot hope to banish domination from human relations entirely. The point is rather that the introduction of law significantly expands our freedom from domination by ensuring we will not be exposed to arbitrary coercive force: to the extent that we solve the problem of social order, only public coercive agents will be able to coerce us; and to the extent that we solve the problem of constitutionalism, the ability of public coercive agents to coerce us will, in turn, be reliably and effectively constrained to the enforcement of known rules of law.

---

[30] Simmonds 2007, pp. 97–104, similarly argues that the rule of law constitutes some degree of freedom from domination, though his conception of law is very different from mine. The connection between the rule of law and freedom from domination is also sketched in Pettit 1997, pp. 174–177, and Krygier 2011, pp. 75–80. Their views (and mine) should be carefully distinguished from the quite different view that defines the rule of law in terms of democracy, and thus links its value to a positive or participatory conception of liberty (see for example Michelman 1988).

[31] Something like this view is commonly attributed to Hayek. See also the discussion in Waldron 1989.

Might the practices of market exchange or the practices of democracy serve just as well as the practices of law in governing the use of coercive force? (Presumably, it is obvious that authoritarian practices will not serve at all.) If our concern is to reduce domination, probably not. Suppose that coercive force were organized according to the method of bargaining, for example. In this case, whether Andrea coerces Bob will depend on her willingness to pay for coercive services. Given some configuration of resources and preferences, Bob might be able to predict whether she will or no, but his predictions will not be reliable in the sense that they will not be robust in the face of perturbations of that configuration: if Andrea receives a windfall gift, or if her attitudes toward Bob change, she might suddenly become willing to pay for coercive services she was not previously. The method of deliberation is not likely to serve much better. If Bob's liability to coercive force were purely a function of the outcome of collective deliberation, he would have great difficulties in forming any expectations at all: everything would depend on the unpredictable twists and turns of future debate. Given the importance of clear and robust public expectations concerning the use of coercive force, it is thus not surprising that these methods have not commonly been employed.

This, then, is the special value the rule of law: the law can govern the use of coercive force effectively and reliably in a way alternative practices cannot.[32] Historically, this connection between freedom and the rule of law was most emphatically extolled in the classical republican tradition. In the famous expression of William Blackstone, "laws, when prudently framed, are by no means subversive but rather introductive of liberty." Indeed, "where there is no law, there is no freedom."[33] This is precisely what we have just shown, and the connection is perfectly clear provided we understand political liberty or freedom in the republican sense as an independence from arbitrary power or domination. The classical republicans often paired their conception of freedom, however, with an implicit natural law jurisprudence. Coincidentally, legal positivism was historically introduced by authors vehemently opposed to the republican conception of liberty – Hobbes and Bentham in particular. On their view, political freedom should be

---

[32] Contrary to Maravall and Przeworski 2003, p. 4, who claim bargaining equilibria are just as good as constitutional provisions. Their discussion considers only the effectiveness of a given constraint, however, not its reliability.

[33] Blackstone 1765, I.1.12: p. 122.

understood simply as the absence of interference. So understood, any connection between freedom and the rule of law is merely contingent: if the legal system happens to protect an expansive private sphere, its net effect on levels of freedom might be positive, but as Hobbes and Bentham took some pains to emphasize, nothing guarantees that this will be the case.[34]

Some have recently suggested that the political commitments of these authors indeed *required* them to advance a positivistic conception of law, since no other view is consistent with the conception of liberty as non-interference.[35] Even if correct, however, it does not follow that a commitment to legal positivism entails rejecting the republican conception of freedom, nor that accepting the latter entails rejecting the former.[36] Quite the contrary; one of the central aims of this book has been to show that the best theory of the rule of law is precisely one built on positivistic foundations. The strong connection between freedom and the rule of law was obscured not by legal positivism, but rather by the non-interference conception of liberty.

The rule of law alone does not guarantee that individuals will lead fully flourishing lives. Nevertheless, as one necessary condition (among others) for the achievement of human flourishing, the rule of law constitutes a significant part of social justice.[37] Only in a society enjoying some measure of the rule of law is it even possible for people to regard one another as free and equal citizens, no one the master of any one else. In the traditional language of the classical republicans, only such a society can be a genuine empire of laws and not of men.

---

[34] If we define freedom as "the silence of the law," then as Hobbes says, there will be "in some places more, and in some less" freedom "according as they that have sovereignty shall think most convenient" (1651, II.21.18: p. 146). "All coercive laws," says Bentham, "and in particular all laws creative of liberty, are, as far as they go, abrogative of liberty" (1843, p. 57). For further discussion, see Pettit 2009.

[35] See for example Dyzenhaus 2010, ch. 8, and Stone 2011.

[36] Technically, 'if Non-interference then Positivism' entails neither 'if Positivism then Non-interference' (fallacy of the converse), nor 'if ~Non-interference then ~Positivism' (fallacy of the inverse).

[37] The difference between my view and that of Bellamy 2007, pp. 54–66, is thus superficial: since he defines domination more broadly to include many distinct obstacles to human flourishing, it is obvious why he believes the rule of law insufficient to combat domination.

4.2.2 *Objections to the Rule of Law*

Not everyone, of course, has been convinced that the rule of law as such is a good thing, and before proceeding we should consider some of the more serious objections that have been raised against this claim.

One objection concerns the possibility that the rule of law might serve as an instrument for evil regimes. Consider the society we imagined at the outset of this discussion: the laws introduced by the powerful ruling group were designed precisely with the aim of securing advantages at the expense of the various subordinate groups. That being so, wouldn't it be better if the ruling group had *failed* in its attempt to introduce a legal system? And if so, how can we regard it as always a good thing to be ruled by law?[38]

This objection rests on two interconnected mistakes. To begin with, it assumes that ruling groups have no alternative methods available for imposing an unfair social order on subordinate groups: it assumes, in other words, that if a ruling group fails to impose an unfair social order *through law*, it will simply fail to impose an unfair social order. But surely this is not the case. In our imagined society, we wondered precisely which of two methods – the rule of law or direct subjugation – was better and which was worse. Better or worse for whom? Herein lies the other mistake, for the objection seems to confuse what is better and worse for subordinate groups with what is better or worse for ruling groups. Clarifying these points, it should be clear that two distinct comparisons are really involved (see Table 4.1). The claim we have made – that, other things equal, the rule of law is a good thing – refers only to the second comparison. Perhaps it would be best if powerful groups simply failed in their efforts to impose unfair social orders, but that is not the issue at hand. Supposing they will succeed one way or another, our claim is simply that things will be less bad for the subordinate groups if the regime respects the rule of law than if it does not. It will be less bad, as we have said, because in that case the subordinate groups will at least have reliable expectations concerning the incidence of coercive force.

Which method is better or worse for the ruling group? Will powerful groups also reap benefits from respecting the rule of law? That is a separate and debatable question. There are both short-run and long-run

---

[38] Versions of this objection are pressed in Hart 1994, pp. 200–202, and Waldron 1999a, pp. 174–181.

Table 4.1

	Rule of Law	Direct Subjugation
Ruling groups	?	?
Subordinate groups	Better	Worse

interests to consider. In the short run it might seem that rulers would reap efficiency gains from imposing standing rules on their subjects, as compared with having to constantly supervise them.[39] But we must be careful here not to confuse genuine rules of law with mere rules-of-thumb, or what in Chapter 2 we described as unreflective habits. Constant and direct supervision is naturally out of the question, but is it better for the master to impose a rule from which he cannot deviate, or is it better for him to rest on habit which he can revise any time at his discretion? Obviously the latter. Apart from the benefit of flexibility, his subjects in the latter case will probably have instrumental reasons to strategically overcompensate so as to not upset habits with which they are at least familiar.[40] The long-run story is murkier. On the one hand, if there really are substantial economic benefits to the rule of law, for example, ruling groups might do best in the long run trying to capture these gains, even if it means enjoying a smaller proportionate share of benefits in the short run. On the other hand, for reasons we shall discuss next, entrenching the rule of law might eventually upset the ruling group's grip on power. Regardless, however, these issues should not be seen as detracting from the main claim that the rule of law is better, other things equal, for subordinate groups.

This leads us to a second objection, familiar from a Marxist and critical theory perspective. Grant that an established rule of law is, at least in some degree, itself beneficial for subordinate groups. One might still plausibly object that it has detrimental ideological side-effects – roughly, that it serves to simultaneously conceal the under-lying unequal power relations in society and lend stability and legitimacy to the existing social order.[41]

[39] So argues Kramer 2004, pp. 67–69.
[40] In Lovett 2010, pp. 243–249, this is demonstrated in a formal model. Stewart 2006, pp. 152–162, presents a different model supporting the same conclusion.
[41] The locus classicus for this sort of critique is probably Marx 1843. More recent versions are pressed by Zinn 1971; Unger 1976, pp. 176–181, 192–223; and Kennedy 1997, ch. 10.

We might helpfully compare the role of a rule of law ideology in supporting an unfair social order with the role of the Horatio Alger myth in supporting capitalism. Of course for the rule of law ideology to be at all effective, it must be the case that the law actually constrains power relations, at least some of the time.[42] Similarly, for the Horatio Alger myth to be at all effective, it must be the case that at least some individuals succeed in pulling themselves up by their bootstraps. Alas, very few do, and they only with good luck. The reality of capitalism is thus far short of what would be required to actually justify it on equality of opportunity grounds, and in consequence the *net* effect of the Horatio Alger myth is to obscure this unfortunate reality. Analogously, while the rule of law may bring some palliative benefit to subordinate groups, the *net* effect is to obscure the unfortunate reality of their subordination. In both cases, progressive change would be better served by unmasking reality, and thus rendering it intolerable.

Against this view, however, we must submit a historical record in which an apparently conservative appeal to the law has frequently been conjoined with a revolutionary resistance to oppression. When the medieval English barons rebelled against King John, their appeal was to the ancient constitution which the latter had usurped; similarly, the Calvinist resistance in sixteenth-century France, the leaders of Parliament in the English civil war of the seventeenth century, and the American and French revolutionaries of the eighteenth century all appealed to rights and liberties thought to be long-established rules of law. These examples could easily be multiplied. More recently, one of the more interesting phenomena during the collapse of the communist regimes in Eastern Europe was the fact that the process of transition was often carried out in strict conformity with the rules set out in the existing communist legal codes. This was not by accident. Václav Havel wrote about the revolutionary use of law in an essay that was widely circulated in Eastern European dissident circles. "A persistent and never-ending appeal to the laws," he said, "does not mean at all that those who do so have succumbed to the illusion that in our system the law is anything other than what it is" – that is, an instrument of subordination. "Demanding that the laws be upheld is thus an act of

---

[42] As Thompson 1975, p. 262, observes, no one is "mystified by the first man who puts on a wig." Recent studies of legal systems in authoritarian regimes have more or less come to the same conclusion: see for instance Ginsburg 2008.

living within the truth that threatens the whole mendacious structure at its point of maximum mendacity." It exposes the unfair social order for what it is. In fact, "to assume that the laws are a mere facade," he writes, "that they have no validity, and that therefore it is pointless to appeal to them would mean to go on reinforcing those aspects of the law that create the facade and the ritual."[43]

Why might this be? Though all ruling groups use ideology to support their rule, not all ideologies are of a like nature. Under a natural superiority myth, for instance, there is no command, no action, no use of force members of the powerful group could undertake that would contradict the official story. By contrast, even under a very unfair system of laws, subordinate groups can always try to escape the reach of the powerful by conforming to the rules – by walking safely on law's causeway. Then, whenever a member of the ruling group attempts to reach beyond the law to dominate them in some way, the ideological veil is lifted, and power relations are revealed for what they are. By appealing to a rule-of-law ideology, ruling groups place themselves on the horns of a dilemma: they must either surrender power outside the laws they themselves have created, or else expose their domination for what it really is. For these reasons, it is unlikely that the rule of law will serve, at least in the long run, as an effective ideological tool for maintaining unfair social orders.[44]

4.2.3 Limits of the Rule of Law

So far, we have been discussing the benefits that may or may not flow from the rule of law to the various groups in society. We have argued that, regardless of the governing regime's aims for good or for ill, it will always be better at least for those subject to that regime if it rules by law rather than by other means.

---

[43] Havel 1992, pp. 189–190. Law was similarly employed in the struggle against South African apartheid: see Abel 1999.

[44] One might then wonder what would ever prompt ruling groups to introduce the rule of law. The short reply, of course, is that not all do. A more sophisticated reply might point to the need for elites to stabilize internal power-sharing arrangements (see North et al. 2009, ch. 5), monitor lower-level officials (see Ginsburg 2008), or raise and finance popular armies (see Holmes 2003). Paradoxically, these needs may cut against their long-run interest in maintaining a hold on power.

Some have suggested, however, that the rule of law operates not only as a constraint on *means* governing regimes might employ, but also as a constraint on the *aims* they might adopt in the first place. It is in the very nature of law, on this view, to frustrate certain sorts of aims and facilitate others. There are two versions of this claim to consider. On the first, the law tends to frustrate the aims characteristic of evil regimes. This claim, most famously advanced by Fuller, has proved controversial, and is still debated.[45] We need not settle the issue here, for if true it would merely strengthen the argument already presented. The second version of the claim is quite different: it is that the law can also frustrate the aims of good regimes. Specifically, will not many worthwhile and progressive causes be obstructed by a fundamentally conservative appeal to the rule of law? Here one might point to the reactionary role legal institutions have sometimes played in the struggle to establish the modern welfare state.[46] This latter issue, unlike the former, should be addressed here since, if true, our argument for the value of the rule of law might thus seem to be weakened.

Later, in Chapter 6, I will argue that the tension between the rule of law and progressive public policy is much less serious than often thought. Nevertheless, it cannot be doubted that there may be cases of genuine conflict. What this illustrates, however, is not that the rule of law should be dispensed with, but rather that the rule of law should not be regarded as a comprehensive political ideal. The rule of law has normative limits. In order to clearly identify those limits, and assess in a responsible manner the relevant trade-offs, it is first necessary to properly understand what the rule of law is and where its value lies. The rule of law, I have argued, is the situation enjoyed by persons and groups to the extent that they will not be exposed to coercive force except as the consequence of their having failed to observe a legally valid prescriptive rule. I have argued that the value of the rule of law, so defined, lies in the fact that it mitigates a particularly significant potential source of domination. But it would be absurd to conclude from this argument that promoting the rule of law should be our only public concern, or even that it should have lexical priority over other concerns. Either conclusion would clearly be false.

---

[45] Fuller 1969, ch. 4; Simmonds 2007, ch. 3; and Dyzenshaus 2010, ch. 9, have all defended versions of this first claim, while legal positivists, esp. Hart 1965; Raz 1979, ch. 11; and Kramer 2004, have generally argued against it.

[46] For a nice review, see Tamanaha 2008, pp. 524–537.

To begin with, an overly rigid adherence to the rule of existing law can militate against expanding its protection to all. Consider the law of slavery, for example. Under this law, slave-masters hold property rights in their slaves, and rights to treat them according to their own discretion. These laws protect the master who beats his slave from external coercive interference, but they do not of course protect his slaves: it was not true that slaves experience coercive force only when they fail to observe legally valid prescriptive rules. On the contrary, slaves are exposed to the use or threat of violence and physical restraint at almost any time, and for any reason. While masters are *legally authorized*, in the sense described earlier, to use coercive force, their slaves certainly do not enjoy the rule of law. Surely, however, it would be no objection to abolishing slavery and extending the rule of law to former slaves that doing so would temporarily upset the rule of law enjoyed by slave masters. Our concern should rather be increasing the sum total freedom from domination, counting the freedom of every person the same.[47] Sometimes, this may require partial departures from the rule of law in the short run, so as to ensure a wider enjoyment of the rule of law in the long run.

Departures may be required for other reasons as well. While uncontrolled coercive force is an especially important source of domination, it is not the only source. There are many other forms of social power we must contend with. Domination might be secured through economic power, for instance, or through cultural exclusion, or through ideological manipulation. Assuming our aim is to reduce domination in all its forms, we might sometime face difficult choices between avoiding a relatively minor degree of coercive domination, on the one hand, and (say) reducing a relatively substantial degree of economic domination, on the other. This might perhaps be the case when it comes to certain forms of antitrust policy, for example. Laws prohibiting specific monopolistic practices need not conflict with rule of law, nor would well-designed standing regulations designed to discourage the formation of monopolies.[48] When dangerous "natural" monopolies form despite such precautions, however, it might not be possible

---

[47] Or at any rate, so I argue in Lovett 2010, pp. 173–179.
[48] Hayek 1960, pp. 264–266, concedes the former; with respect to the latter, I have in mind regulations that scale up minimum reserve requirements for banks as they grow larger, for example.

to break them up without violating the rule of law.[49] If this would substantially reduce economic domination, it would be folly to let a mere slavish devotion to the rule of law as such prevent us from doing so.

Finally, there will be cases in which the value of freedom from domination itself runs up against other values. Freedom from domination is important, but it is certainly not the only thing we should care about.[50] For example, suppose there is a trade-off between the rule of law and national security: in emergency circumstances, it might be reasonable for some societies to give up some of the former in order to get more of the latter.[51] In cases of transitional justice, similarly, adherence to the strict rule of law might run up against broader moral claims. Evil regimes often legally permit or even require actions that are regarded in retrospect as morally abhorrent. Subsequently, justice cannot be done to the victims of those actions without violating the strict rule of law – that is, without the perpetrators being subject to public coercion for reasons not relating to their having previously failed to observe what was at the time a legally valid prescriptive rule.[52] By no means should it be assumed that the rule of law always trumps other considerations. While it does always have value, that value must be weighed against other values in a reasonable manner.[53]

Many other examples could easily be cited, but the main point is clear. As important and valuable as the rule of law is, it is certainly not a comprehensive political doctrine.

4.3 Rule of Law Principles

In Chapter 1, we observed that there is little agreement in the contemporary literature on how to specify the principles of legality: this is because, I suggested, the principles are usually discussed as if they were

---

[49] Even if such actions must violate the rule of law, they need not be *arbitrary*, provided the implementing agents are suitably controlled. This is a topic for another time, however.

[50] I argue this at greater length in Lovett 2010, pp. 140–147, 187–189.

[51] Of course not everyone agrees there is such a trade-off: the contrary view is argued in Dyzenhaus 2006, for example.

[52] Just such a case was debated by Hart 1958, pp. 615–621, and Fuller 1958, pp. 648–657. Transitional justice is further discussed in Chapter 7.

[53] Raz 1979, pp. 226–229, makes a similar claim.

free-floating standards legal systems might exhibit to a greater or lesser degree. On my view, the principles of legality should instead be derived from our underlying conception of what it means for a society to be ruled by law and not by other means.[54]

Laws are social rules provided direct or indirect support by a public coercive agent. Not every pattern in social behavior counts as a genuine social rule, however. Because the rule of law means ruling by law and not by other means, and because law is a species of social rule, it follows that any existence conditions for effective and reliable social rules must carry over into our idea of the rule of law. These conditions, as it happens, are the real substance underlying the virtues or principles traditionally associated with the rule of law. In a round-about way, we can say that the rule of law "requires" or "demands" that we respect these principles, so long as we properly understand what is meant by that expression: what is meant is that when the principles of legality are violated, people will experience a given application of coercive force as something other than the public sanction attached to a known rule – in other words, they will experience it as something other than law.

Since so many contemporary discussions of the rule of law focus on enumerating the principles of legality, it may be useful to sort them out in a rigorous manner.[55] In doing so, however, we must remind ourselves that the principles represent a conclusion derived from our theory and not its starting point. We cannot infer that a society enjoys the rule of law merely from the fact that its legal system answers to the principles of legality, for we must also know the scope of law in that society. As noted in Chapter 1, societies in which the legal system fails to govern most uses of coercive force, or in which it governs only the use of coercive force among elites, do not enjoy the rule of law as we have defined it. Properly understood, the rule of law requires that all uses of coercive force by all persons and groups – both public and private – be governed by law so far as possible.

---

[54] Here the argument follows Lovett 2002, pp. 60–62, in overall strategy, though correcting several significant errors in detail. A similar strategy for grounding the traditional rule of law principles is followed in Hadfield and Weingast 2014 – see below.

[55] Among the more commonly cited discussions are Fuller 1969, ch. 2; Raz 1979; and Fallon 1997. See Appendix A for an overview of the various principles proposed.

4.3.1 *The Principles of Legality*

A society is ruled by law when no member of that society need fear
being subject to coercive force, except as the public sanction attached
to a known rule. This can only be the case when, roughly speaking,
three broad criteria are satisfied, as follows:

(1) Every use of coercive force in that society is governed by *rules*.
(2) The rules governing the use of coercive force in that society must be
     effective and reliable.
(3) It must be *common knowledge* in that society both (a) what rules
     govern the use of coercive force, and (b) that those rules are
     effective and reliable.

To the extent that these criteria are satisfied, it will be possible for
persons and groups to avoid being exposed to violence or physical
restraint by observing the relevant rules, and this is what it means to
enjoy the rule of law as we have defined it. Let us elaborate on these
criteria as follows.

The first criterion is obvious enough, though its scope is not always
fully appreciated. This is because there are in fact two directions from
which individuals might experience coercive force, and accordingly
there must be two different sets of rules governing its use – namely,
rules that prohibit the private use of coercive force, on the one hand,
and rules that limit the public use of coercive force to the enforcement
of social rules, on the other. As mentioned previously, most contemporary discussions of the rule of law focus on the latter, but surely the
former are just as much or more significant: no society can be said to
enjoy the rule of law unless murder, assault, rape, and so forth are
prohibited.

Let us suppose that these sorts of private uses of coercive force have
indeed been successfully controlled in one way or another, however.
What sorts of further constraints must be in place so as to ensure that
people will not experience public coercion except as sanctions attached
to known rules? Many of the traditional rule of law principles discussed in the literature can be accounted for as attempts to answer this
question. At a minimum, the rules governing public coercion must
restrict its employment to securing future compliance with open-ended
and mutually consistent laws that persons of ordinary talent and
commitment can observe. The conditions of prospectivity, consistency,

and performability here are reasonably straightforward, and under some description or other find their way into nearly all discussion of the rule of law.[56] More troublesome has been the distinction – usually reasonably clear in practice, but obscure in theory – between an open-ended rule, on the one hand, and a particular instruction or command, on the other. Prescriptive rules recommend an open-ended course of conduct to their participants, such as 'drive on the right', 'wait in line for service', 'perform contracts made', 'don't commit assault', and so forth. The course of conduct they recommend is typically characterized *abstractly* (at the level of concrete particular actions, many things might count, so to speak, as 'waiting in line' in the recommended sense) and *indefinitely* (one should wait in line at each relevant opportunity, now and in the future). By contrast, many direct applications of coercive force – robbery at gunpoint, say, or the government's interning of Japanese-Americans during the Second World War – are clearly not contingent responses to the breach of some legally valid prescriptive rule. But what of the instruction that 'on the first of March in each of the next 5 years, the members of group *A* should pay an indemnity to the members of group *B*'? There seems to be a continuous range between pure cases of prescriptive rule and pure cases of arbitrary command.[57] This need not be a problem for our discussion, however. Rather than insist on a precise threshold, we can simply say that the degree of rule of law enjoyed varies more or less continuously with the degree to which public coercion is employed in support of rule-like instructions rather than command-like instructions.

The second criterion is pragmatic rather than formal. It is of course not enough that there exist rules formally governing the use of coercive force, unless those rules are effective and reliable in practice: the rules prohibiting robbery, say, or the rules prohibiting police arrest without due cause must actually do the job of protecting individuals from the

---

[56] See for example Fuller 1969, pp. 51–62, 65–79; Rawls 1971, pp. 236–238; or Finnis 1980, pp. 270–271. Less often discussed, since it has not been a major issue in the modern era, is the challenge of securing consistency among legal systems with overlapping jurisdictions. Federalism solves the problem by ranking the systems, but when such rankings are absent – as they often were in medieval Europe – the problem is more serious. With the reemergence of regional law (in the European Union, for instance) these issues may return to prominence.

[57] An early attempt to distinguish general rules from particular commands can be found in Austin 1832, pp. 17–24, and more recent attempts in Neumann 1937, pp. 106–108; Hayek 1960, pp. 149–151; or Fuller 1969, pp. 46–49, 209–210.

arbitrary application of coercive force. To reiterate our earlier discussion, rules are *effective* when there is a high degree of probability that they will be observed, and they are *reliable* when that effectiveness is robust across a reasonably wide range of changes in circumstance. There are many technologies that might ensure effectiveness and reliability in the relevant sense, though not all of these will be consistent with other values. (Imagine for instance that every citizen and every public official is given a brain implant that shocks them whenever they contemplate straying from strict compliance with the law.) For the most part, modern liberal democracies rely on a two-pronged approach to constraining the public and private use of coercive force. On the one hand, there are institutional strategies for combining a system of professional law enforcement with a politically independent judiciary and constitutionally entrenched rights of due process.[58] On the other hand, there are civic education strategies for generating a widespread respect for the law and legal processes in the general population.[59]

Since these topics have been extensively discussed by others, we may pass over them here.[60] It might be worth briefly remarking, however, on the view of some authors that the rule of law should itself be defined in part with reference to the various institutional devices mentioned above. Jeremy Waldron, for instance, points out that when people express concern regarding the integrity of the rule of law – as many did after *Bush v. Gore* and the indefinite detainment of prisoners at Guantánamo Bay, for instance – it is often precisely because judicial independence and due process rights have been threatened.[61] This suggests that the principles of legality should include such specific procedural requirements as the right to legal representation, the right

---

[58] Included here are the requirements that the judiciary be accessible to ordinary citizens, and that it be able to hold public officials to account for their conduct.

[59] Civic education can only go so far in generating the required respect if legal institutions do not also generate their own support, as I will discuss in Chapter 5.

[60] As an aspect of the rule of law, the need for strategies to secure effectiveness and reliability is noted in Fuller 1969, pp. 81–91; Rawls 1971, pp. 238–239; Raz 1979, pp. 216–218; and Finnis 1980, pp. 270–271. One controversial issue concerns whether the rule of law also requires democracy: Barros 2003, for example, argues that it does not. In Chapter 6 I suggest that some degree of democratic accountability may in practice be necessary to reconcile the rule of law with the need for legal change, however.

[61] *Bush v. Gore*, 531 U.S. 98 (2000).

to an open trial, the right to be tried in an independent court, and so forth. The point of these procedures, he further argues, is not so much to secure effectiveness and reliability as it is to respect the freedom and dignity of human beings, especially by providing them an impartial forum for presenting arguments – an opportunity to "make their case," so to speak.[62]

We should, however, exercise caution in tethering our conception of the rule of law to any specific institutional devices, insofar as doing so might lead us to underestimate the achievements of societies having legal systems very different from ours. Imposing the standard devices with which we are familiar on radically different legal systems might in some contexts undermine rather than enhance the rule of law.[63] This is not to diminish the value of the various procedures highlighted by Waldron, of course, nor to deny their connection to the rule of law as implemented in modern liberal-democratic societies. But when people in such societies quite sensibly express concern about threats to judicial independence, due process, and so forth, it is simply because experience suggests that these are the most pragmatically effective devices for securing the rule of law as already defined. No more elaborate explanation is required. That these devices might in turn produce further benefits on top of those we have already discussed certainly does not detract from our previous argument.

So much for the first two criteria. The third complements and reinforces the first two. Except under highly unusual circumstances, it is unlikely that a schedule of rules could be effective and reliable unless the content of those rules is common knowledge. Likewise, the common knowledge that those rules are effective and reliable itself reiteratively enhances their effectiveness and reliability.[64] What is more, people cannot enjoy many of the benefits of the rule of law – the benefits of freedom from domination – except in the secure knowledge that they will not be subject to arbitrary coercion.

What establishes the relevant common knowledge? Again, the answer invokes many familiar principles. First, it is obvious that the rules governing the use of coercive force must be promulgated: it must

---

[62] See esp. Waldron 2008 and 2011.

[63] Rodriquez et al. 2010, p. 1458, and Hadfield and Weingast 2014, p. 33, voice similar cautions.

[64] Hadfield and Weingast 2014, pp. 33–34, emphasize the importance of common knowledge in securing effectiveness and reliability.

be announced in advance which prescriptive rules the public coercive agent intends to support. In effect, this means that the rule of recognition (see Chapter 3) employed by that agent must be public in its operation.[65] Second, the rules must be sufficiently clear as to be understandable by the relevant parties. This does not always mean that everyone must be able to understand every aspect of the rules: only civil engineers, for example, need fully understand the regulations governing the design of public works. Often, however, a general understanding is important. Not only must *we* understand the rules so as to follow them ourselves, but also we must have confidence that *others* understand the rules so *they* can follow them. It is thus beneficial that everyone have some reasonable understanding of the rules governing police conduct, for example. Third, the system of rules governing the use of coercive force should be reasonably stable. If the rules changed too rapidly, it would presumably be difficult for people to form reliable expectations as to what those rules require. These three principles of publicity, clarity, and stability find their way into nearly every discussion of the rule of law.[66]

4.3.2 Legal Equality and the Rule of Law

At this point, it may seem we are well on our way to merely restating what many writers on the rule of law have said before, albeit within a new framework. Even if this were the case, we would have performed a service in placing the traditional principles on a more secure footing: no longer would they represent merely free-floating standards, but rather a detailed specification of the necessary conditions of being ruled by law and not by other means. Doing so, moreover, enabled us to discuss not only the value of the rule of law, but also the limits of that value.

As it happens, however, not all the principles commonly found in the literature can be so grounded. Conspicuously absent from our discussion to this point has been any mention of generality in the sense of legal equality – i.e., in the sense that all persons and groups are to be treated more or less the same. The classic statement of generality in this sense derives from J.-J. Rousseau:

[65] Raz 1979, pp. 215–216, and Finnis 1980, pp. 270–272, both note this point.
[66] See for example Fuller 1969, esp. pp. 49–51, 62–65, 79–81; Rawls 1971, pp. 237–238; or Raz 1979, pp. 214–216.

When I say that the object of the laws is always general, I have in mind that the law considers subjects as a body and actions in the abstract, never a man as an individual or a particular action. Thus the law can perfectly well enact a statute to the effect that there be privileges, but it cannot bestow them by name on anyone. The law can create several classes of citizens, and even stipulate the qualifications that determine membership in these classes, but it cannot name specific persons to be admitted to them.[67]

Notice here an initial blurring of generality in the sense of a rule that is open-ended in respect of the course of conduct it recommends, and generality in the sense of a rule that is open-ended in respect of the persons to whom it applies. This imprecision has persisted, and has encouraged many authors to attempt to extract varying degrees of legal equality from a bare commitment to the rule of law. Dicey, for example, describes the rule of law as requiring that "every man, whatever be his rank or condition" be subject to "one law administered by the ordinary Courts." Similarly, Hayek argues that true law consists of "general rules that apply equally to everybody." Just as the law "should not name any particulars, so it should not single out any specific persons or group of persons."[68] Many other examples of this conceptual fudge could easily be cited.[69]

In my view, this confusion ought to be avoided, and our conception of the rule of law not thereby burdened with normative commitments it cannot bear. We have defined the rule of law as the rule by law and not by other means – as a situation in which persons and groups do not experience coercive force expect as the public sanction attached to legally valid prescriptive rules. As a normative ideal, the rule of law answers to a specific and important value: roughly, the value of knowing where you stand in relation to powerful others. However, we earlier cautioned that this is by no means the only thing we should value, morally or politically. It follows that the rule of law cannot and should not be made to serve as a comprehensive political doctrine. Essaying to shoehorn the value of legal equality, say, into the rule of law serves only to obfuscate and undermine the credibility of both

---

[67] Rousseau 1762, II.6.6: p. 161.

[68] Dicey 1915, p. 114, and Hayek 1960, pp. 153–154, respectively. More recently, Bingham 2010, ch. 5, has urged including legal equality in our conception of the rule of law.

[69] Though it is notable that both Austin 1832, pp. 21–23, and Fuller 1969, p. 47, explicitly consider and decline to make the fudge.

commitments.[70] It is interesting, in this regard, to observe that those who attempt to elevate the rule of law into a comprehensive political doctrine, such as Dicey and Hayek, are particularly prone to this error.

Before concluding this discussion, however, it is worth pausing to consider a recent and clever attempt by Gillian Hadfield and Barry Weingast to incorporate some measure of legal equality into our conception of the rule of law after all. Their effort merits special attention because they do not rely on fudging the meaning of generality. Rather, they proceed in what I have argued is the correct way – namely, deriving rule of law principles from the necessary conditions of ruling by law and not by other means. There is no rule of law, we have seen, unless the rules governing the use of coercive force are effective and reliable. What Hadfield and Weingast try to show is that the effectiveness and reliability of these rules "requires eliminating systems of privilege that differentiate among people" and impose particular legal requirements on each.[71]

They suggest two reasons for believing this. Suppose a legal system will only be effective and reliable provided it can count on the decentralized support of ordinary citizens, for instance in expressing disapproval of law-breaking and boycotting law-breakers. Since "incentive capacity is required for every agent who is essential to the enforcement mechanism," it follows that no citizen's "interests can be ignored." Some degree of legal equality may thus be necessary to incentivize decentralized enforcement. This is the first reason; the second is that general rules are economizing. It will be easier for people "to predict the classification of novel sets of circumstances," and plan their activities accordingly, when legal rules are "general" and "impersonal."[72]

There is nothing wrong with their argument, so far as it goes, but it depends on the assumption that the law will be effective and reliable only if it can count on the decentralized support of ordinary citizens as well as public coercion. Is this a sound assumption? The historical durability of some highly particularized legal regimes, such as European feudalism and the Indian caste system, might suggest otherwise.

---

[70] Interestingly, the ambitious recent effort of Gowder 2013 to connect the rule of law with equality involves abandoning the connection we have drawn with political freedom.

[71] Hadfield and Weingast 2014, p. 34.

[72] Ibid., pp. 34–36. Note that their derivation of legal equality from the rule of law was more explicit and forceful in earlier, unpublished papers.

A better way to interpret their result, in my view, is to suggest that they have demonstrated a contingent relationship between decentralized enforcement and legal equality: *if* one wants to have a decentralized legal system that is effective and reliable, *then* one must design a broadly egalitarian legal code. If decentralized legal systems are more efficient on the whole than centralized ones, then there might be some comparative advantage to be secured via legal equality.

This is a significant finding, and an encouraging one for those who, like myself, value legal equality. But other technologies for securing effective and reliable compliance are no doubt available, and thus it does not seem correct to conclude that the rule of law as such requires legal equality.

4.4 Conclusion

This concludes our basic argument for the rule of law's value. In order to claim that the rule of law is a good thing, I have insisted that we must start with a strictly descriptive conception of the rule of law – we must know what a thing *is* before we can judge whether and to what extent it is a *good* thing. The rule of law is the rule by law and not by other means. It is, in other words, to have a society so organized that persons and groups will not experience coercive force except as the public sanction attached to legally valid prescriptive rules. Other things being equal, it is good when societies are organized in this way: it is good because it secures at least some significant measure of freedom from domination, and thus constitutes a significant part of social justice. This is not to say that the rule of law is the only thing we should care about, or that the rule of law can serve as a complete political doctrine, but it does have real and important value.

Our argument has so far rested, however, on a simplified equilibrium model of a static legal system largely free from disagreement. Real-world legal systems are obviously not like this, and so the obvious question is whether our argument will hold up once the dynamic aspects of the law are fully appreciated. That is the question to which we turn in Part II.

PART II

Legal Dynamics

5 | *Adjudication and the Realist Challenge*

Societies enjoy the rule of law, we have argued, to the extent that every use of coercive force in those societies, both public and private, is governed by law. But many people are skeptical about the law. This is not to say, of course, that anyone denies the existence of lawyers, judges, legal code books, published opinions and dissents, and so forth. Rather, it is to say that many people do not believe these sorts of things – the material components of a legal system – really have the meaning and significance they are often purported to have. The law is not an objective body of formal rules, discoverable through diligent study of the relevant statutes and case histories, mechanically applied by impartial courts to particular cases. Rather, in terms of our practical felt experience at any rate, the law is simply whatever judges say it is.[1] Something like this view and its implication is famously expressed by Oliver Wendell Holmes as follows:

The reason ... people will pay lawyers to argue for them or to advise them, is that in societies like ours the command of public force is intrusted to the judges in certain cases, and the whole power of the state will be put forth, if necessary, to carry out their judgments and decrees. People want to know under what circumstances and how far they will run the risk of coming against what is so much stronger than themselves, and hence it becomes a business to find out when this danger is to be feared. The object of our study, then, is prediction, the prediction of the incidence of the public force through the instrumentality of the courts.[2]

In other words, the law is just another form of ordinary political power. Judges are merely individuals empowered in certain circumstances to render decisions regarding the public use of coercive force, which they do according to their personal inclinations or ideological beliefs. Others obey their decisions, or are compelled to obey, accordingly.

---

[1] Of course this can only be true of legal systems that have judges, strictly speaking, but the familiar slogan could be generalized without much difficulty.
[2] Holmes 1897, p. 991.

The view just sketched has come to be known as *legal realism*. In its various guises, legal realism has exercised an enormous influence over the past century or so.[3] The first aim of this chapter, accordingly, will be to consider how far legal realism presents a serious challenge to our argument for the rule of law presented in Part I. In one way, it is curious that skepticism about the law has not often been extended to skepticism about social rules generally. Many people firmly believe in the efficacy of social rules to constrain individual behavior. Indeed, some do so strongly they are concerned lest the matrix of norms and conventions become so dense as to leave no appreciable individual freedom of choice (this was one of J. S. Mill's concerns, for example). My argument will be, in part, that it is difficult to reconcile our belief in the efficacy of social rules with legal realism. If we believe that social rules really can constrain individual behavior, then we will have little reason to doubt that a genuine rule of law is possible.

In the process of answering the challenge of legal realism we will have to consider the nature of adjudication, the process of appellate review, and the significance of legal indeterminacy. Unfortunately, some discussions of these topics confuse empirical questions with normative ones. Thus, in addition to the fundamentally empirical question of how far a genuine rule of law is possible, there are two entirely separate normative questions – the first concerning the institutional role various legal officials should be given in a well-designed political system, and the second concerning what moral and political duties properly fall on those officials. The latter two issues are, of course, logically independent from the former. Only after having addressed the challenge of legal realism, therefore, does this chapter proceed to sketch a framework for addressing them.

5.1 Realism and the Rule of Law

How far does legal realism present a challenge to the theory developed in Part I? In certain respects, it presents no challenge at all. The existence and content of law, I have argued, ultimately depends on

---

[3] The critical legal studies movement, the attitudinal model of judicial politics, and the so-called naturalized jurisprudence all derive inspiration from legal realism. For recent representatives of each, see Kennedy 1997, Segal and Spaeth 2002, and Leiter 2007, respectively. Similar views have also been held by Marxists and various other leftist critics.

social facts. It follows that legal systems are indeed properly understood as constituted by social behavior we can and should study descriptively. To this extent, legal realism is perfectly consistent with the positivist conception of law developed in Part I.[4]

We must part company with legal realism, however, when it comes to identifying and describing the nature of the relevant social facts. Centrally important to our theory is the claim that legal systems are built on conventional social rules. The rule of law exists, we have said, to the extent that people can only experience coercive force as the public sanction attached to legally valid prescriptive rules. In order to realize this state of affairs, public coercion must itself be governed by reliable and effective social rules that are common knowledge among those affected.

This is precisely what the legal realist denies is possible. On the legal realist view, the behavior constituting our experience of law is only the more or less predictable behavior of judges, governed by their personal inclinations or ideological beliefs. Just how predictable that behavior turns out to be is of course an empirical question, on which the classical realists sometimes disagreed.[5] But that is neither here nor there for our purposes: the relevant claim is that, from the point of view of those who would experience its effects, there are no normatively relevant differences between law, on the one hand, and ordinary politics or power relations, on the other. Properly studied and analyzed, the former can be reduced to the latter. It follows that any talk of the rule of law as a normative ideal – as an empire of laws and not of men – must be meaningless. The notion that the laws can rule is an illusion. In reality, the rule of law is always just another sort of direct personal rule: it is the rule of men in robes, so to speak.

Recall from Chapter 2 that with any social rule, the various strategies of the participants in that rule must necessarily form a Nash equilibrium. At equilibrium, no one can do better according to her own lights changing her strategy unilaterally, because that strategy represents her best response to the (possibly different) strategies adopted by each of the others.[6] Some social rules – what we called

---

[4] Put another way, legal positivists and legal realists both subscribe to what we termed the social fact thesis in Chapter 1: see Leiter 2007, ch. 4.

[5] Leiter 2007, pp. 21–30, discusses the different views of the realists on this point.

[6] To reiterate what was said in Chapter 2, it does not follow that all existing social rules are Pareto optimal. Obstacles to coordination might hinder the transition from one equilibrium to another, even if the latter is better for everyone.

social norms – are maintained in part with the help of sanctioning behavior in the event of noncompliance with the base rule. In our earlier discussion, we noted that this sanctioning behavior must itself also be in equilibrium. That is to say, in the event that one person has deviated from the expected equilibrium path somewhere along the line, it must be the optimal response of others to sanction him, given what all the others are doing.

Social norms generate a special sort of experience. If we consider a social norm from the point of view of each individual participant, we find that the base rule expressed in that social norm presents itself as a sort of impersonal standard. If one participant contemplates deviating from the base rule, he can expect other participants to sanction him, even if he knows little about their personal psychology or private circumstances, because doing so represents their equilibrium response to that deviation. Social norms are thus experientially different from a situation in which one person or group has the power simply to rule over another – to tell them what to do or not do directly, according to their personal whim or pleasure. In the latter case, the empowered person simply chooses a desired outcome according to her preference, and the others are compelled to obey.

In Chapter 4 we observed that the difference here is not entirely one of predictability. People often have stable preferences. With access to the private preferences and circumstances of a powerful individual, one might understand her well enough to effectively predict her choices. But this requires special knowledge, and in any case the preferences and circumstances of others are always liable to change. The experience of social norms is different. Although we may observe some people sanctioning others, the former are not ruling over the latter in the same sort of way: rather, the sanctioners are themselves conforming to a social norm whose various provisions are all common knowledge. Without knowing much about them, we can reliably assume their behavior will be in equilibrium – sanctioning us if we stray from the equilibrium path, and not otherwise.

Now consider the hypothetical contract dispute between Andrea and Bob referred to in earlier chapters. It is a mistake, I argued in Chapter 3, to regard what happens in court as the most significant aspect of the law. On the contrary, far more significant is the normal course of events in which people stick to the equilibrium path, so to speak – that is, they perform whatever contracts they have agreed to, do not end up in court, and are not subject to sanction. Alas, this observation is unlikely to reassure the legal realist. To see why, we must delve into the example a bit more deeply.

We have supposed that, contrary to the usual expectation, Andrea and Bob end up in court. How might this happen? There are three different scenarios to consider. The first and perhaps most obvious possibility is that there is some uncertainty as to what happened – i.e., as to whether Bob departed from the equilibrium path or not. Such disputes of fact, however, are the least important scenario for our present topic, since they do not represent any deep challenge to the rule of law. Disputes of fact are inevitable in social life, which is why we have conventional procedures for resolving them as best we can.[7] More important is the second possibility, that Bob simply reneged – i.e., departed from the equilibrium path, or the third, that there is some uncertainty as to what the relevant legal rule actually requires – i.e., as to where the equilibrium path itself lies. The second and third scenarios, as it happens, correspond to two very different doubts we might have regarding the possibility of a genuine rule of law.[8]

On the one hand, our doubts might be practical. We might plausibly believe that since one power or force can be constrained only by another equal or greater power or force, there is no sense in which we can describe merely formal rules as such as having any real effect – as exercising any real constraint. This might be called *efficacy skepticism*. Efficacy skepticism corresponds to the scenario in which Andrea and Bob find themselves in court because Bob simply departed from the equilibrium path. It is presumably clear what the judge *should* do in such cases: our concern is that the legal rule as such cannot *constrain* him to do it. "What man, that has his natural senses," wonders Hobbes, "believes the law can hurt him; that is, words, and paper, without the hands and swords of men?"[9] Why would we expect mere words on paper to actually constrain judges to apply the law?

---

[7] Roughly speaking, we might think of those procedures as themselves social rules requiring that we accept the judgments of trial courts in disputes of fact.

[8] The two varieties of skepticism considered in what follows are both examples of what Leiter 2007, pp. 68–69, terms "empirical skepticism" – that is, skepticism with respect to the possibility that law can actually govern. What he terms "conceptual skepticism" concerns the existence of laws purporting to govern (whether they succeed or not). Leiter persuasively argues that legal realism is best understood as pressing the former rather than the latter.

[9] Hobbes 1651, IV.46.36: p. 454.

On the other hand, our doubts might be conceptual. We might plausibly believe there is something in the nature of rules such that, at least in many cases, they are not capable of determining their own application. This corresponds to the scenario in which it is uncertain where the equilibrium path lies: the meaning of the rule as it applies to the facts is not altogether clear. Judges cannot be governed by rules of law that are indeterminate. In such cases, any disposition of the case must necessarily be an act of discretion. As contrasted with efficacy skepticism, this might be called *indeterminacy skepticism*.

Often, these two varieties of skepticism are blurred together. Those who challenge the possibility of a genuine rule of law often rely on indeterminacy skepticism to deflect reasonable responses to the efficacy problem, and on efficacy skepticism to deflect reasonable responses to the indeterminacy problem, thus creating the illusion that the challenge is much stronger than it really is. It is therefore essential to keep the two issues distinct in our discussion: until both problems have been separately addressed, the realist challenge cannot finally be put to rest.[10]

5.2 The Efficacy of Law

Let us suppose it is clear that Bob departed from the equilibrium path – that he simply reneged on his contract with Andrea. This isolates the problem of efficacy skepticism, which we will address first. Our aim here is to figure out what ensures that rules of law will actually constrain the relevant legal officials.

5.2.1 Constraints on Adjudication

The specific worry of efficacy skepticism is that, once Andrea and Bob find themselves in court, the trial judge can simply decide the case according to her personal will or pleasure. This is equivalent to saying, in our terms, that the judge is not constrained to sanction Bob as, according to the general understanding of the legally valid prescriptive rule in question, she ought to do. She might have private motives for enforcing it, of course, which (if her personal preferences and

---

[10] Not only the supporters, but also sometimes the critics of rule skepticism muddle the two separate issues: this is one of the problems with the famous discussion in Hart 1994, pp. 136–147.

circumstances were sufficiently known) could form the basis for an accurate prediction of her likely judgment. Her private motives might even include moral or ethical considerations – she might, for example, personally believe that fairness requires her to enforce the rules as formally expressed in the published legal code. But however *effective* such predictions might be, in the language of Chapter 4, they will not be *reliable* in the required sense. Andrea and Bob will experience the judge's power to decide their dispute according to her private motives alone as a form of direct personal rule, and not as the public sanction attached to a legally valid prescriptive rule.

Judicial discretion thus seems to create a loophole that threatens to unravel our entire enterprise. The rule of law requires that every use of coercive force in society be channeled so far as possible in directions people can be reasonably expected to anticipate. This can be done so long as everyone knows what will happen at the end of the game tree, so to speak, and thus will be able to select their best-response equilibrium strategies accordingly. But if the game tree ends in an exercise of unconstrained judicial discretion, it may be hard to see how reliable expectations could be formed in the first place.[11]

Fortunately, it is easy to see how this worry might be allayed. First, recall from Chapter 2 the distinction between coordination conventions and social norms. When it comes to the former, there is no problem of enforcement: the mere fact that others behave in some particular way (driving on the right, say) gives us a compelling reason for doing likewise ourselves. Social norms such as 'perform contracts made', however, are not like this. The fact that others perform their contractual obligations does not by itself give us compelling reason for performing ours (although it might give us private reasons if we believed it the right thing to do – that is, if we have adopted 'perform contracts made' as a personal rule for ourselves). Some sort of sanctioning mechanism is necessary to maintain social norms, and that

---

[11] Suppose, however, that judges decide cases brought before them perfectly randomly. Going to court will thus impose a similar cost on both parties (where the net expected cost = legal expenses + cost of an adverse judgment × probability of an adverse judgment). Private individuals might then be able to maintain social norms with the threat of triggering this mutual expected cost whenever someone deviates from the equilibrium path. This threat would have to be credible, of course. For an analysis of contract law along these lines, see Posner 2000, ch. 9. In reality, judges are not random outcome generators, and so the problem remains.

sanctioning mechanism must itself be incentive compatible: i.e., carrying out the sanction when others violate the base rule of a social norm must be our best-response equilibrium strategy.

Also recall from Chapter 2 that social rules need not be symmetric. Often there is a division of labor in the various equilibrium strategies adopted by participants. In the example of campers searching for firewood, for instance, an equilibrium might consist in one person searching to the east and another to the west. By extension, a social rule might involve a division of labor when it comes to the administration of sanctions. Here we must think of judges as participants in the relevant social rule, not as exogenous parties – albeit participants whose strategy options are different from those of ordinary citizens. Contract law can thus be described as a game with three players: Andrea, Bob, and a judge. To simplify, we might imagine the judge has a set of available actions, including 'find for the plaintiff' and 'find for the defendant', and that the relevant history is whether the defendant reneged or not on his contractual obligations (recall that, for the time being, we are assuming the history is clear). Thus, a possible strategy for the judge could be, 'find for the plaintiff if the defendant reneged, and not otherwise'.[12]

In order to alleviate the worry of efficacy rule skepticism, then, we need only combine these two observations, and show that enforcing the base rule expressed in a law is the equilibrium best-response strategy for the judge, much as conforming to the base rule is the equilibrium best-response strategy for everyone else. If and when this is the case, the felt experience of individuals facing the law will be different from the felt experience of being subject to direct personal rule. Although legal officials will punish those who break the law, in doing so they will simply be following their own equilibrium strategies – observing the sanctioning clause of a known social rule for publicly accessible reasons. Without knowing much about the private psychology of a particular judge, we can reliably assume her behavior will conform to our expectation that she will sanction us if we stray from the equilibrium path and not otherwise. Judicial power will thus be experienced, from the point of view of those it affects, as the rule of law and not of men. Notice that it is the actual felt experience of those

---

[12] To simplify here, I ignore cases in which the legal rules themselves direct judges to exercise discretion. Discretionary authority is discussed in Chapter 6.

potentially subject to coercive force that matters: it does not matter what actually *motivates* judges, provided their decisions are experienced *as if* they were governed by known rules of law. Judges need not be motivated by respect for the law as such, for instance. In order to vindicate the possibility of a genuine rule of law, it is thus only necessary to secure incentive compatibility. How difficult is this to secure?

In the introduction to this chapter, I pointed out that while many doubt the efficacy of law, few doubt the efficacy of other sorts of social rules. What makes this curious, on reflection, is that incentive-compatibility is probably *easier* to achieve when it comes to the law. Consider the social norm of waiting in line at the bank, or the norms of etiquette. In cases like these, it is up to the participants themselves to perform any sanctioning behavior. Often, this is costly (no one likes to make a scene, etc.), so we must figure out how sanctioning deviations from the equilibrium path are worth the cost for enough people to maintain the equilibrium. The law makes things easier, not harder. This is because, having specialized the job of imposing sanctions, we need only incentivize the specialists. When it comes to judges, for example, fixed salaries, secure tenure, and conflict of interest rules can remove the usual sorts of disincentives; opportunities for promotion, the appeals process, and competition for legal reputation can supply positive incentives.[13]

Much of the business of law enforcement – the great majority of it, perhaps – consists in the straightforward sanctioning of citizens by legal officials for departures from the base rules of the legal system. Typical traffic law cases, for example, involve some departure from a base rule (improper parking, speeding, etc.) followed by a sanction (usually a fine). Many criminal law cases follow the same pattern. Very few such cases are seriously contested or appealed, no doubt in large part because it is obvious to all concerned what the eventual outcome will be.[14] If we add to these typical cases the countless instances in which people simply observe the base rules to begin with, we will have accounted for nearly all of the practical experience of law.

---

[13] The desire for leisure might also be a positive incentive: devising novel or controversial interpretations of the law can be hard work.

[14] According to the Court Statistics Project (www.courtstatistics.org), traffic cases account for about one half, and criminal cases another one fifth, of all state-level court activity. Overall, fewer than one in three hundred cases generate any appeals.

In civil law, the picture is perhaps a bit different. Civil cases such as breach of contract often end up in court not so much because someone has clearly engaged in non-equilibrium behavior, but rather because it is not clear whether someone has done so or not. Sometimes, criminal cases (or even traffic cases) can also be like this. This complicates our picture, as we shall see below. Much of the plausible grounds for skepticism about the law rests on this complication. The possibility of a genuine rule of law, it is sometimes believed, depends entirely on our ability to tie up this loose end. Before attempting to do so, however, I should remark on how odd it is to make the whole issue hinge on what is ultimately the exception. Such complaints ignore the countless instances in which people perform their contracts, refrain from theft and assault, pay their speeding tickets, and so on. The real argument for the rule of law, I would suggest, hinges on the day-to-day normal experience of the ordinary citizen. Needless to say, these observations refer to the operation of law in reasonably well-ordered societies. Only in such societies is the rule of law in this everyday sense undervalued: in many places around the world, however, its elusiveness constitutes an absolutely central political concern. But let us leave such observations aside for the moment.

5.2.2 The Judicial Hierarchy

The determined legal realist might object that our analysis in the previous section was too quick, and that serious difficulties remain. Two lines of attack, in particular, present themselves. According to one, it might be objected that we have merely assumed the case was clear – that Bob clearly reneged on his contract agreement with Andrea. But what if the case is not clear? I will address this objection in the next section. First, I want to address another possible objection, namely, that no account has been given of the appeals process. Why might this be an issue?

In the contract dispute between Andrea and Bob, we assumed that Bob had clearly departed from the equilibrium path (and that this is why the dispute ended up in court), and tried to show that when properly incentivized, the equilibrium best-response strategy for the judge is to sanction him. But what if the trial judge departs from the equilibrium path for some reason? Presumably, Andrea appeals. Ideally, we want an appellate court that is properly incentivized to compel the trial court to properly enforce the base rule of the relevant social norm (in this instance, 'perform contracts made'). If we suppose that judges do not like having their decisions overturned on appeal, then the possibility of appellate review positively enhances the incentive structure facing the trial judge. So far, so good. Next we must consider the incentives facing appellate judges. These are the same as those facing trial judges, including the prospect of being overturned on appeal if they (the appellate judges) depart from *their* equilibrium best-response strategy of compelling trial judges to properly enforce the base rule.[15]

But at some point, this particular incentive mechanism runs out: specifically, it runs out in the court of final appeal, as for example the Supreme Court of the United States, or (until recently) the House of Lords in the United Kingdom. Unfortunately, this is precisely where another incentive mechanism also runs out: opportunities for promotion. Understandably, many worry that the incentives which remain – primarily, reputational incentives – are too weak to perform the work demanded of them.[16] Does this unravel the whole enterprise?

To answer this question, we must first properly frame it. Sometimes the issue is presented as the problem of ensuring *fidelity to the law* on the part of judges – especially, those from whom there is no further avenue of appeal. This way of presenting the problem, however, suggests that there exists an already-present, abstract formal structure called "the law," against which fidelity might be measured or evaluated. But I have rejected this naïve view. The law is a social fact. To vindicate the genuine possibility of a rule of law and not of men we need only show that when the system is properly engineered, people will experience the law as a body of impersonal rules rather than as a meaningless gloss on the direct personal rule of the powerful. This will be the case, roughly speaking, when people know what the rules are in advance and can form reliable expectations that the rules will actually govern – in particular, expectations that do not depend on their having special insight into the private psychology of whoever holds power.

---

[15] For a sophisticated technical model of the hierarchy of justice, see Lax 2003.

[16] These worries are understandable, though not necessarily sound. Clark 2011 argues that the comparatively weak institutional position of high-level courts demands that they carefully cultivate their own perceived legitimacy, without which their decisions are unlikely to be implemented by other government officials.

Imagine that in some legal system the final judge is a single individual. Absent some further configuration of institutional constraints, we might indeed worry that the hierarchy of law simply degenerates into an expression of his whim or pleasure. The structure of incentives set up by the appeals process would then operate, more or less efficiently, to transmit those whims or pleasures down the ladder of legal authority to private individuals, who would experience what is called "law" in that society as merely an expression of the personal will of the final judge. Perhaps this is what happens in a totalitarian dictatorship.

But let us suppose the final court is instead a panel of justices. Let us further suppose there are no constraints on this panel except, first, that they must decide according to majority vote; second, that they must publish their decisions and dissents; and third, that they can decide only disputes brought before them, on a case-by-case basis. (This almost certainly understates the actual constraints on Supreme Court justices, but we may leave that aside and consider the worst-case scenario in our model.) Subject to these constraints, the justices are free to decides cases according to whatever reasons or preferences they happen to have without adverse consequence – that is, they cannot be removed from office by voters or other political actors, and their salaries are fixed.[17]

The first thing to observe here is that our justices, so described, face a commitment problem. In other words, it would seem they cannot engage in log-rolling agreements from one case to the next because, when each new case comes before them, there is no reason for a given judge not to vote his or her sincere preference in that new case. This follows from the fact that there are no personal consequences attached to deciding particular cases one way rather than another (unlike, say, legislators who must face reelection, and thus can be rewarded with committee appointments, spending for their districts, etc.). No punishments can be attached to reneging on a prior deal.[18]

Now what is interesting is that, even in the relatively unconstrained scenario described, the *by-product* of a series of cases decided by

---

[17] They need not serve life terms, however: they might for example serve fixed terms without the possibility of reappointment.

[18] Naturally, there can be plenty of bargaining in constructing a particular majority decision, as discussed in Murphy 1964, esp. ch. 3; or more recently in Maltzman et al. 2000. The point here is only that there is no mechanism for enforcing the trade of a vote in one case for a vote in another.

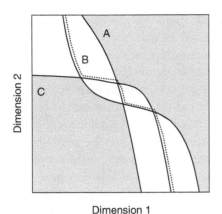

Figure 5.1. A two-dimensional fact space.

majority vote according to the sincere preferences of the justices may often turn out to be what is in effect an impersonal rule. To understand why, let us consider Figure 5.1.[19] In this figure, each point represents a possible case as a combination of two fact dimensions. Thus the horizontal axis might represent the degree to which there is evidence of legal capacity in a disputed contract, while the vertical axis represents the degree to which there is evidence of consideration. When a case presents itself in this "fact space," each justice votes whether the contract is valid or not. Regardless of the basis of his or her votes (even if they are purely ideological, for example), and provided that his or her preferences are reasonably coherent, the sum of a particular judge's various rulings will generate a partitioning of the fact space in two. For example, Justice A in Figure 5.1 upholds contracts to the left of the line A, and invalidates those to the right; the shape of this line suggests that she regards legal capacity as considerably more significant than the element of consideration. The other justices, as we can see, have different preferences over the disposition of contract cases, and thus partition the fact space differently.

Now imagine the panel of justices hears a series of cases one by one and votes sincerely on each. The dotted line in Figure 5.1 indicates the official position of the court induced by this process: provided that

[19] The argument here closely follows a remarkable paper by Lax 2007, which demonstrates these results formally.

none of the judges changes his or her mind, we can expect contracts to be upheld in cases arising to the left of that line, and invalidated otherwise. Some of these determinations are admittedly less certain, in that they rely on the preferences of a single median justice.[20] To the extent that the median judge is genuinely unconstrained in such marginal cases, our experience coming before the court may indeed be one of direct personal rule. Fortunately, this is not the whole story. More important than the central band of uncertainty are the two shaded areas to the lower left and upper right. In these areas, decisions of the court are highly reliable, since *no one justice can change the opinion of the court by changing his or her vote unilaterally.* Thus we have what is in effect an impersonal rule not depending on the whim or pleasure of any specific individual: while not perfect, it may be good enough for most practical purposes. To expand on Kahn's metaphor cited in Chapter 4, even if we do not know exactly where to find the railing, law's causeway can be sufficiently broad to ensure safe passage.[21]

From our point of view, the actual basis of the judges' determinations in whatever cases come before them hardly matters. What matters is that people subject to the law generally experience its effects as that of an impersonal body of rules, rather than as the personal will of those holding power. Here we have seen that this experiential effect can be engineered, in most cases, by the structure of the final court itself.

5.3 Legal Indeterminacy and Hard Cases

In order to deflect responses to the efficacy problem, legal realists and their followers may shift ground to indeterminacy skepticism. When the facts are clear and it is obvious where the equilibrium path lies, perhaps it is reasonable to expect everyone will follow that path, at least most of the time. But what if the law is indeterminate? And worse, what if indeterminacy is common – or even endemic – to legal systems? Here we face a very different challenge. In order not to confuse the two issues, let us now assume that the relevant legal officials are all suitably motivated to respect the law when it is clear what the law requires, and focus our attention specifically on the

---

[20] Notice, however, that there is no one median justice, even in a single area of law: the swing vote depends on the facts of the case: See Lax 2007, pp. 595–597.

[21] Kahn 2006, p. 354.

possibility that the law is *not* clear. This will enable us to isolate the challenge of indeterminacy skepticism.

Legal positivists are sometimes accused of believing there are no serious cases of legal indeterminacy – of holding what Ronald Dworkin famously called a "plain facts" view of the law.[22] Put crudely, if the existence and content of law must ultimately depend on social facts alone, as the legal positivist claims, then isn't there always a fact of the matter as to what (if anything) the law requires? If so, how can there be any genuine disagreement about the law? As it happens, something like the plain fact view does seem to have been held by the so-called *legal formalists*.[23] According to legal formalism, the law necessarily constitutes a complete and internally coherent system that, in principle, supplies to every possible legal question a determinate answer discoverable through the rigorous application of deductive or inductive legal reasoning. So described, legal formalism is deeply implausible, and was justly ridiculed by the realists as "mechanical jurisprudence." It is easy to see why mechanical jurisprudence of the sort the legal formalists apparently envisioned must fail.

The most obvious reason it must fail is practical. Modern societies have enormously complex legal systems, and legislators are only human. Some mistakes are thus inevitable. For example, legislators might issue laws that contradict one another; or they might issue laws that are clearly self-defeating according to their own aims; or they might issue laws whose provisions are simply underspecified or prove unworkable; and so forth. Let us set aside such mundane sources of legal indeterminacy, however, which could perhaps be reduced by crafting legislation with greater care. The deeper source of indeterminacy is inherent in the nature of rules themselves. As we observed in Chapter 2, any finite statement of some rule in ordinary language can in principle instantiate an infinite number of logically possible rules. Suppose you observe Andrea going for a walk every Tuesday and Thursday morning several weeks in a row. It is possible she is following the rule, 'always go for a walk on Tuesday and Thursday mornings', but it is also possible she is following the rule 'always get moderate exercise several times per week', or the rule 'go for a walk

---

[22] Dworkin 1986, pp. 6–11, 33–35; cf. Dyzenhaus 2010, esp. pp. 192–205.

[23] Whether legal formalism existed as a coherent tradition is a matter of some dispute: see Sebok 1998, esp. ch. 3, and Tamanaha 2010, esp. chs. 2–4, for further discussion.

two mornings per week for one month, then rest for one month, and so on', or any number of other theoretically possible alternatives. It follows that one cannot mechanically derive from a given statement of some rule what that rule must require in every possible future circumstance.

This simple fact about the nature of rules can manifest itself in a variety of ways when it comes to law. Three manifestations in particular have attracted much attention. The first is the problem of ambiguity. In any particular case, we are presented with a bundle of discrete facts which can only be brought under the purview of a rule through an act of interpretation. A popular example is the rule 'no vehicles allowed in the park'. Does this rule apply to emergency vehicles? or bicycles? etc. No matter how carefully detailed, rules cannot eliminate the possibility of such ambiguities. The second is the problem of internal contradictions. Since it is impossible to foresee all the implications of a given rule, it is likely that any reasonably complex legal system will encompass conflicting principles. In contract law, for example, we might imagine that principles of fairness underlie the requirement of consideration, while principles of moral responsibility underlie the requirement of legal capacity. Since it is not obvious that these principles can be definitely ranked or reduced to a single master rule, it is possible that in a given case judges will simply have to choose which principle they want to use to determine the outcome. The third is the problem of incompleteness. This is the problem that new situations might arise in which it is unclear how to extend an existing rule. Suppose Andrea is following the rule 'always take a morning walk Tuesdays and Thursdays', but one day the local park where she walks is closed. Does the rule indicate that she should walk somewhere else, or that she should suspend her walks until the park reopens?

Legal positivists are not formalists, and they have long recognized that the existence of indeterminacy in law renders mechanical jurisprudence impossible.[24] The model of adjudication sketched above can easily represent the three cases of indeterminacy as follows. We might think of ambiguity as cases presenting fact that lie at or very near the

---

[24] For example, Kelsen 1960, pp. 348–352, observes that the law must always be interpreted to be applied, and Hart 1994, pp. 124–136, emphasizes the "open texture" of law. The confusion of legal positivism with legal formalism is further discussed in Sebok 1998, chs. 2–3, and Shapiro 2011, ch. 8.

dotted line in Figure 5.1. Internal contradictions can be illustrated with reference to the figure's two dimensions: notice that the induced rule of the court (the dotted line) does not track the view of any one particular justice regarding how the two principles are best balanced, and thus might not itself constitute a logically coherent reconciliation of the principles. Finally, the problem of incompleteness is apparent in that the induced rule of the court as shown will not help in a new case that adds a third (or fourth, fifth, etc.) dimension to the fact space.

How widespread is indeterminacy? Some apparently believe it is pervasive. But if that were so, what explains everyday social norms and conventions like waiting in line for service and other rules of etiquette? It is odd to be skeptical about rules of law when one is not skeptical about social rules generally. As we observed in Chapter 2, some combination of natural instinct and cultural background usually ensures that new situations present few challenges. In many cases, interpretations of a given rule in a given community will tend to converge.[25] That the law sometimes *appears* permeated with more indeterminacy than, perhaps, in practice it actually contains might largely be explained by selection bias. Knowing what the law requires of them, most people conform to the rules of law most of the time. Knowing that appellate courts will uphold the law when its requirements are clear, most people do not bother with appeals. Other things equal, the comparatively rare cases presenting genuine problems of indeterminacy are more likely to find their way into the courts. Restricting our attention to those disputes which end up in court, and especially those which end up in the highest courts, begets an extremely biased view of the system as a whole.

Nevertheless, it cannot be denied that there will be cases in which varying circumstances and experiences are such that interpretations of some rule do not converge in a given legal community. When this happens the law is genuinely indeterminate, and courts face what is sometimes called a *hard case*.[26] There may be some confusion about this term, however. Significantly, there are at least two rather different

---

[25] Both Tamanaha 1997, pp. 231–236, and Marmor 2001, pp. 73–78, correctly observe this point with respect to legal interpretation: as the former observes, many judges describe a sense of "going with the flow" of law (ibid., p. 231). Of course the situation is more complex when rules of law are imposed across cultural boundaries: see Cover 1993, esp. ch. 3.

[26] Following Dworkin 1977, ch. 4.

respects in which a particular case might present serious challenges to conscientious legal officials.

First, a case might present challenges because a strict application of the law would be objectionable on broader moral or ethical grounds. This may often occur in unjust legal systems, for example: South African judges during the period of apartheid were presented with many cases in which the law demanded results repugnant on moral or ethical grounds.[27] But such unfortunate dilemmas can arise even within a reasonably just legal system: the law is in many ways a crude instrument that cannot take every morally or ethically significant detail into account. It follows that even well-meaning laws will occasionally have objectionable results if applied strictly: mandatory sentencing regimes in criminal law, for example, give rise to many such cases. When this happens, it will not be easy for a legal official to implement the law, insofar as doing so may conflict with her broader moral and ethical obligations as a human being. But while they impose unenviable responsibilities on legal officials, such dilemmas do not arise out of legal indeterminacy per se. In order to keep our ideas straight, let us term these *difficult* cases, and set them aside.

Hard cases, in contrast, are those in which it is genuinely unclear what the law as such demands. (Of course some hard cases are also difficult, and some difficult cases are also hard, but that does not detract from underlying distinction.) Dworkin provides a nice illustration using the 1983 case of *McLoughlin v. O'Brian*.[28] In English law at the time, there had been a number of cases establishing that individuals could win compensation for emotional injuries received on being exposed to the victims of accidents caused by negligence. In each of these cases, however, the exposure had been more or less immediate at the scene of the accident. In *McLoughlin*, a wife suffered emotional injury later and away from the scene, on arriving at the hospital and discovering that her daughter was dead and her husband seriously injured. The outcome in the latter case seems to depend on which rule we take the earlier cases to instantiate. Both 'award emotional damages to those exposed at any time to the victims of accidents' and 'award emotional damages to those immediately exposed to the victims of

[27] Such cases are discussed in Dyzenhaus 2010, esp. chs. 2–6.
[28] *McLoughlin v. O'Brian*, 1 A.C. 410 (1983), discussed in Dworkin 1986, pp. 23–29.

accidents' are consistent with the earlier cases. For that matter, so too is 'award emotional damages to those immediately exposed to the victims of accidents, and close family members exposed at any time thereafter'.

Dworkin argues that legal positivists do not have a conception of hard cases that is true to experience: they cannot explain the fact that when legal disagreement arises, it is often felt to be a disagreement about what the law requires rather than a mere political debate regarding how to fill in some legal gap. In Chapter 2, I responded to this complaint. People are conditioned through instinct and experience to feel that certain extensions of indeterminate rules are natural, and when disagreement does arise it is due to local variation in conditioning and experience. There is a second level to Dworkin's critique, however, which we could not address at that time. Sometimes our disagreements about law do not concern extending rules to new cases, resolving unforeseen ambiguities, or other such marginalia, but rather the central or core meaning of law. Dworkin illustrates this sort of fundamental disagreement with *Riggs v. Palmer*.[29] In this case, an elderly man in New York had recently remarried, and his grandson – the primary heir under the elderly man's existing will – feared the will would be rewritten so as to leave him with nothing. In order to forestall this eventuality, he poisoned his grandfather. The question before the court was whether, having done so, the grandson should be prohibited from inheriting according to the existing will, given that the statute of wills in New York at that time indicated no such prohibition. Not surprisingly, there was disagreement among the judges. Judge Gray, writing for the minority, believed the law required following a strict reading of the New York statute of wills, however imperfectly written, with the result that the grandson should inherit. Judge Earl, writing for the majority, had a different view: he believed that the statute of wills should be interpreted in the context of general legal principles, which included the proposition that no one should profit from his own wrongdoing.

According to Dworkin, this disagreement concerns not merely how to fill in some gap at the margins of law, but rather the central meaning of law. It is not clear, however, why he believes the legal positivist

---

[29] *Riggs v. Palmer*, 115 N.Y. 506, 22 N.E. 118 (1889), discussed in Dworkin 1977, p. 23, and 1986, pp. 15–20.

cannot explain foundational disagreements of this sort. As we have seen, all rules by their nature contain the possibility of indeterminacy. Surely this fact applies not only to ordinary rules of law, but also to the rule of recognition itself. *McLoughlin* presented an unforeseen indeterminacy in the existing rule on emotional injury. *Riggs*, by contrast, presented an unforeseen indeterminacy in rule of recognition for New York law. To simplify greatly, both the rule 'acts of the New York legislature count as law' and the rule 'acts of the New York legislature, as interpreted through generally accepted legal principles, count as law' were presumably consistent with the court's prior rulings.[30] The difference between them was only revealed when the Riggs case presented itself to the court. Obviously, disagreement arising from indeterminacy in a rule of recognition will be experienced as more fundamental than other ordinary legal disputes. For a positivist conception of law, however, they pose no great theoretical mystery.

Granting the existence of hard cases, then, how serious a problem do they pose? For the legal officials who must adjudicate hard (or difficult) cases, of course, they pose very serious challenges indeed. These challenges are discussed in the following section. From a rule of law point of view, however, not all manifestations of legal uncertainty are equally problematic. The problem of ambiguity, for instance, need not be a major concern so long as there is a broad area of legal certainty within which one can comfortably live without fear of being subject to violence or physical restraint. As we have said, provided law's causeway is sufficiently broad, it is less important how much pressure the railings can withstand. Similarly, the problem of internal contradictions need not be very troubling in practice: it hardly matters whether the induced official rule of the final court (the dotted line in Figure 5.1 above) is coherent or not, so long as it is known approximately where that rule cuts the fact space in two.

The problem of gaps, on the other hand, is more serious. Continuing with our earlier example, let us suppose that a case arises in which it is not clear whether Bob reneged on a contractual agreement. Perhaps this is because Andrea inferred acceptance from Bob's actions, rather than from any explicit statement on his part. If two parties discuss

---

[30] Here I postpone until Chapter 6 the dispute among positivists as to whether moral or ethical principles, when generally accepted in a legal community, should themselves count as law.

terms, and one of the parties undertakes actions that clearly seem to
imply acceptance of those terms, has a valid contract been created? If
so, then Andrea should presumably be compensated, but not otherwise. We may further suppose that no such case has previously arisen
in the community, and that the scenario is not contemplated in the
existing statute of contracts. When there is genuine indeterminacy like
this, it is not clear what the law requires – or, put another way, where
the equilibrium path lies. Indeed, we might say there *is no equilibrium
path* to find. What then will happen? Andrea and Bob will go to court,
and either ruling is possible. Of course we might regard particular
outcomes as better or worse all things considered: it might be that
Andrea properly deserves to win on moral grounds, for instance.[31] But
we cannot assume that such considerations will effectively and reliably
constrain courts in the sense required to secure freedom from domination, as discussed in Chapter 4.

Fortunately, precisely because the requirement of law is indeterminate, the losing party can appeal. Thus, we would usually expect uncertain cases to climb to the final court (which can rule either by deciding
the case itself or by affirming the lower court's decision).[32] The upshot
is that the problem of indeterminacy basically turns out to be the same
as the problem of finite appeals discussed in the previous section: there
it was wondered what ensures the final court will be faithful to the law,
here what ensures there will be a law for the final court to be faithful
to. It should be clear, however, that the second question is improperly
posed for the same reason as the first. The real issue is not fidelity, but
rather the extent to which we can generate the *experience* of law as a
body of impersonal rules. It doesn't really matter what judges do, or
why they do it, so long as people generally experience coercive force
only *as if* it is the public sanction attached to known rules.[33] From this
point of view, the solution discussed in the previous section works

---

[31] Normative theories of adjudication, which aim to guide legal officials in cases of
indeterminacy, are discussed below.

[32] Provided, of course, that the litigants have the necessary resources for appeal.
When they do not, the de facto final court will be the court they are in when their
resources run out. This creates a problem when the de facto final court is the
trial court: there thus might be a rule of law argument for the public provision
of legal resources sufficient to appeal at least one step up the legal hierarchy.

[33] Thus Tamanaha 1997, p. 235, remarks that "if judges act (behave) as if the law
is determinate," then pragmatically speaking they "have in effect created ...
law-based determinacy in their actions despite the indeterminacy of legal rules."

nearly as well.[34] Regardless of what the final court decides, (the *by-product* of their ruling will be a new impersonal rule for similar future cases.)

Admittedly, this might not be a comfort for the *particular* litigants, Andrea and Bob: they will experience that first ruling as an expression of the whim or pleasure of the final court. This is unfortunate. Perhaps in response we should extend public compensation to parties that lose hard cases in final courts, so that in effect the ruling fully determines only future cases. In practice, of course, determining when compensation is appropriate would be difficult, and such a policy might encourage excessive appeals. The perfect rule of law might not be possible, but we can get close, and there are good reasons for aiming to get as close as we feasibly can.

5.4 Adjudication and Legal Office

It is often complained that legal positivism offers a theory of adjudication that is either useless or else pernicious.[35] This charge rests on a misunderstanding. Legal positivism aims only to describe the law – to provide an accurate report of the various practices distinctively characteristic of the law as an approach to managing expectations and motivating cooperation. Such a report can be extremely useful, I have argued. Among other things, it can help us clearly and fairly assess both the value of the rule of law, and also its limits. But this is not the same as offering a theory of adjudication, if by this we mean a normative account of how legal officials such as judges, public prosecutors, police, agency administrators, and so on should interpret and apply the law in particular cases. We misunderstand legal positivism in complaining that it does not provide a workable theory of adjudication, for it does not aim to do so.[36]

---

[34] Of course in this instance, unlike the previous, the final court will in truth be *making law*. Chapter 6 considers the issue of judicial lawmaking.

[35] These seem the main complaints animating Dyzenhaus 2000 and Dworkin 2002 in their critiques of positivism, for example. See also Fuller 1958, pp. 646–648.

[36] As correctly pointed out in Gardner 2001, pp. 211–214. Despite this, Shapiro 2011, chs. 12–13, attempts to derive such a theory from positivism. His argument hinges on the implicit assumption that if individuals are participants in a special sort of social practice – roughly, one designed to serve joint intentional aims – they have a normative obligation to further those aims. It is not clear to me, however, why positivism requires that assumption.

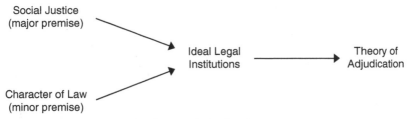

Figure 5.2. Derivation of a theory of adjudication.

This is not to say, however, that a normative theory of adjudication would not be useful to have, or that legal positivism cannot assist in constructing one. On the contrary, legal positivism supplies a necessary minor premise in building any such theory: only given an accurate descriptive report on legal practices can we derive a sound normative theory of adjudication from some broader account of social justice. In this section, I briefly consider what such a theory might look like, if we take as a major premise the broader account of social justice referred to in Chapter 4, according to which we should understand our central political aim as the optimal realization of freedom from domination. The theory's derivation will necessarily be somewhat indirect, insofar as the problem of adjudication is mediated by the problem of institutional design. Thus a complete argument must have something like the structure suggested in Figure 5.2. The first step in our argument will be to ask: *given* the particular character legal practices happen to have, what configuration of legal institutions would best realize freedom from domination? And the second to ask: *given* a configuration of legal institutions realizing social justice in some degree, what duties fall on individual legal officials in interpreting and applying the law to particular cases?

Once laid out in this way, it should be obvious that the problem of adjudication is closely intertwined with broader social and political considerations, for the best configuration of legal institutions will obviously depend on the role we expect those institutions to play within the framework of a well-ordered society's overall political system.[37] Since this topic is far too broad to be addressed here, I will provide no more than a suggestive sketch in the sections that follow.

[37] Ward 2002, pp. 55–62, correctly observes that many accounts of adjudication fail to recognize this dependence.

5.4.1 Two Models of Legal Institutions

Suppose our aim is to realize freedom from domination. From this point of view, we must balance two distinct considerations in designing a political system.[38] On the one hand, we will want that political system to be a force for social justice, identifying and mitigating instances of domination as they appear in society at large. On the other hand, we will also want to ensure that the political system does not itself become an agent of domination in the process. These two considerations may obviously cut against one another to some extent: the more powerful and centralized the political system, the greater a force for social justice it can be, but also the greater a potential source for domination; conversely, a weaker and more decentralized political system will be not only less threatening, but also less of a force for social justice.[39] Conventional wisdom holds that, whatever the appropriate balance between these considerations, our overall institutional scheme must include some sort of independent judiciary – that is, a political sub-system within with disputes can be settled in a predictable manner by legal officials who are not themselves party to those disputes and who are at least partially insulated from the pressures of ordinary politics. No society in which the coercive capacities of the political system are not at least constrained by an independent judiciary in this manner can plausibly be described as well-ordered on the republican view.[40]

Let us simply grant that this conventional wisdom is roughly correct. Given that a well-ordered society must have some sort of independent judiciary, we can narrow our focus to the particular role we expect that judiciary to play within the political system as a whole. What criteria,

---

[38] The framing that follows is due to Pettit 1997, ch. 6, and has since been adopted by many contemporary civic republican writers.

[39] This tension might be articulated theoretically as a tension between legitimacy and justice. The most *legitimate* political system, on the civic republican view, would be the one least likely to itself inflict domination on its citizens. A somewhat less legitimate state, however, might be more *just* if it manages to reduce more domination in society at large than it introduces through its own activities. Pettit 2012, pp. 130–132, believes the tension unlikely to materialize in most cases.

[40] Here I merely gesture toward a broader republican account of institutional design. Historically speaking, the classical republicans generally advocated dispersing political authority over multiple agents via what they described as a "mixed constitution." For further discussion, see Pettit 1997, pp. 177–180.

then, would we want an independent judiciary to satisfy if soundly designed? Three come to mind. The first, and most obvious, is that we would expect the judiciary to make some positive contribution to the overall aims of the political system – namely, the realization of social justice. Suppose, however, as is very plausible, that the overall aim of realizing social justice will be best served through some sort of division of labor, according to which each of the different parts of the political system is assigned a portfolio tailored to its particular institutional strengths and weaknesses. In this case, it will be a second criterion of a soundly designed independent judiciary that its assigned portfolio be well tailored to the characteristic features of legal systems which it necessarily shares. If certain important tasks are not easily accommodated to courtroom hearings, say, it would be counterproductive to assign those tasks to courts.

In addition to these first two criteria, there is also a third: namely, that whatever design we implement, we will want it to be stable in something roughly like Rawls's sense of this term.[41] The idea here is simply that we cannot regard an independent judiciary as soundly designed unless we can reasonably expect it to continue to perform its job well over the long run. To be stable in this sense, the design of the judiciary must be such that its continued institutional health does not depend on the heroic virtue of its office-holders, the exceptional wisdom and patience of ordinary citizens, or both. Rather, imagining that legal officers will be well meaning if not heroic, and that citizens will have a reasonable if not exceptional understanding of the legal system, the judiciary will be stable if its ongoing operation according to its assigned portfolio tends to solidify, rather than undermine, its own institutional health. Later, we shall see that stability in this sense depends on securing a sort of congruence between legal institutions, on the one hand, and the ideas and the theories of adjudication those institutions tend to engender, on the other.

As stated, these criteria should not be controversial. What sort of independent judiciary do they recommend? Consider first what we might call an *activist* model. On this model, the job of the judiciary would be to strive to realize social justice directly so far as it reasonably can: the law should be regarded as an all-purpose instrument for advancing freedom from domination. Accordingly, institutional rules

---

[41] See Rawls 1971, pp. 453–458, 567–570.

regarding jurisdiction, venue, standing, and so forth should be permissive and flexible so as to create as wide a portfolio for legal officials as possible. In order for these various efforts to have real and lasting effects, of course, judicial determinations concerning the demands of republican justice and legitimacy must be treated as final and beyond the authority of other political institutions to revise or reverse: thus courts should have expansive powers of judicial review, at least when it comes to advancing republican aims.

How does this model fare according to our criteria? On the plus side, it will surely to do very well by the first: not only will the judiciary make a positive contribution to the overall project of achieving social justice, it will indeed strive to maximize its contribution to that project. Unfortunately, the activist model is not so likely to score well on the second criterion. If the aim of the judiciary is simply to realize social justice *simpliciter*, it is not clear what its distinctive contribution to that project is supposed to be vis-à-vis the other parts of the political system. The activist model is not well tailored to the particular strengths and weakness of legal systems, regarded as distinctive social formations composed from a characteristic bundle of specific practices. Realizing social justice will often require settling extremely complex and highly controversial issues of socio-economic policy, for example. Such issues are much more likely to be addressed in a successful manner through public deliberation and bargaining in legislative assemblies than they are through the legal process.[42] The nature of law is such that courts are usually presented with problem cases, and (as the saying goes) hard cases make bad law. It is unlikely that the optimal design of national health care policy, for instance, is best determined by a high court's ruling on some singular and highly unusual local dispute.

Therefore, let us consider instead we might call a *restraint* model. On this second model, the portfolio of the judiciary would be strictly limited to the resolution of formal legal disputes – that is, disputes about what the letter of the law as such demands. As the institution specifically charged with the job of resolving such disputes, its determinations on formal legal questions should be treated as final and beyond the authority of other political institutions to revise or reverse: thus courts must have absolute, though narrow, powers of judicial

---

[42] Among others, Waldron 1999b, ch. 5, and Bellamy 2007, ch. 2, have made this point. Similar claims can found in Fuller 1969, pp. 170–178.

review. But in no way should it aim to realize social justice, or even take social justice considerations into account when resolving legal disputes: that job is left to the other parts of the political system whenever possible. Indeed, institutional rules regarding jurisdiction, venue, standing, and so forth should be strict and precisely adhered to so as to reduce temptations in an activist direction.[43]

In contrast with the activist model, the restraint model will certainly score very well on the second criterion. Building on a strict interpretation of the famous separation of powers doctrine, according to which the various functions of government (legislative, executive, judicial) are assigned to different government branches, this model would design a judiciary that maximally respects the portfolios of the other parts of the political system. Moreover, the restraint model seems to play to the institutional strengths of the judiciary as an impartial arbiter of formal legal disputes. But alas, it just as clearly falls short on our first criterion, for a judiciary so-designed would make little contribution to the project of realizing social justice. Indeed, it might sometimes hinder that project. In cases of clear legislative error, for instance, the judiciary would be charged with consistently enforcing the bad policy as literally written, regardless of the consequences. Knowing that policies will be so interpreted, the other parts of the political system might waste tremendous resources on policy details, attempting to anticipate each and every possible contingency in advance.

5.4.2 The Republican Model

We have found that the activist and the restraint models each fail according to one of our first two criteria. Consideration of the third criterion will be postponed, for reasons that will be clear when we return to it below. In the meantime, the failure of these two models prompts us to seek some sort of alternative. What might a better model be? One possibility is to start with the thought that a well-designed independent judiciary should indeed have a portfolio tailored to its particular institutional strengths and weakness, but suggest that this portfolio be limited by its practical aims rather than by its formal jurisdiction. Let me explain as follows.

---

[43] Something like this restraint model is proposed by Bellamy 2007, esp. pp. 15–17, 83–88.

Suppose we regard promoting freedom from domination as our central political aim. Throughout this book, I have insisted that uncontrolled coercive force is an important, though not the only, source of domination. While many other forms of domination (economic, cultural, etc.) are perhaps better addressed through democratic political processes, coercive force is special: it is crucial that people be able to form reliable expectations as to the circumstances under which they are likely to experience coercive force. Now the distinctive value of the rule of law, I have argued, lies precisely in its constraining and channeling the use of coercive force in such a way that it is not experienced as arbitrary, and thus does not constitute domination. Legal practices are particularly well adapted to this task, insofar as they are based on the method of convention: social rules can constrain the exercise of coercion both effectively and reliably. Therefore, it is natural to think that a well-designed independent judiciary might be built on the premise that it will be assigned the specific portfolio of tending to the rule of law. In other words, the job of legal officials should be to strive to realize and maintain the rule of law so far as possible – to ensure that people will not experience coercive force except as the public sanction attached to known rules. Notice that determinations of the judiciary need not, on this view, be regarded as final, beyond the authority of other political institutions to revise or reverse.[44] Rather, on this model the judiciary is understood to be an equal partner with other political institutions in the overall project of realizing freedom from domination, albeit one with a distinctive area of specialization. Let us call this the *republican* model.

How does the republican model fare according to our criteria? With respect to the first, it certainly does well indeed. The rule of law constitutes an important part, though not the whole, of social justice. In advancing the rule of law, the judiciary will therefore be contributing to the overall project of promoting freedom from domination.[45]

---

[44] Cf. Ward 2002, pp. 73–99, who argues that courts are well suited to deciding controversies, but not to permanently fixing constitutional meaning.

[45] Or at any rate, it will at least in passably decent political regimes. By contrast, it is possible that upholding the rule of law in an especially evil regime will do little good, in which case the broader moral obligations of legal officials might assume priority over their institutional obligations. There is some evidence, however, that this path should not be taken hastily: authoritarian regimes can bypass courts altogether when they are found insufficiently compliant, in which case it will no longer matter what legal officials do: see Pereira 2008.

Notice that its portfolio on this view is defined by its practical aims rather than its formal jurisdiction. On the restraint model, the job of the judiciary is understood to be the resolution of strictly formal legal disputes – that is, disputes about what the letter of the law as such requires. On the republican model, the job of the judiciary is more flexibly understood to be ensuring that individuals generally experience coercive force only as the public sanction attached to legally valid prescriptive rules. Sometimes this will require moving beyond the so-called letter of the law, so as to take into account broader social expectations. In any given legal community, a combination of background culture and natural instincts will strongly condition how people interpret ambiguous or incomplete rules of law, for example, and legal officials should respect these interpretations when they can.[46] It follows that the republican model will score better than the restraint model on this criterion.

The republican model nevertheless places definite limits on the role of a well-designed independent judiciary within the political system as a whole. Specifically, the judiciary should concentrate on attending to that aspect of social justice it is most naturally suited to address – namely, the maintenance of the rule of law. This tailors the portfolio of the judiciary to its particular institutional strengths and weaknesses. While courtrooms might not be the best forums for debating the intricacies of controversial issues of socio-economic policy, they are ideally suited to revealing public understandings and expectations with respect to ambiguous or incomplete rules of law: the legal process provides an opportunity for individuals to cast their interpretations as reasonable; legal argument often involves drawing out the good or bad consequences of competing interpretations; and so forth. These aims are not so likely to be well served by deliberation or bargaining in large public assemblies. It follows that the republican model will score better than the activist model on the second criterion. So far, so good.

5.4.3 Theories of Adjudication

Our initial discussion has revealed some advantages for the republican model of judicial institutional design over either the activist or the

---

[46] Note that in multicultural societies, this might entail being sensitive to local variations in expectations: see Cover 1993, ch. 3.

restraint models. The argument is not complete, however, until we consider what all this means for a theory of adjudication.

Let us define a *legal official* as any individual in a given society charged with some degree of responsibility for implementing the laws of that society. Legal officials thus obviously include judges, but also perhaps public prosecutors, the police, some agency administrators, citizens in their capacity as jurors, and so forth. For our purposes, nothing much hangs on how we define this term, and in any case its scope will vary according to the institutional design of various societies. What is important to observe, however, is that every legal official necessarily wears two hats, so to speak. In her capacity as a legal official, on the one hand, she has certain institution-specific obligations, while in her capacity as a human being, on the other, she also has broader moral and ethical obligations. Of course this situation is hardly unique. Indeed, it arises in every case where a person fills an office – the office of mayor, of doctor, of movie critic, and so on. Every office comes with its own institution-specific obligations. Unfortunately, there is no guarantee that our institution-specific duties as the holder of some public office will always coincide with our general moral and ethical duties as human beings. The problem of how to balance these two sets of obligations when they conflict can only properly be addressed within a broader account of moral philosophy, and thus lies beyond the scope of this study.

Despite this, much mischief has been caused by confusing these two sets of obligations, and it is thus important to keep them carefully distinct. Accordingly, let us stipulate that a *theory of adjudication* is a normative account of how legal officials should interpret and apply the law in particular cases according to their institution-specific obligations. In other words, our topic concerns the duties that fall on legal officials *as* legal officials – as the holders of a particular office in a legal system such as the office of judge.[47] It does not, therefore, include an account of how these "duties of adjudication," as we might call them, should be balanced against other broader moral or ethical considerations.

Now it is precisely in this connection that our earlier-mentioned third criterion – the criterion of stability – comes into play. Particular

---

[47] Note that a complete theory of adjudication need not assign the same duties to all legal officials (judges, prosecutors, police, jurors, etc.), but the discussion here will gloss over such details.

institutions, we might naturally suppose, have a tendency to engender particular constellations of values and beliefs among those individuals whose behavior the institutions govern. Thus for instance, economic institutions organized along pure free market lines might tend to generate instrumental and competitive attitudes among their participants, whereas economic institutions governed by Rawls's difference principle might tend to foster attitudes of reciprocity and fair cooperation.[48] It follows that, assuming we care about stability, our choice among possible theories of adjudication is severely constrained: specifically, in selecting a particular model for the design of judicial institutions, we are in effect constrained to select as well whatever theory of adjudication the institutions answering to that model would tend to engender. Why so? Simply because any other theory would not be congruent with those institutions in the long run. We might imagine, perhaps, a judge of heroic personal character who persistently observes principles of restraint in the face of judicial institutions designed to encourage activism (or vice versa). From a practical point of view, however, we cannot expect the long-run stability of judicial institutions to rely on many individuals exercising a more than reasonable degree of personal virtue.

Accordingly, we shall compare the distinct theories of adjudication naturally engendered by legal institutions designed according to the three models. Any plausible theory would agree, presumably, that judges and other legal officials should respect and apply the law whenever it is reasonably clear and not inconsistent with the demands of social justice.[49] In healthy legal systems, these will constitute the great majority of cases, especially at lower levels of the judicial hierarchy. The theories diverge, however, in those cases where the law is indeterminate or problematic. These are precisely the cases, of course, that are most likely to ascend the judicial hierarchy and receive the most attention.

Consider the activist model first. On the theory of adjudication most congruent with this model, legal officials in the judiciary should strive to advance social justice and political legitimacy when presented with

---

[48] These sorts of issues are central to Rawls's concerns in 1971, part three.

[49] Less plausible theories, of course, might disagree. For example, certain ideological approaches to adjudication (fascist, communist, etc.) might hold that political considerations should sometimes trump legal considerations even in easy cases.

indeterminate, incoherent, or otherwise problematic rules of law.[50] Indeed, to the extent that it is able, the judiciary should aim to increase its portfolio by turning easy cases into hard ones so as to give a greater scope its efforts.[51] In hard cases like *Roe v. Wade* or *Brown v. Board of Education*, we should ask what outcome would be normatively best according to our preferred account of social justice, and then interpret the law accordingly.[52] By this criterion, we may suppose that both cases were rightly decided, if not necessarily rightly reasoned. But would we expect a judiciary operating along these lines to be stable? Probably not. In the process of crowding out the portfolios of other branches, an activist judiciary will in the long run tend to undermine its own institutional legitimacy and good will.[53] If the judiciary is imagined to be no different from the other parts of the political system, what justifies its independence and insulation from ordinary political processes? Such a judiciary will likely provoke strong resistance to its efforts, while at the same time exposing itself to politicization.

So what about the restraint model: will it fare any better? Probably not. On a theory of adjudication congruent with this model, legal officials in the judiciary should always follow the strict letter of the law as such whenever they can.[54] This would suggest that *Brown* and *Roe* were wrongly decided, since both involved significant departures from what was explicitly required by the relevant legal materials.[55] In many problematic cases, adhering to a narrowly literal interpretation of the legal materials will moreover generate absurd or counterproductive consequences. Consider for instance a simple safety ordinance that

---

[50] It is less clear on this theory what duties of adjudication fall on other legal officials. For instance, should the police likewise strive to see that justice is done whenever rules they are charged with enforcing are unclear or ambiguous?

[51] One example of an activist theory might be the pragmatist approach discussed and critiqued in Dworkin 1986, esp. ch. 5; the integrity approach Dworkin himself prefers (ibid., esp. chs. 6–7) represents a more moderate activism in which legal officials resolve hard cases in light of the best normative justification for the legal materials available.

[52] *Roe v. Wade*, 410 U.S. 113 (1973); *Brown v. Board of Education* 347 U.S. 483 (1954).

[53] Here see Rosenberg 2008.

[54] Textualism, originalism, and doctrinalism are examples of this sort of theory. As in the case of an activist theory, we might again wonder whether the duty of restraint is supposed to apply to all legal officials, including the police, public prosecutors, and so forth.

[55] Bellamy 2007, pp. 43–44, expresses doubts about both decisions, as we would expect given his support of the restraint model.

requires pedestrians to walk against traffic. What about those occasions when this is clearly the more dangerous option? Is the correct interpretation of the ordinance 'always walk against traffic, even when this is clearly more dangerous'; or 'always walk against traffic, except when this is clearly more dangerous'? On a restraint theory of adjudication, it would seem we must believe the court in *Tedla v. Ellman* erred when it concluded the latter.[56] What is worse, confined by its own institutional portfolio to acting as an impartial mouthpiece of law, the judiciary will be unable to address problems of genuine indeterminacy in good faith. Legal officials will be institutionally pressured to conceal indeterminacy and pretend there are no gaps in the law. Since courts cannot help but sometimes engage in discretionary interpretation, an ideology denying this will in the long run be self-defeating. Especially when it comes to high-level constitutional questions, over which the judiciary claims final authority on the restraint model, the court's bad faith will be most egregious.[57]

This leaves us with the republican model. A theory of adjudication congruent with this model of judicial institutions need not pretend that the law is always determinate or that some issues are not genuinely political. It can acknowledge in good faith that legal officials must engage in discretionary interpretation when faced with hard cases. However, it directs that interpretation toward the particular aim of maintaining and enhancing the rule of law: judges and other legal officials should strive to ensure that people will experience coercive force only as the public sanction attached to known rules.[58] What might this mean in practice? By definition, of course, the law itself provides no determinate result in a hard case, but it does not follow that people were acting without expectations of any kind. This suggests that we try to work out whose expectations were most reasonable, extending ambiguous or incomplete rules in the direction that an unbiased person in the relevant community might find most natural.

---

[56] *Tedla v. Ellman*, 280 N.Y. 124, 19 N.E.2d 987 (1939).

[57] This problem of "bad faith" is analyzed extensively in Kennedy 1997.

[58] With suitable refinement, the republican theory of adjudication might be extended to all legal officials: it is more plausible in my view to say that the police, for instance, should strive to ensure that people generally experience coercion only as the public sanctions attached to known social rules, than it is to say either that they should strive to realize justice directly or that they should strive to enforce the letter of the law regardless of circumstances.

When faced with hard cases, in other words, we should strive to respect as best we can the reasonable expectations of the various parties affected, whether those expectations are fully merited in the existing legal materials or not.[59]

For example, suppose the existing rule is clear, but its proper extension under new or unanticipated circumstances is legally indeterminate. If natural instinct and background culture tend toward convergent expectations in the relevant legal community, the rule should be extended accordingly. Thus the court in *Tedla* decided correctly that the most sensible and natural interpretation of the safety ordinance favors the extension 'always walk against traffic, except when this is clearly more dangerous', since this furthers rather than frustrates the obvious purpose of the ordinance. When variations in instinct and experience produce serious disagreement rather than convergence, of course, the issue is more difficult. The best courts can do under such circumstances is respect those disagreements so far as possible, either by not imposing a specific interpretation through judicial fiat or, when this is unavoidable, by minimizing its scope. It may follow, on the republican theory of adjudication, that *Roe* was decided wrongly.[60] The Supreme Court faced a very different problem in *Brown*, however, since a series of previous cases attempting to clarify and refine the "separate but equal" doctrine had degenerated into incoherence and confusion: in effect, there was no longer a clear rule to follow. The republican theory may thus regard the ruling in *Brown* as correct less because it advanced social justice (though of course it did) than because it dramatically clarified expectations in a natural and sensible way, indeed explicitly stating the new rule the high court was by that time already following in practice, though until then not officially.[61]

---

[59] It is by this mechanism that custom has often become a source of law: see Watson 2001, ch. 4.

[60] It does not follow, however, that *Roe* should be overturned. Having been declared and repeatedly reaffirmed, reasonable expectations have now been built around abortion rights. Insofar as the republican theory of adjudication directs legal officials to respect reasonable expectations, it will place considerable weight on the principle of *stare decisis*.

[61] Here I follow the illuminating discussion of *Brown* in Straus 2010, pp. 85–92. One might read the line of cases culminating in *Obergefell v. Hodges*, 576 U.S. ___ (2015) in a similar manner.

Importantly, legal officials need not have the final authority to settle questions of law or policy on a republican theory of adjudication.[62] They may claim to be the final arbiter of any particular dispute, but this need not be the same thing. The portfolio of the judiciary centers on enhancing the rule of law – one aspect of the broader republican conception of social justice. Other parts of the political system, however, will presumably have their own portfolios. Recall that our overall aim is to realize freedom from non-domination, and our initial assumption was that this aim might be realized most effectively through a sort of division of labor granting distinct portfolios to different political sub-systems. The various parts of the system should be regarded as mutual partners in the overall scheme. To the extent that a well-designed independent judiciary advances its particular portfolio so defined, it will thus contribute to the overall project of realizing social justice in a way that enhances, rather than detracts, from its own institutional legitimacy.[63] Unlike either of the other theories, it seems to me that the republican theory of adjudication will tend to support the long-run stability of legal institutions.

Before concluding, let me briefly remark on the issue set aside above: the general moral and ethical obligations of those individuals who happen to occupy offices in the legal system. These obligations presumably include, for example, some sort of duty to realize social justice, as well as humanitarian obligations such as duties of charity and rescue. Their existence obviously complicates our picture. Broadly speaking, there are two sorts of difficult cases to consider. In the first, an individual holds legal office in a bad political system – that is to say, a political system which is to some significant degree unjust. Here we might think of South African judges under apartheid, for instance: these judges frequently faced cases in which the rule of law seemed to dictate seriously unjust or inhumane outcomes. In the second situation, an individual holds legal office in a good – that is to say, reasonably just – political system, but faces a bad case. The case is bad in the sense that, despite the well-meaning best efforts of the political system as a whole, the peculiarities of the case are such that the rule of law seems to dictate seriously unjust or inhumane outcomes.

---

[62] It is beyond the scope of this discussion to consider what this means in terms of the details of judicial review, but it would certainly involve limiting the scope of that authority considerably.

[63] Or at least it usually will if the political regime is passably decent: see n. 45.

In either situation, legal officials face an unenviable choice. However, we cannot say what they should do without answering much broader questions of moral philosophy.[64] My point here is simply to observe the possibility that such situations might arise, and caution that they present problems distinct from the problems theories of adjudication are meant to address. It is important to do this so as to not confound our theory with intuitions more properly addressed elsewhere.

5.5 Conclusion

In Chapter 4, the rule of law was defined as that situation in which individuals are never exposed to coercive force except as the consequence of having failed to observe legally valid prescriptive rules. Insofar as uncontrolled coercive force is an especially serious source of domination, it was argued that achieving the rule of law, other things being equal, would significantly advance the project of social justice. That argument, however, relied on a simplified picture of legal systems. To what extent does legal indeterminacy and judicial discretion present a serious challenge to our earlier argument?

In order to answer this question, we focused on two distinct issues. The first was efficacy skepticism – the worry that formal rules as such do not really constrain legal officials. If this were so, then people would not experience the law as an impersonal body of rules, but rather as the mere expression of the private whim or pleasure of legal officials. This worry was answered, however, by showing how legal officials are themselves participants in the network of social norms and conventions constituting a legal system. Provided the network is properly engineered, there is no reason to believe that arbitrariness cannot be reduced to an acceptable minimum. The second issue was indeterminacy skepticism – the worry that in many cases existing rules cannot constrain legal officials because the rules are indeterminate. If there is no rule to govern, then whatever legal officials do in such cases, their decisions will be experienced as an expression of private whim or

---

[64] Solum 1994, however, points out that we might consider how different approaches to such difficult cases might affect a legal official's settled disposition to respect his duties of adjudication in normal cases. To the extent that he is right, we might indeed extract some guidelines for difficult cases from our theory of adjudication.

pleasure. This worry was answered by pointing out that indeterminacy is in practice much less troublesome than sometimes feared. Provided that legal actors behave *as if* the law is reasonably clear in most cases, the subjective felt experience of those it governs will largely be one of an impersonal body of rules. Accordingly, there is no need to abandon our earlier normative argument for the rule of law.

We have lifted only one of the assumptions underlying our simple model of legal systems, however: namely, the assumption that the law is always clear. What about the other assumption, that the law does not change? In Chapter 6 we will address the challenges presented by lifting this assumption as well.

6 | *Legislation, Administration, and Discretion*

Part I of this study relied on the simplified model of a legal system as a serene equilibrium, free from disagreement about what the law is and what it should be. Part II complicates the simple model. In Chapter 5, we dropped the assumption that it is always clear what the law requires, and considered problems arising from indeterminacy and the need for interpretation. In this chapter, we drop the assumption that it is always agreed what the law should be, and consider problems arising from legislation, discretion, and regulation. Our aim will again be to demonstrate that, suitably addressed, these problems need not pose an insurmountable challenge to our understanding of the rule of law and its value.

What animates the somewhat disparate issues addressed in this chapter might be characterized as an underlying worry that there exists some deep tension – or worse, contradiction – between the traditional ideal of the rule of law, on the one hand, and the modern social-democratic state, on the other. Is it possible, for example, to achieve social justice under modern conditions without resorting to deliberate legislation, discretionary authority, government planning, and so forth? And if not, can these devices be reconciled with the rule of law? In answering these questions, we face a dual challenge. First, in order to avoid the stark conclusion that we must choose between the rule of law and social justice, we will need to show that there is no necessary contradiction between the rule of law and many of the methods of governance commonly employed by modern social-democratic states. Second, however, in order to avoid proving too much, we will need to show that the rule of law is not a vacuous ideal compatible with anything modern social-democratic states might do, but rather that it generates significant and useful guidelines for constraining state activity.

Before proceeding, let me stress (as I have repeatedly throughout this study) that the rule of law should not be understood as a comprehensive political ideal. My hope in this chapter is to further illustrate not only the enduring value of the rule of law, but also its limits in relation to other things we might reasonably care about.

6.1 The Rule of Law and Legal Change

The value of the rule of law, we have argued, lies in its reliance on what Chapter 4 termed the method of convention. It is crucially important for human flourishing that people know they will be exposed to coercive force only under specific and determinate conditions not subject to the arbitrary whim or pleasure of others. These conditions can be secured when the use of coercive force is effectively and reliably governed by the rules and procedures embodied in a reasonably well-ordered legal system. But our argument to this point has relied on a static model of legal systems. No existing legal system is, or could ever be, perfectly static. Once we have suitably adjusted our characterization of law to account for this fact, as we shall below, must our argument for the value of the rule of law be substantially revised?

6.1.1 Endogenous versus Exogenous Change

The method of convention secures coordination through reliance on an established schedule of public rules. Now it may at first seem that the method of convention does not contain within itself any mechanism for effecting change in the schedule of rules. This is not entirely correct. As we have discussed, the necessarily open-ended and indefinite character of all prescriptive rules is such that they cannot cover in advance every possible circumstance that might arise in the future. It follows that whenever new and unexpected circumstances arise, existing rules must be adapted and extended through interpretation. At least to the extent that this ongoing process of adaption and extension at the margin is oriented toward the natural expectations of the relevant parties, it constitutes an integral part of the method of convention itself rather than a distinct practice.[1] Accordingly, we might describe

---

[1] The republican theory of adjudication outlined in Chapter 5 advocates precisely this approach to legal interpretation.

it as a form of *endogenous change*. Precisely because endogenous legal change is gradual and marginal, static characterizations of legal systems such as the one presented in Chapter 3, while not strictly accurate, nevertheless approximate reality tolerably well for many analytic purposes.

All legal systems – as indeed all systems of social norm and convention more generally – exhibit endogenous change. This is most conspicuously evident, perhaps, in the common law tradition, which has historically developed extensive bodies of legal doctrine through the gradual accretion of precedent. The emergence of English contract law in the early modern period represents a particularly famous example of endogenous legal change: though to some extent English and American contract law has now been formally codified, codification was merely the conclusion of a lengthy process in which the legal doctrine of enforceable voluntary agreements based on mutual consideration gradually emerged out of traditional tort law through incremental extension and revision.

Some less conspicuous examples might be equally significant, however. For instance, it is surely remarkable that case law seems to creep into even the French and German civil law systems, despite the fact that those systems officially refuse to acknowledge judicial precedent as an independent source of law. This only goes to show that endogenous change is an unavoidable aspect of the method of convention itself. Even when judges conscientiously ignore past rulings in deciding present controversies, their similar social background, education, professional experience, and so forth virtually ensure that customs of interpreting particular statutes this way rather than that will tend to emerge. The evolution of these customs over time then gives rise to what is, in effect, endogenous legal change.

Endogenous legal change has some significant advantages. First, by hewing as closely as possible to the internal logic of the method of convention, the process of incremental extension and revision minimizes both the occurrence and severity of upset expectations. This is beneficial on rule of law grounds – namely, that the incidence of coercive force be channeled so far as possible in directions people can be reasonably expected to anticipate. Second, as Hayek observed, by relying on a decentralized process of marginal adaptation, an immense quantity of differentiated local knowledge can be processed and integrated into the system as a whole. From this point of view, the process of endogenous legal change parallels to some extent the operation of decentralized free markets.[2]

Despite these advantages, there are at least three important difficulties with relying on endogenous mechanisms for legal change alone. The first, and most obvious, stems from the fact that endogenous change is by its nature gradual; when confronted with conditions of rapid social or economic change, it is unlikely to keep pace. This limitation can indeed prove fatal to societies not equipped with alternative mechanisms for effecting change more rapidly.[3] The second arises from the problem of path dependence. Sometimes the line of endogenous development followed in some area of law, while initially promising, leads through unanticipated future contingencies to a dead end. Not only is this inefficient, it can also be self-defeating from a rule of law point of view: often, the upshot of such dead-end developments is a confusing tangle of half-measures and mitigating strategies that obfuscate rather than clarify legal expectations.[4] One famous example illustrating both of the first two difficulties might be the nineteenth-century privity of contract doctrine, which shielded manufacturers from product liability claims unless their product was "inherently dangerous," as for instance a bottle of poison. While this rule may have served when first introduced, with the advance of modern commerce it quickly degenerated into incoherence: scaffolding, elevators, and large coffee urns were held by various courts to be inherently dangerous, whereas flywheels and steam boilers were not. By the time a case involving a defective automobile arose, it was clear the doctrine no longer provided any guidance at all – is an automobile more like an elevator or a steam boiler? – and needed drastic revision.[5]

These first two difficulties are, of course, largely practical. Even if they could be avoided, however, there is a third and decisive objection

---

[2] Hayek 1973, esp. chs. 4–5. Cf. Dicey 1915, pp. 115–120, who argues that legal rules developed organically through the courts will be more efficacious in practice than abstract principles pronounced in deliberate legislation.

[3] In this connection it is interesting to reflect on the communities discussed in Diamond 2005 that collapsed due to an inability to revise their customary ways of doing things in the face of changing circumstances.

[4] Hayek discusses this problem at 1973, pp. 88–89.

[5] Accordingly, in *MacPherson v. Buick Motor Co.*, 217 N.Y. 382, 111 N.E. 1050 (1916), Judge Benjamin Cardozo dispensed with the privity of contract doctrine and introduced a new foreseeability doctrine. For a nice discussion, see Strauss 2010, pp. 80–85.

to relying exclusively on endogenous mechanisms for legal change. This is the fact that the process of incremental extension and revision at the margin, if it does not always exacerbate, will at least often tend to track the existing balance of power and influence in society.[6] Of course, local decisions can sometimes favor culturally or economically disadvantaged parties, but in aggregate it is exceedingly unlikely that a legal system will of its own accord naturally evolve toward greater cultural or economic equality. This is partly due to the superior resources the advantaged will be able to deploy in navigating the legal process, and partly due to the class affiliation of many members of the legal profession. Note that the law is hardly unique in having a conservative bias: while all systems of social norm and convention spontaneously evolve with changing conditions, in the absence of deliberate intervention they only rarely do so in a broadly egalitarian direction.

For these reasons, it is important to have additional mechanisms for effecting deliberate legal change. One reasonably straightforward mechanism might involve what in Chapter 4 we termed the method of deliberation: the members of the relevant legal community might in assembly explicitly debate possible changes to their laws, and effect such changes through consensus or voting. Another straightforward, but much less appealing option would be to designate some individual or committee as having the authority to unilaterally introduce legal change. In complex modern societies, of course, the mechanisms for legal change are considerably more complex. Usually, they involve not only representative national assemblies exercising primary legislative authority, but also extensive delegation to administrative agencies, legal commissions, local governments, and so forth. Notice that in each case, from the point of view of the legal system as a distinctive social formation – that is, as a bundle of practices characteristically built on the method of convention – we can regard these sorts of mechanisms as *exogenous* rather than endogenous. We are therefore bound to wonder whether exogenous legal change might present a problem for our account of the rule of law.

---

[6] Interestingly, Hayek 1973, pp. 88–89, was equally aware of this problem. Cf. Galanter 1974.

6.1.2 *Characterizing Legal Change*

In order to sort through the implications of legal change for our account of the rule of law, let us consider the various forms legal change might take, since some of these will pose a more serious challenge than others.

Our starting point is the simple equilibrium model of Chapter 3: a society governed by a wide range of social rules, some subset of which is regularly supported by a public coercive agent and thus constitutes a legal system. Now suppose that change in that configuration is wanted – either because shifts in underlying socio-economic conditions have rendered the existing system of norms and laws suboptimal, or because there is a push for greater equality, or for some other reason. What might change look like from the point of view of our model? As a rough schematic, we might suppose that any particular change in the law will have the aim of either:

(a) introducing a new social rule,
(b) modifying an existing social rule, or
(c) eliminating a social rule no longer desired.

Following this schematic, we might first consider a few scenarios in which legal change presents little or no problem from a rule of law point of view.

As we have seen, the method of convention is at root a method for securing coordination through clarifying expectations and motivating cooperation. When there are mutual gains to be captured through coordination, new social norms or conventions sometimes emerge spontaneously. Nothing ensures they will, however. Especially when it comes to coordination problems that are very complex or asymmetric in the distribution of potential benefits, people may fail to settle on an equilibrium. The law can solve such problems by simply announcing a coordination point, as it does in setting public standards (for rail gauge, for weights and measures, etc.). In other cases, social norms or conventions might indeed emerge spontaneously, but turn out to be suboptimal, either through historical accident or changes in the background socio-economic conditions. Despite the fact that some other equilibrium would be better for some or all parties, and worse for none, the assurance problem may present an obstacle to transition. As in the case of equilibrium selection, the law can facilitate transition by simply announcing a new coordination point.

In these first two scenarios, legal change will present no particular problem for the rule of law. This is because in either case, the benefits of coordination alone are sufficient to motivate the parties to observe the new social rule: once it is known that others will be ϕ-ing, everyone will want to ϕ themselves. (Of course, publicity is required here, but then if the new law is not made public, it will not solve the coordination problem in the first place!) The law's role here, we might say, is primarily expressive.[7] Legal change will also present no problem in a third scenario. Through changes in ideas or circumstances, it may happen that a once-serviceable law becomes objectionable or unnecessary, by which time people might observe the underlying social rule (if they still do) only to avoid the coercive sanctions the law itself imposes. The repeal of such laws raises no problem because, presumably, no one will be exposed to coercive force once the law is repealed.[8]

We have said that, in these scenarios, legal change poses few difficulties from a rule of law point of view, but this is not to say it will not often be controversial and thus politically challenging to undertake. When the anticipated benefits of coordination will be shared unequally, for example, it may be especially hard to secure agreement on the specific direction legal change should assume. Even cases of repeal can be ideologically controversial, as when legal prohibitions on abortion or punishments for sodomy are lifted. But these are different topics, unrelated to the rule of law per se. Here we are concerned narrowly with the extent to which legal change might clash specifically with the rule of law.

The value of the rule of law lies in its capacity to channel the incidence of coercive force so far as possible in directions people can anticipate. The rule of law is secured when people have effective and reliable expectations that they will be exposed to violence or physical restraint only in the event of their failure to observe a legally valid prescriptive rule. The special difficulty presented by legal change thus arises when people have reasons to resist that change. To be sure, once a new law is in place, and the corresponding social rule generally observed, even those who opposed the change will at least know what they have to do in order to avoid being coerced in the future – they will

[7] See McAdams 2005 on the expressive functions of law.
[8] Here I leave aside the special case in which repealing a law would create opportunities for coercion in the sphere of private relations. Such repeals would be objectionable on rule of law grounds for obvious reasons.

know where law's causeway lies. Nevertheless, from their point of view *the transition itself* may in effect be experienced as a command (roughly, 'Switch from this equilibrium behavior to that!') backed by the use or threat of coercive force.

In any of the scenarios delineated by our rough schematic people may find they have reasons to resist change. The most common difficulties will arise in efforts to modify existing social rules; for it is probably not often the case that the best reform, all things considered, will constitute a strict Pareto improvement on the status quo, better for some and worse for no one. Existing social norms or conventions often distribute benefits and burdens unfairly, and it may not be possible to arrive at a fair distribution without making at least a few people worse off. Thus, for example, progressive reforms in the tax code or the introduction of new welfare benefits obviously involve transfers from some people to others. But many policies not intentionally redistributive will nevertheless have indirect redistributive effects. Workplace safety regulations, for instance, benefit workers by reducing injuries, but cost consumers by raising prices; the Americans With Disabilities Act expands opportunities for the disabled, but imposes facility improvement costs on the non-disabled; modifications in zoning laws can raise some property values while lowering others; and so forth. The other two scenarios of legal change can present difficulties as well, however. On the one hand, new social rules are not always universally welcomed, and thus take time to become widely accepted (sexual harassment law, for instance). On the other hand, long-standing social rules can sometimes stubbornly resist even concerted attempts to stamp them out (dueling, for instance).

The point here is not that these sorts of reforms cannot be normatively justified, all things considered. Quite the contrary, it is precisely because endogenous change is unlikely to secure a fair distribution of benefits and burdens that we feel the need to introduce exogenous mechanisms for legal change. Rather, the point is a narrower one: namely, that insofar as some persons or groups might not abandon the status quo for some new equilibrium that will leave them somewhat worse off but for the coercive inducement provided by the law, those specific persons or groups might experience the transition itself as what is in effect a coercive command. Whatever the overall balance of arguments in favor of the reform in question, this seems at least potentially problematic from a rule of law point of view. Our next question, then, is whether exogenous mechanisms for legal change can be designed in such a way as to mitigate this problem. In the following section I will argue they can.

Before turning to that discussion, however, there is one loose end worth addressing regarding our account of legal systems. In actual instances of legal change, it is often not the case that the underlying social rule changes in perfect lock-step with the change in the law. Particularly when many persons or groups in society have reasons to resist reform, the law can find itself moving well out in advance of social norm and convention. When this happens, a gap opens between what the law requires, on the one hand, and what social rules dictate, on the other.[9] Historically, the consequence of this has usually been that considerable time, effort, or both were required to bring social rules into conformity with the law. It took centuries, for example, before European states finally managed to stamp out the practice of dueling among the aristocratic classes. In the United States, it was only through tremendous political effort and extensive social mobilization that explicit policies of segregation were finally abolished.[10]

In the meantime, the gap raises a puzzle for our account of legal systems, for we have defined law as a social rule regularly supported by some public coercive agent. But during such a time as the gap exists, there is no underlying social rule corresponding to the requirement of law. In the technical language of Chapter 3, we must say that the prescriptive rule is *legally valid*, but apparently *not a law* strictly speaking. This may seem like conceptual hair-splitting, but there is actually some intuitive sense to expressing the situation in this way. Consider America circa 1960, for instance. After *Brown v. Board*, the prescriptive rule of desegregation was legally valid throughout the United States.[11] However, if five or six years later we asked someone in the South – particularly someone black – whether desegregation was or was not "the law," we would understand perfectly well what she meant if she answered, "No it isn't." Questions of ultimate legal

---

[9] Gaps can also emerge when, through an absence of legal change, social customs and norms advance ahead of law. This creates a different challenge, here set aside, insofar as it may become hard for many people to continue obeying increasingly outdated legal rules.

[10] Interesting further examples of resistance to legal change can be found in Galligan 2007, ch. 17.

[11] *Brown v. Board of Education*, 347 U.S. 483 (1954).

validity aside, it was at that time not yet a fact on the ground. From this point of view, desegregation was *not* the law, in the fullest and most concrete sense of that expression, until after much struggle actual institutions and practices were dragged into conformity with what had been legally required for some time.[12]

Apart from definitional quibbles, however, there is a substantive issue to resolve here. If coercive force is directed toward a person who fails to comply with a legally valid prescriptive rule that is not (yet) a social rule, does this violate the rule of law? The best answer is no. Pragmatically speaking, the value of the rule of law rests in securing effective and reliable expectations concerning the future incidence of coercive force: it is immensely important for human flourishing that people understand the conditions under which they will be exposed to the use or threat of violence or physical restraint. Does this always require not only that the incidence of coercive force tracks a legally valid prescriptive rule, but also further that there exists a corresponding social rule on the ground, so to speak? It does not. Provided sufficient public notice has been given, of course, the former should be sufficient to secure the relevant expectations, and thus make it possible for individuals to avoid being exposed to the use or threat of violence or physical restraint. This explains why, in Chapter 4, our definition of the rule of law was framed in terms of "legally valid prescriptive rules," not more simply "laws."

6.2 Designing Legislative Authority

There are many ways exogenous mechanisms for effecting deliberate legal change might be designed. Which way is best? Unfortunately, there is no simple answer to this question. Particular institutional configurations might be judged better or worse according to a range of normative criteria that do not always agree. Those configurations most conducive to efficiency, for instance, may not be the same as those most likely to advance equality. This section will consider only the

---

[12] Some of this story is related in fascinating detail by Brown-Nagin 2011. Of course, we are here considering only explicit policies of segregation, not the various sorts of informal segregation that have arisen through residential housing patterns, for instance. While the latter clearly give rise to significant injustice, they do not do so in a way contrary to any existing law, and are thus beyond the scope of present discussion.

extent to which possible institutional configurations are congenial to
the rule of law. Since, as we argued in Chapter 4, the rule of law
constitutes an important part of social justice, such congeniality must
itself count as a virtue in those institutions. The difficult task of
weighing this virtue against others, however, is a task we must leave
for another time.

Let us term the institutional authority to exogenously change the law
legislative authority. Now imagine a legal community in which legislative authority is vested entirely in the hands of a single individual or
insular committee. Suppose the authority is unlimited in scope and
unaccountable to the community at large: at any time, the individual
or committee can simply decide that the law from henceforth will
require some new or different thing. From a rule of law point of view,
this could hardly constitute a desirable state of affairs. The difficulty is
not simply that the specific laws of that community might be liable
to frequent change, thus making it difficult for people to form depend-
able expectations concerning the conditions under which they will be
exposed to coercive force – though that might indeed be the case.[13] It is
further that, in such a community, people will in effect be subject to
uncontrolled or arbitrary coercion. Even if the laws remain reasonably
stable, that is only by the good graces of the legislative authorities.
At any time and for any reason, the latter might simply rewrite the laws
so some person or group must go here or there, do this or that, or be
subject to thus and such new burden – and the very next day rewrite
the laws again to suit some other whim. If our aim is to ensure that
people are exposed to coercive force only according to known and
determinate conditions not subject to the arbitrary whim or pleasure
of others, this will not do at all.

How then might we design institutions for effecting deliberate legal
change differently, so they would be more congenial to the rule of law?
Let us imagine an institutional configuration (much more familiar to
contemporary democratic societies) in which legislative authority is
primarily vested in a national assembly with a rotating membership.
Let us further suppose the national assembly sometimes enacts specific

---

[13] There is, presumably, some limit as to how rapidly the law can change before its
capacity to serve as a basis for reasonable expectations would collapse, but this
limit might be a good deal further off than is sometimes supposed. There was no
general collapse of law and order during the extraordinarily rapid creation of the
American welfare state, for example.

legal change directly, but other times legislates only in broad outline, assigning most of the details to professional administrative agencies or commissions that presumably have the advantage of specialized expertise and local knowledge. Thus, for instance, the national assembly might create a traffic safety commission, and instruct the latter to craft specific rules of the road. Taking this familiar institutional framework as our rough starting point, then, how might we ensure that the process of exogenous legal change remains congenial to the rule of law?

Our aim, to reiterate, is to ensure that people experience coercive force only according to known and determinate conditions not subject to the uncontrolled or arbitrary whim or pleasure of others. From this point of view, we must ensure that the process of exogenous legal change itself constitutes a rule-governed process – that legislative authority be brought under the cover of law, so to speak. This entails at a minimum that there should exist:

(1) public and orderly procedures legislative authorities must follow in order to change the law.

Furthermore, those procedures should

(2) clearly define and limit the scope of the relevant legislating authority, and
(3) indicate the broad aims or goals it is meant to serve.

Finally, there must be

(4) some mechanism for holding the relevant legislative authority accountable in the event that it fails to respect the above conditions.

Together these might be termed conditions of *legislative due process*.[14] How the principles of legislative due process are best met will obviously depend on the institutional context.

In the case of administrative agencies or commissions, we might say that the specific scope and limit of their legislating authority should be given in the relevant enabling statute or organic act, together with explicit objectives and purposes they should aim to realize in using

---

[14] Following the suggestion of Waldron 2007, p. 107. As an aspect of the rule of law, analogous principles are mentioned in Raz 1979, pp. 215–216, and Finnis 1980, p. 270.

that authority.[15] A traffic safety commission, for instance, could be granted the limited authority to promulgate rules of the road with the aim of reducing accidents at a reasonable cost. Some orderly and public procedure must be followed in promulgating such rules: perhaps the commission must first conduct independent research, then announce its recommendations together with their rationale, next provide for a period of community notice and comment, and finally publish the new rules in the relevant volume of statutes.[16] In order to ensure that these various constraints are not merely empty formalities, it is essential that there be some institutional mechanism for holding the agency or commission accountable; perhaps individuals subject to the new rules should be permitted to challenge them in court.

In the case of national assemblies, by contrast, the conditions will probably have to be satisfied in a very different manner. The scope and purpose of a national assembly's legislative authority might be specified in a constitutional document, or simply implied in the conventional understanding that it serve the common good of the relevant legal community. More often given some explicit statement are the limits on such authority, as for instance in bills of rights. The public and orderly procedure for exercising legislative authority might involve proposing new laws, conducting debates on their merits, and holding public votes. Accountability might in part be achieved through judicial review, but most probably must be secured ultimately through regular elections.[17]

Here of course I have only sketched a framework for how to reconcile the need for exogenous legal change with the rule of law. Among other topics, the optimal allocation of legislative authority to national versus federal institutions, or to elected assemblies versus agencies and commissions, has not been considered. The main point is simply that when the conditions of legislative due process suggested above are

---

[15] In American constitutional law, the U.S. Congress is required by the so-called non-delegation doctrine to provide specific guidance when it delegates to agencies; Article 80 of the German Constitution states a similar requirement explicitly.

[16] These sorts of requirements are embodied in the Administrative Procedures Act of 1946 (Pub. L. 79-404, presently codified at 5 U.S.C. 500 et seq.), for example.

[17] For further discussion, see Waldron 2007, esp. pp. 104–108. Pettit 1997, pp. 183–200, discusses the role of democratic contestation specifically in supervising legislative authority.

effectively and reliably met, people should not experience the exercise of legislative authority as a form of arbitrary power. To reiterate, however, congeniality with the rule of law is only one institutional virtue among others. It is also important that legislative authorities be responsive to needs, that they advance social justice, and so forth.[18] Often it may be possible to respect many or all of these virtues simultaneously. But to the extent that these other virtues are better served by institutional configurations differing from those we have discussed, we will face hard choices indeed, which are unfortunately beyond the scope of present discussion.

Before concluding our discussion of legislation, however, it is perhaps worth considering the issue of judicial lawmaking. As observed above, courts inevitably generate endogenous legal change at the interpretive margin, so to speak. This process can be relatively overt, as in the common law tradition, or relatively covert, as in the civil law tradition, but it does not properly amount to an exercise in legislative authority as we have defined it. Likewise, as discussed below, courts must sometimes exercise discretion in applying specific rules of law to particular situations. The degree of such discretion can vary according to the specificity of the legal materials available, but again this does not itself constitute what we have termed legislative authority. Here I am interested in something else: namely, the possibility that political systems might in some instances implicitly or explicitly grant courts – rather than assemblies, agencies, or commissions – the institutional authority to *exogenously create or change law*.[19]

The most interesting instance of courts exercising legislative authority arises whenever a community's generally accepted legal sources include statements of moral principle.[20] For example, the Eighth Amendment to the U.S. Constitution prohibits "cruel and unusual

---

[18] This might require designing agencies and commissions exercising legislative authority so they are more democratically accountable and less vulnerable to capture by special interests. For further discussion, see Richardson 1999.

[19] Hayek 1973, esp. ch. 5, aims to minimize any such authority; on very different grounds, so do Waldron 1999b and Bellamy 2007.

[20] Though the most interesting, it is not of course the only such instance. Especially in the common law tradition, courts may have the authority to effect significant exogenous legal change, especially when (as discussed earlier) the process of gradual endogenous development leads to a dead end. Cardozo's reform of product liability law in *MacPherson* (see n. 5 above) might be an example. Many others could be found in the history of American Supreme Court jurisprudence.

punishments." Similarly, Section 2–302 of the Uniform Commercial Code renders "unconscionable" contracts unenforceable. As it happens, the proper meaning and significance of such statements has been the subject of extensive debate among legal positivists.[21] When lawyers refer to these moral principles in presenting arguments, are they appealing to law? When judges draw on these moral principles in issuing rulings, are they applying that law? Roughly speaking, soft or inclusive positivists answer yes: whenever the generally accepted legal sources in some community include statements of moral principle, those principles count as law in more or less the same way as any other legal rule. Thus, for instance, when a court finds that cross-collateral agreements in an ordinary retail context are unconscionable, that court is simply *applying the law*.[22] Hard or exclusive positivists, by contrast, answer no: moral principles, even when explicitly enumerated among other generally accepted legal sources, do not themselves count as law. When a court finds that cross-collateral agreements are unconscionable it is in truth *creating law*.[23]

The conception of law developed in Part I of this study is more congenial to the second view. This can be seen through the following analogy. Suppose some national assembly creates a traffic safety commission and grants it the authority to create rules of the road with the stated aim of "reducing accidents at a reasonable cost." Further suppose everyone in the community agrees that setting a 55-mile-per-hour speed limit would indeed reduce accidents at a reasonable cost, and thus fully expects the commission to issue such a rule in due course. Until it does, however, we would surely not say the speed limit was already law. Now by analogy, before any court in the United States had ruled on the issue of cross-collateral agreements, it is unlikely

---

[21] Note that the legal sources of a given community *need not* include such moral principles, thus satisfying the separability thesis as discussed in Chapter 1. Likewise, such moral principles are so included only when they are generally accepted in the relevant community, thus satisfying the social fact thesis as well.

[22] See *Williams v. Walker-Thomas Furniture Co.*, 350 F.2d 445 (D.C. Cir. 1965). In a cross-collateral agreement, the purchaser does not repay the balance owed on any one purchased item until all payments are made on every purchased item.

[23] Leading inclusive positivists include Coleman 1982, 2001; and Waluchow 1994. Leading exclusive positivists include Raz 1985, 2009; Shapiro 1998, 2000, 2011; and Marmor 2001. The postscript to Hart 1994 is generally read as embracing the inclusive view.

anyone would have said they were in fact legally invalid. Certainly, there was no underlying social rule to that effect; at best, some particularly prescient legal expert might have predicted a court would someday decide they were. But until that happened, there was simply no law on the question.

How then are we to understand what a lawyer is doing when she appeals on behalf of her client to Section 2–302 of the Uniform Commercial Code (or to the Eighth Amendment of the U.S. Constitution, etc.)? Such statements of moral principle in the legal sources are best understood as procedural requirements that courts engage in directed moral reasoning.[24] In this sense, they serve a purpose analogous to the procedural requirement that the traffic safety commission consider what will reduce accidents at a reasonable cost (or that revenue bills originate in the House of Representatives, or that agencies provide for a period of notice and comment on proposed new regulations, and so on). The stated principles instruct courts to consider whether this or that type of contract is unconscionable, whether this or that form of punishment is cruel or unusual, and so on.[25] Just as we would not be tempted to say that the principles of cost–benefit analysis themselves count as law merely because the traffic safety commission has been instructed to consult them, so we should not be tempted to say that moral principles themselves count as law merely because courts have been instructed to consult them.[26] Especially when statements of moral principle appear in common law legal systems, where the ruling of the court will subsequently serve as a legally authoritative precedent, we should understand the court in such cases as creating law.

There are advantages and disadvantages to assigning courts some share of legislative authority in this manner.[27] On the one hand, including moral principles among a community's legal sources builds into the law a certain element of flexibility. The Eighth Amendment,

---

[24] Here I basically follow the suggestion of Marmor 2001, pp. 67–69.

[25] When enforceable, the procedural requirement might count as a law for judges, but presumably this is not what inclusive positivists have in mind.

[26] Raz 2009, pp. 190–202, uses references to foreign law to make a similar point, but such examples are vulnerable to the response in Waluchow 1994, pp. 155–163: roughly, that the Eighth Amendment to the U.S. Constitution is obviously a part of American law in a way that references to foreign law usually are not.

[27] For arguments in favor of including moral principles among a community's legal sources, see Waluchow 1994, ch. 8, and for arguments against, MacCormick 1985.

for instance, presumably creates a space for legal change, corresponding to the evolution of moral sentiment, without resort to the cumbersome process of constitutional amendment.[28] On the other hand,
including moral principles among the legal sources may render the
law less clear or predictable, especially in instances of deep moral
disagreement. From a rule of law perspective, however, our central
concern should be that the conditions of legislative due process be
observed. Thus judicial lawmaking should proceed through public
and orderly procedures, and its scope and aims should be clearly
defined and respected, and so forth.[29] The most important challenge
will be ensuring that some mechanism exists for holding courts
accountable for properly exercising whatever legislative authority
they may possess. Such mechanisms are unfortunately lacking in the
American system.

6.3 Discretion and Economic Justice

In the previous section, we tried to reconcile legal change with the rule
of law. However, there is another issue that has sometimes been confused with the problem of legal change – not *whether* the rule of law
permits legal change, but rather *what sorts* of change it permits. Here
the worry has been that the rule of law might condemn in advance
many worthwhile and important substantive political aims. Hayek famously argued that economic justice (that is, roughly, justice in the organization of economic activity and in the distribution of economic
goods) cannot be pursued without departing from the rule of law. While
he of course welcomed this purported conflict, many others have not.

Now throughout this study, I have emphasized that the rule of law
should not be conceived of as a comprehensive political ideal. Rather,
it is only one part – albeit an important part – of social justice. It
follows that, even if there is some deep conflict between the rule of law
and economic justice, this does not necessarily mean our theory is
flawed. It may simply be that the rule of law represents one value

---

[28] Or, at any rate, it does so provided we ignore implausible originalist theories of
constitutional interpretation.

[29] Included here is the thought that judicial lawmaking should to the extent
possible be governed by the republican theory of adjudication discussed in
Chapter 5, at least so far as this is consistent with the terms of any specific grant
of legislative authority to the courts.

and economic justice another, in which case we must sometimes make difficult choices between them.[30] If they are genuinely irreconcilable, however, it would certainly be disheartening. Fortunately, I will argue, they are not.

6.3.1 The Rule of Law and Economic Justice

To begin with, let us consider the usual grounds for believing the rule of law cannot be reconciled with economic justice. Roughly speaking, the argument has two interrelated parts. On the one hand, it is often argued that a just distribution of goods cannot be secured and maintained except through continuous public interventions and ex post adjustments in our private affairs. There is simply no telling in advance what the outcome of a process of free exchange is going to be, and there can be no assurance that it will match any particular pattern in holdings thought to represent economic justice. In order to secure a just pattern in holdings, therefore, we must wait and see how things develop, and then coercively intervene to correct those particular outcomes failing to conform to the desired pattern.[31] But this is precisely what the rule of law condemns – namely, the use of coercive force merely to direct human beings in this or that particular direction. The rule of law instead requires that we establish open-ended rules in advance, and subject individuals to public coercion if and only if they fail to observe those rules, regardless of the unpredictable results flowing from their various activities under the auspices of those rules. It is therefore impossible to expect that we could secure or maintain economic justice without violating the rule of law.

On the other hand, it is further argued that modern economic systems are incredibly complex and dynamic, far beyond the capacity of even the most diligent experts to fully understand in detail. It is thus impossible to predict the effects economic legislation will have in particular cases. Rules that seem to serve reasonably well at first will almost certainly turn out to have perverse, self-defeating, or unfair consequences in unanticipated future circumstances. In order to secure or maintain economic justice in particular cases, therefore, it will be

---

[30] Roughly speaking, this seems to be what Neumann 1937, esp. pp. 122–132, 138, ultimately concluded.

[31] This point was not only made by Hayek 1944, pp. 83–93, and 1960, pp. 231–233; but also later, and more famously, by Nozick 1974, pp. 153–164.

necessary to delegate wide discretionary authority to administrative agencies so they can tailor sensible and fair policy responses to particular problems as they arise.[32] But once again, this is precisely what the rule of law condemns: those individuals subject to such agency determinations will not experience coercive force only when they fail to observe some legally valid prescriptive rule, but rather according to the whim or pleasure of agency officials. For this reason also, therefore, we cannot expect to secure or maintain economic justice without violating the rule of law.

This argument has proved extremely influential. Indeed, it has been lent further credibility by some progressives who, granting the alleged incompatibility between the rule of law and economic justice, suggest that we therefore abandon our attachment to the rule of law.[33] In my view, by contrast, the argument is largely (though perhaps not entirely) mistaken.

The first part of the argument can be addressed more easily, for it rests entirely on a crucial assumption – namely, that economic justice is correctly understood as the achievement of a specific pattern in economic holdings. In other words, for a society S with members $\{1, 2, 3, \ldots, n\}$, the assumption maintains that there is a specific schedule of entitlements to goods and services represented by the vector allocations $x_1, x_2, x_3, \ldots, x_n$ that represents economic justice for S. This pattern might be, for example, a perfectly equal distribution of all entitlements, or it might be something else more complex. Were this assumption correct, then it would indeed be difficult to see how securing and maintaining that specific pattern could be reconciled with the rule of law.

But this is not the only, nor even the most widely accepted understanding of economic justice. John Rawls, for example, rejects precisely this view as both infeasible and, in any case, undesirable. Economic justice, on his view, should rather be understood as an instance of what he terms "pure procedural justice."[34] Here the idea is that what we

---

[32] Concerns about expanding agency discretion in the pursuit of economic justice were raised by Dicey 1915, pp. lv–lxi; Hayek 1960, pp. 227–230; and Lowi 1969, ch. 5. Many of their arguments have been recently recycled in Epstein 2011.

[33] See for example Unger 1976, ch. 3, or Habermas 1988; for a nice review, see Scheuerman 1994.

[34] Rawls 1971, esp. § 14, but see also the often overlooked §§ 47–48. If Nozick read these sections, he apparently misunderstood them.

assess as just or unjust are alternative configurations of basic economic institutions such as property rights, legally enforceable contracts, the tax structure, rules of inheritance, workplace regulations, and so forth. These institutions represent what we might term the "ground rules" of an economic system.[35] Once we decide which particular configuration of ground rules is most fair or just, we permit individuals in that society to live out their lives according to those rules. While we cannot predict the specific allocation of entitlements that will result (i.e., whether Andrea will end up with more or fewer apples than Bob), we can nevertheless regard the outcome as representing economic justice *because the ground rules followed in producing that outcome were themselves fair.*

Once we clarify that economic justice is best understood in this way, it should be immediately obvious that it can be pursued using strategies fully consistent with the rule of law. For example, consider the sorts of collective insurance programs widely employed in developed nations. The base rule underlying such programs might be 'everyone contribute to a national retirement fund' or 'all employers contribute to a fund for unemployment insurance', and such rules are a part of a legal system insofar as they are directly or indirectly lent support by a public coercive agent. But so long as the rules are clear and public, and their enforcement effective and reliable, individuals will be exposed to public coercion if and only if they fail to observe the base rule. Such programs therefore present no difficulty from a rule of law point of view. The same can be said for progressive taxation or inheritance taxation. Here the underlying base rule is roughly, 'everyone contribute their fair share to public projects', and the tax code merely spells out in complex detail what counts as a fair contribution and the particular form that contribution must take. Again, there is no necessary conflict with the rule of law.[36]

None of this is to say, of course, that the rule of law places no constraints at all on the pursuit of economic justice. On the contrary,

---

[35] This useful expression is due to Pogge 1989, p. 16 and *passim.*

[36] As an aside, a similar strategy might be used to show that, properly implemented, military conscription need not conflict with the rule of law: here the base rule might be something like, 'everyone do his or her part to contribute to the community's security'. Of course, actual conscription policies have often been highly problematic. Hayek 1960, p. 143, notably argues that both taxation and conscription can be reconciled with the rule of law.

in order to adhere to the rule of law, we should limit ourselves to the procedural approach just outlined, and strive to ensure that the ground rules of the economic system are indeed clear and reliable. No doubt many other strategies cannot be reconciled with the rule of law, and here perhaps lies the element of truth in Hayek's critique of economic justice: specifically, the rule of law is probably not consistent with the sort of active economic planning pursued extensively in command economies and sometimes in others. But we have as yet no good reason to believe economic justice and the rule of law inherently incompatible.

6.3.2 *Discretion, Rules, and Standards*

Having dismissed the claim that economic justice is somehow deeply irreconcilable with the rule of law, we may now turn to the second part of the argument. Does the dynamic complexity of modern economic systems require that those interested in advancing economic justice concede to the state extensive discretionary authority? In truth, the question is a general one. Modern states have responsibilities not only for regulating economic activity, but also for protecting consumers, for defending the environment, for ensuring transportation safety, for managing immigration, for safeguarding public health, for reducing crime, and much more besides. Can these manifold responsibilities realistically be discharged without extensive discretion? If not, how can that discretion be reconciled with the rule of law?

First, a clarification. It is important to distinguish between the discretion to create a rule, on the one hand, and the discretion to determine a specific outcome, on the other. Sometimes these two sorts of discretion are linked, as for example when common law courts establish a future-oriented legal precedent and dispose a specific case simultaneously. They need not run together, however, and often they do not. Modern national legislative assemblies often delegate wide-ranging discretion to administrative agencies – as for example the U.S. Congress has delegated responsibility for governing traffic safety to the Department of Transportation. Much of that delegated authority, however, is employed in issuing regulatory code rather than in adjudicating particular cases. Since the provisions of this code have the force of law, the exercise of such discretion is better understood as a form of decentralized legislation. Here we are concerned only with the second sort of discretion, the first having been addressed in our discussion of legal change above.

The discretionary authority to determine specific outcomes can be exercised by administrative agencies, but also by courts and other public officials. Examples might include the discretion of administrative agencies to resolve labor disputes, the discretion of immigration courts to dispose applications for asylum, the discretion of public prosecutors to grant immunity, or the discretion of central banks to raise and lower interest rates. It is inconceivable that modern states could function without exercising such discretionary authority, but, at least initially, hard to see how that discretion authority does not necessarily fall afoul the rule of law. The rule of law requires that individuals be able to form sound expectations concerning the likely incidence of coercive force; this, in turn, requires that the use of coercive force be effectively and reliably governed by public rules. How can these conditions be satisfied in the case of discretionary authority?

First, let us consider some different types of discretion. One type of discretion arises from the nature of prescriptive rules themselves. As discussed in Chapter 2, all prescriptive rules involve partitioning the set of possible circumstances or histories H and the set of possible action responses A into categories, and then drawing a map between the two sets. The social rule 'wait in line for service and criticize others who don't wait in line', for example, gathers all situations in which a person has jumped the line together (regardless of whether she was in a hurry or not, etc.) and assigns criticism as the appropriate response. Now these partitions can be given various degrees of specificity along a more or less continuous range. At one end of the range we might have relatively specific *bright-line rules*, such as 'drive at 55 miles per hour or less' or 'don't drink until you are 21', while at the other end we might have relatively less specific *standards*, such as 'drive a reasonable and prudent speed' or 'don't drink until you are sufficiently mature'. Of course, given the immense diversity of possible circumstances, few rules could ever be so detailed and specific as to render their implementation strictly mechanical in all possible cases. It follows that at least some discretionary judgment will often be necessary to apply a given rule to a particular situation. Let us call this *rule-implementing discretion*. The degree of such discretion will presumably be less in the case of bright-line rules, more in the case of standards. Later we will consider the advantages and disadvantages of designing rules that permit greater or lesser degrees of discretion in implementation.

Notice, however, that the degree of rule-implementing discretion tracks the content of the rule in question, not its effectiveness or reliability. In order for a rule to be effective and reliable, there must exist some mechanism for holding the relevant parties to account for observing it, and thus a very different sort of discretion can emerge when the required mechanism is absent or ineffectual. Let us call this *accountability discretion*. While it is true that excessive rule-implementing discretion can give rise to accountability discretion, they are nevertheless distinct.[37] This can be seen if we imagine a community in which, although there is a bright-line rule 'drive at 55 miles per hour or less', speeding tickets issued by the police cannot be challenged in court: here the police may in principle have little rule-implementing discretion, but in practice they have extensive accountability discretion. Dicey, in his review of nineteenth-century French administrative law, was very concerned about the accountability discretion created when agents of the state are granted broad legal immunities in the conduct of their official duties.[38] To some extent prosecutors in the United States enjoy a similar immunity, and thus accountability discretion in the exercise of their charging authority.[39] Even when a formal accountability mechanism is in place, it may prove ineffectual if the content of a rule is so poorly formulated that there is no general agreement among reasonable persons as to what counts as observing the rule. This might happen because the terms of the rule are excessively vague, inconsistent, or politically controversial. Current asylum adjudication in the United States might be an unfortunate example.[40]

Finally, distinct from either rule-implementing or accountability discretion, there is the sort of perfect or *strong discretion* that exists in the absence of constraint all together.[41] This sort of discretion might

---

[37] Some argue, for instance, that the loose interpretation the U.S. Supreme Court has given to the "public use" standard for eminent domain amounts in effect to a grant of accountability discretion: see Epstein 2011, pp. 109–113.

[38] Dicey 1915, ch. 12.

[39] Krug 2002, pp. 647–649. For a classic critique of such discretion, see Davis 1969, esp. ch. 7; Epstein 2011, pp. 23–27, is more sanguine.

[40] Legomsky 2007 argues that the shocking inconsistency in current U.S. asylum adjudications stems in part from deep ideological differences.

[41] Dworkin 1977, p. 32. Whereas Dworkin contrasts strong discretion with the other two sorts of what he terms "weak discretion," it will turn out on our

be explicit, as for example when an autocratic ruler is granted the legal authority to condemn or pardon prisoners of the state purely according to his pleasure. It might also arise implicitly from the failure to create governing rules, as for example when masters hold wide discretionary authority over their slaves in the absence of laws or norms explicitly governing their treatment. At least in modern democratic societies, pure cases of strong discretion when it comes to the use of coercive force are probably rare, though extreme accountability discretion may in effect be subjectively experienced as strong discretion.

Which sorts of discretionary authority, if any, can be reconciled with the rule of law? The rule of law requires that individuals be able to form expectations concerning the likely incidence of coercive force which, in turn, requires that the use of coercive force be effectively and reliably governed by public rules. Now it is easy to see that neither strong discretion nor accountability discretion meet these conditions: in neither case will it be possible to form reliable expectations concerning the incidence of coercive force. Recall our imagined community in which police-issued speeding tickets cannot be contested. Despite the existence of a bright-line rule on paper, drivers in such a community would in reality be vulnerable to coercive force simply at the whim and pleasure of the police.

The same is not necessarily the case when it comes to rule-implementing discretion, however. Suppose that some rule is reasonably clear, in the sense that most people agree on what it requires in a wide range of circumstances. This means, in the case of a bright-line rule, that reasonable people agree on the same thing being required in nearly every circumstance, while in the case of a standard, that reasonable people agree on what different thing is required in different circumstances. Further suppose that there is an effective and reliable mechanism for holding the relevant parties accountable for observing the rule. To the extent that these conditions are met, it will indeed be possible for people to form sound expectations about how rule-implementing discretion will be exercised, and thus sound expectations concerning the likely incidence of coercive force.[42] Pragmatically speaking, that is what matters for the rule of law.

analysis that the more significant cut is between rule-implementing discretion and the other two.

[42] Thus, contrary to Scalia 1989, standards as well as bright-line rules can be consistent with the rule of law.

Now we have said that it is inconceivable that modern states could function without discretionary authority. But discretionary authority of which sort? Given the dynamic complexity of the social and economic world, it will not be possible to rely on bright-line rules alone: many public policy regimes are better crafted in the more flexible and general language of standards.[43] It follows that, in order to discharge its many responsibilities, the state will often have to possess rule-implementing discretion. Fortunately, this is precisely this sort of discretion, as we have seen, that can be reconciled with the rule of law. This is not to say, of course, that modern states do in fact limit themselves to rule-implementing discretion. Quite the contrary. However, it is to say that – at least from a rule of law point of view – they ought to, and that in doing so they will still be able to discharge their proper responsibilities.

6.4 The Rule of Law and the Modern State

The rule of law is an old idea. It was developed at a time when state capacity was far less extensive than today, and when the law consisted primarily of first-order rules of conduct that did not change very much. In this chapter we have been concerned with whether the rule of law can be adapted to modern political conditions – conditions under which the law must change more rapidly, and rely on discretionary standards much more extensively. I have argued it can.

There remains one further challenge, however. The rule of law is fundamentally concerned with governing the incidence of coercive force. Modern states, however, do considerably more than coerce people. Indeed, on reflection, overt coercion may constitute a decreasing share of the state's overall activities. To a large extent, the activity of modern states consists in directing the conduct of public personnel and the use of public resources. For example, modern states distribute funds accumulated in public social insurance schemes, conduct scientific and medical research, manage public property (national parks, strategic oil reserves, foreign exchange accounts), dispatch military forces, undertake public projects (building bridges, combating homelessness, exploring outer space), and so on. According to Hayek, "service activities" like these, involving no more than the use and

---

[43] Reasons for this are discussed in Davis 1969, pp. 15–21.

direction of public resources, are trivially consistent with the rule of law simply because they do not, or at least not in the first instance, involve imposing coercive force on ordinary citizens.[44] But if such non-coercive service activities constitute an increasing share of what modern states do, then must not the importance of the rule of law as a political value correspondingly diminish?[45]

There is one very important rejoinder to this thought. Whether the bulk of what modern states do is constituted by non-coercive service activities or not, it remains the case that modern states have at their disposal significant coercive capabilities. So long as this is true, it is surely important to have political values governing the use of those capabilities. The worry here arises from the mistaken assumption that the rule of law is supposed to constitute a comprehensive political ideal. It does not. Provided it addresses *an* important concern, it remains *an* important aspect of our complete account of social justice.

That point aside, it is worth exploring the issue a bit more deeply. Two observations, in particular, come to mind. First, it is possible that, while not coercive in the first instance, the service activities of the state might in certain circumstances coerce people indirectly. (In this one area, Hayek was perhaps a bit too sanguine.) The most obvious way the state might inflict indirect coercion is through the deliberate withholding of expected public goods. Robert Moses, for example, was reputed to have cut off power and water to recalcitrant neighborhoods so as to force their residents into moving. Similar scenarios are easy to imagine, given the extent to which modern communities are built on a dense network of interconnected public goods. The rule of law therefore demands that, whenever some service activity of the state becomes a part of the baseline expectations of the community, its distribution must be governed by effective and reliable public rules. Another, less obvious way in which non-coercive service activities of the state might involve indirect coercion is through its failure to protect individuals against the private use of coercive force. If public goods are poorly distributed, perhaps, some persons and groups might find themselves vulnerable to exploitation.[46] In this way, it may turn out that, far from

---

[44] See Hayek 1960, pp. 212–214, 222–224. Note that we here set aside the fact that such activities can involve some agents of the state coercing others to perform their respective official responsibilities.

[45] Rubin 1989, for instance, argues that it must.

[46] See Lovett 2010, pp. 190–203, for an argument to this effect.

conflicting with the rule of law, some degree of economic justice is a necessary background condition to securing it for everyone.

The second observation is that, even when the service activities of the state involve no coercion at all – not even indirectly – they can nevertheless impose serious costs or burdens on individuals. For example, whenever the central bank raises or lowers interest rates, some investors gain while others certainly lose; whenever state-sponsored medical research is redirected, some patients benefit while others no doubt suffer. In Chapter 4 we observed that such conse-quences of government activities are unavoidable, and thus cannot be regarded as incompatible with any useful conception of the rule of law: hence our restriction of the latter to the problem of coercive force. Still, we may have good independent reasons to insist that such deci-sions not be made capriciously or arbitrarily.[47] Perhaps principles parallel to the conditions of legislative due process discussed earlier should guide the service activities of the state: thus, to the extent possible, decision-making procedures should be public and orderly, with clearly defined limits and aims, and subject to formal accountabil-ity mechanisms.[48] Whether one wants to regard these principles as themselves a part of the rule of law ideal or not, the main point of the present discussion stands – namely, that the rule of law is a political value worth holding on to.

---

[47] Significantly, we may have similar reasons when it comes to the decisions made by powerful private organizations, which can impose serious costs and burdens on individuals in much the same way. This only goes to show that a complete political doctrine must supplement the rule of law with other principles.

[48] I am grateful to Chad Flanders for this suggestion.

7 | Conclusion

[The] freedom of men under government is, to have a standing rule to live by, common to every one of that society ...; a liberty to follow my own will in all things, where the rule prescribes not; and not to be subject to the inconstant, uncertain, unknown, arbitrary will of another man ....[1]

This book has argued for the intrinsic value of the rule of law. To achieve the rule of law, I have argued, is to achieve, in some significant degree, social justice. Societies enjoy the rule of law to the extent that no individual in that society will be exposed to coercive force at the hands of any other person, group, or organization except as the consequence of her having failed to observe some legally valid prescriptive rule. The value of the rule of law, so understood, lies in its capacity to mitigate an especially worrisome source of domination: the capacity some persons or groups might have to wield coercive force over others. Having achieved the rule of law, we have "a standing rule to live by" together with our fellow citizens. Provided we are willing to understand political freedom or liberty in the traditional republican sense – as independence from arbitrary power or domination – then we can readily agree with Locke and Blackstone that the rule of law introduces, rather than restricts, our freedom. Surprisingly, this argument for the rule of law is best made on the foundations of legal positivism, and not (as many believe) on a theory in which legal systems necessarily possess certain normative merits.

In contrast with many other contemporary accounts, this study has emphasized that the rule of law has two important aspects: on the one hand, the use of coercive force must be reserved to public coercive agents alone, so citizens will not experience the use or threat of violence or physical restraint at the hands of other citizens; and on the other hand, public coercive agents must be reliably and effectively governed by rules,

---

[1] Locke 1690, § 22: p. 17.

so the use or threat of violence or physical restraint by those agents is confined exclusively to providing remedial support to legally valid pre-scriptive rules. So understood, the rule of law has no necessary connec-tion to legal equality, as some authors have claimed. While this might seem a disadvantage, it is so only if we insist on regarding the rule of law as a comprehensive political doctrine. I have argued we should not. While the rule of law constitutes a significant part, it does not constitute the whole of social justice. Domination has many potential sources, and we cannot expect the rule of law alone to address every one of them. Nevertheless, it does address an especially important source of domin-ation, and it may therefore have a certain pragmatic priority: it is difficult to see how we might achieve the other aspects of social justice without having first, at least to some extent, achieved the rule of law.

Throughout this study, however, we have considered only the relation-ship between the rule of law and social justice, where the latter expression refers to justice or injustice in the design of the basic institutions and practices of an ongoing and independent society. Can our account of the rule of law and its value be extended beyond this sphere? In particular, might it have anything useful to contribute with respect to the problems of transitional justice, on the one hand, and global justice, on the other?

The problem of transitional justice can arise whenever less just configurations of institutions or practices in some society are replaced with more just configurations. Most often discussed are transitions from autocratic political regimes (Nazi Germany, military rule in Argentina) to democratic ones, and from unequal social regimes (slavery or segregation in the American south, apartheid in South Africa) to more equal ones. Such transitions raise special challenges with respect to justice in general, and the rule of law in particular. Two challenges stand out. First, it is often the case that under the previous dispensation many people engaged in conduct now seen as substan-tially unjust and illegal, but which at the time was legally permissible or even legally required. The case of the German informant debated by Hart and Fuller illustrates this first difficulty: a women who wanted to rid herself of her husband reported him to the Nazi authorities in 1944, and after the war was charged with depriving him of his freedom; in defense, she argued that her conduct was perfectly consistent with the law at that time.[2] Second, it is often the case that under the previous

[2] See Hart 1958, pp. 615–621; Fuller 1958, pp. 648–657.

dispensation some people benefited at the expense of others in ways now seen as substantially unjust. Justice may now seem to require that the former (or their descendants) compensate the latter (or their descendants) in some measure. The ongoing debate concerning reparations for American slavery illustrates this second difficulty.

In either case, our intuitive sense of what justice requires seems to cut against the rule of law. Punishing people or imposing reparation payments on them now in correction for past injustices would seem to involve exposing individuals to coercive force for something other than their having failed to observe a legally valid prescriptive rule. In my view, we cannot avoid this conflict, and we should not pretend otherwise. Instead, we should recognize that the value of the rule of law has limits: the rule of law is a part, but only a part, of justice, and it follows that its value can and sometimes should be outweighed by broader considerations. Nevertheless, in realizing transitional justice, it is important that we respect the interest individuals have in being able to form reliable expectations concerning the incidence of coercive force. Among other things, this suggests that transitional justice should be pursued only through processes meeting the conditions of legislative due process described in Chapter 6.

The problem of global justice raises a very different set of concerns. Our lives are affected not only by the configuration of domestic institutions and practices, but also in many ways by the configuration of global institutions and practices. Now the rule of law ideal is addressed specifically to the problem of uncontrolled or arbitrary use of coercive force. Whether and to what extent we are exposed to arbitrary coercive force can, as it happens, be influenced by the configuration of global institutions and practices both directly and indirectly. On the one hand, it should be obvious that possible sources of coercion are not limited to the domestic sphere: indeed, a wide variety of global agents (states, terrorist and revolutionary organizations, multinational corporations, etc.) might potentially coerce us. Their capacity to do so, however, is directly influenced by the configuration of global institutions and practices – for instance, by the effectiveness and reliability of those institutions and practices in preventing military aggression, policing global terrorism, and so forth.[3] On the other hand, even when

---

[3] Influenced, though not determined, of course: also relevant is the relative power of your own state and the effectiveness of the security it can provide. Even great powers, however, are vulnerable to coalitions, and in any case many people are not citizens of a great power.

it comes to domestic sources of coercion, global institutions and practices may have a less obvious, though not always less important, indirect relevance. This is because the configuration of global institutions and practices may influence the likelihood that a domestic rule of law will be successfully introduced and maintained in various societies around the world. Thomas Pogge and others have argued, for instance, that the borrowing and resource privileges presently enjoyed by all de facto sovereign governments might encourage local despots, and certainly help them maintain power.[4] Extending the rule of law, therefore, suggests designing global as well as domestic institutions and practices so as to optimally protect individuals from uncontrolled or arbitrary coercive force, regardless of its source.

Would the optimal configuration of global institutions and practices necessarily include a system of international law? Perhaps, perhaps not. Here we might usefully distinguish between the international rule of law, the rule of international law, and the global rule of law.[5] The international rule of law means governing the behavior of states by rules of law – for instance, rules prohibiting aggression and requiring the performance of treaties. The rule of international law means the supremacy of international law over conflicting domestic law – as expressed, for instance, in the recognition that certain basic rights of the European Union trump the legislation of member states. And finally, the global rule of law means extending security against all sources of uncontrolled or arbitrary coercive force, domestic or otherwise, to persons and groups everywhere in the world. My interest is primarily in the last of these. The rule of law has value for people because people can subjectively experience domination as an obstacle to their flourishing. States as such do not have subjective experiences, though we may as a sort of metaphorical shorthand collectively refer to the shared experiences of their members in this way.[6] It follows that we should only be interested in governing the behavior of states by law, or in subordinating domestic law to international law, instrumentally – that is, only insofar as doing so will actually help secure freedom from domination for individuals around the world.

Conveniently, focusing on the third rather than either of the first two issues means we can largely sidestep the ongoing controversy as to

---

[4] See Pogge 2002, esp. ch. 6.   [5] Following Chesterman 2008, pp. 355–356.
[6] Cf. Bingham 2010, ch. 10, who seems to regard the international rule of law as the natural extension of the domestic rule of law.

whether international law counts as law in the relevant sense. In order to coherently address the pros and cons of the international rule of law or the rule of international law, it would seem, one must first establish that there exists (or at any rate, could exist) something properly counting as international law. There is, of course, no obstacle to developing a positivist account of international law. Suppose, for example, there exists a group agent (the set of great powers, for example) with the capacity to coerce any state in the world (including any one of its own members). Further suppose that the strategy of coercive enforcing (through military intervention) certain prescriptive rules (no aggressive wars, perform treaties made, etc.) forms a sub-game perfect Nash equilibrium among the members of that group. According to the analysis presented in Chapter 3, these rules would then properly count as international laws. Whether and to what extent international law exists, however, must be an empirical question.[7] With respect to extending the global rule of law, we can avail ourselves of any useful instruments to the purpose. If those instruments include effective international laws, so much the better.

As with the domestic rule of law, the global rule of law cannot serve as a comprehensive political doctrine. Only some of the many injustices experienced around the world are due specifically to the fact that people are frequently exposed to the use of uncontrolled or arbitrary coercive force. Another, and in many instances more serious, injustice concerns the staggering levels of socio-economic inequality and poverty around the world. Such concerns must be addressed in another place. This should not detract, however, from the rule of law's very real contribution to justice. The rule of law, both domestic and global, is perhaps inevitably underrated. This is because, by its own nature, it is least noticed precisely where it is most effective. It is my hope that this work may help to continue to remind us of its value, by forcefully articulating its meaning and significance in a way that avoids the challenges and objections that have been raised against it in the past.

---

[7] Kelsen 1960, ch. 7, argues that a system of international law along these lines does in fact exist, though its rules do not necessarily correspond with what everything we conventionally refer to as "international law." Hart 1994, ch. 10, is more doubtful.

APPENDIX A

The Principles of Legality

Table A.1 represents an attempt to catalog the rule of law virtues or principles of legality proposed by various authors, here organized according to the general framework discussed in Chapter 4. Obviously, interpretation is required to properly assign some principles to a given box. For example, I have here interpreted the principle that "similar cases be treated similarly" as another way of saying that the application of public coercion is governed by rules rather than case-by-case judgments; interpreted substantively as a requirement of legal equality, it would fall outside the scope of the rule of law on my view. Similarly, I have here interpreted the principle that "no man is above the law" as the requirement that public officials be accountable for their conduct in ordinary courts, which may help more effectively to control public discretion.

Two further observations are worthy of comment here. First, with the partial exception of Fallon, none of these authors apparently regards the regulation of private uses of coercive force as falling under the scope of the rule of law. For reasons discussed in Chapter 4, I view this as a serious shortcoming. Second, what in Chapter 6 are termed the conditions of legislative due process appear in Raz and Finnis as a part of the rule of law itself. While my preference is to regard the former as an adjunct to the latter, nothing in principle bars our adopting an expanded definition of the rule of law so as to include them.

Table A.1 *The principles of legality*

	Dicey 1915, pp. 110–116	Hayek 1944, p. 80	Fuller 1969, pp. 46–91
I(A): Private uses of coercive force governed by rules, and			
I(B): Public uses of coercive force governed by rules ...	(1) No man punishable except for breach of law	(1) Government actions bound by rules	
... which are:			
• general,			(1) Generality
• prospective,			(3) No retroactive laws
• performable, and			(6) No requiring the impossible
• consistent.			(5) No contradictions in the laws
II(A): Rules governing private coercion effective and reliable, and			
II(B): Rules governing public coercion effective and reliable.			(8) Congruence between official action and rule
Effectiveness and reliability often most secure when:			
• judiciary is independent,			
• rights of due process are respected,			
• legal system is accessible to ordinary citizens, and			
• public officials accountable to ordinary courts.	(2a) No man above the law		
III: Existence of rules governing coercive force common knowledge.			
This requires that:			
• rules are published,		(3) Rules announced	(2) Promulgation
• rules are clear, and			(4) Clarity of laws
• rules are reasonably stable.		(2) Rules fixed beforehand	(7) Constancy of law through time
Other principles proposed:	(2b) Legal equality (3) Constitutional principles result of judicial decisions		

Table A.1 (*cont.*)

Rawls 1971, pp. 236–239	Raz 1979, pp. 214–218	Finnis 1980, pp. 270–271	Solum 1994, p. 122	Fallon 1997, pp. 8–9
(2) Similar cases treated similarly			(5) Similar cases treated similarly	
			(1) No extralegal commands	
(3c) Statutes general			(4) Legal rules general	
(3e) Penal laws not retroactive	(1a) Laws should be prospective	(1) Rules prospective		
(1) Ought implies can		(2) Rules possible to comply with	(7) Ought implies can	(1b) People able to comply with law
		(5) Rules coherent with one another		
				(2) Law actually guides people
	(8) Discretion not allowed to pervert the law	(7) Discretion guided by rules		(4) Law should rule officials
		(8b) Rules actually applied		
(4c) Judges independent	(4) Independence of judiciary guaranteed			
(4b) Procedures of due process	(5) Natural justice observed		(6) Fair and orderly procedures for deciding cases	(5b) Courts employ fair procedures
(4a) Provisions for orderly trials	(7) Courts easily accessible			(5a) Courts available
	(6) Courts have review powers		(2) Officials not above the law	
(3a) Laws known and promulgated	(1b) Law must be publicized	(3) Rules promulgated	(3) Laws known and promulgated	
(3b) Laws clearly defined	(1c) Law must be clear	(4) Rules clear		(1a) People able to understand law
	(2) Laws should be relatively stable	(6) Rules sufficiently stable		(3) Law should be reasonably stable
(3d) Severe offenses strictly construed	(3) Making of laws guided by general rules	(8a) Rule-making authority accountable to rules		

Measuring the Rule of Law

Societies enjoy the rule of law to the extent that no individual in that society is exposed to the use or threat of violence or physical restraint at the hands of any other person, group, or organization except as the consequence of her having failed to observe some legally valid prescriptive rule. How might the rule of law, so understood, be measured?

Roughly speaking, first, we would start by adding up for a given period every instance in which people experienced coercive force at the hands of any public or private agent. Second, from this total we would then subtract those cases which might have been avoided had the individual observed some legally valid prescriptive rule. So far, so good. Third, however, we must count all those instances in which coercive force was avoided only through self-abnegation or ingratiation. In a dictatorship, for instance, many sensible people stay out of politics to avoid exposing themselves to the dictator's wrath, and thus the observed level of coercion may appear low; nevertheless, since there are many ways to expose oneself to coercive force in such a society apart from violating legally valid prescriptive rules, we cannot say that it enjoys the rule of law.[1] Adding this total to the previous (and dividing by population size) gives us an approximate measure of the rule of law.

In theory, the first two steps seem feasible; much less so the third, for it is difficult to even imagine how we might measure the amount of strategic anticipation in a given society. In practice, of course, even the first two steps present formidable obstacles. Perhaps not every instance of coercive force is equally serious, for example, and thus we would want to weight each according to its severity. Assigning appropriate weightings to different classes of coercion, however, involves a substantial degree of qualitative judgment. Likewise, not every legally valid prescriptive rule is on a par: the best rules are general, easily

---

[1] Similarly, in highly corrupt political systems, people might frequently avoid coercion through a combination of flattery and bribery. This too would be a departure from the rule of law.

performable, stable, well publicized, clear, and so forth. Once again, appropriately discounting lower-quality rules will necessarily involve significant qualitative judgment. To these challenges we must add that of collecting an enormous amount of raw data, sometimes under less-than-favorable circumstances. In short, accurate measures of the rule of law remain a long way off. Meanwhile, we must make do with various indirect proxies.

As it happens, there have been many attempts to generate something like a rule of law index.[2] For the most part, in my view, these efforts are unsatisfactory. No doubt influenced by the list-based rule of law accounts common in the contemporary literature, they usually define the rule of law as a cluster of virtues or principles of legality, and in an effort to measure each cobble together a heterogeneous jumble of instruments, few of which directly capture an aspect of the rule of law as such. Often they attempt to measure the presence or effectiveness of institutions and practices commonly thought essential to securing the rule of law – judicial independence, political transparency, procedural due process, the security of contracts, and so forth. There are many objections to such an approach.[3] First, the very diversity of measures used raises serious aggregation problems. How well or badly a given society scores on the index will thus be particularly sensitive to how the various measures are weighted and combined. Second, institutions and practices defy easy measurement. For example, if we measure judicial independence with a survey of experts, our results may be subjective; but objective measures of judicial independence derived from explicit constitutional provisions often do not capture political reality. Third, we should not in any case assume that the institutions and practices best securing the rule of law will be the same in every context. This is especially important to keep in mind when comparing the rule of law across societies with very different legal traditions and social or political environments.

It is beyond the scope of the present work to develop a satisfactory instrument for measuring the rule of law, and in any case doing so fall well outside my scholarly competence. The following preliminary suggestions are therefore offered merely in the hope that they might prove useful to others more able than myself.

---

[2] For a good recent survey, see Skaaning 2010.
[3] Some of these difficulties are discussed in Skaaning 2010, pp. 455–458; and Haggard and Tiede 2010, pp. 675–678.

First, we might evade the problem of measuring strategic anticipation by sorting countries into groups we believe on some independent grounds to be roughly similar in that respect. For example, let us suppose that the scope for extra-legal public coercive discretion in the OECD countries is relatively limited; comparisons among them can thus to some extent ignore the degree to which public coercive force is avoided merely through self-abnegation or ingratiation. This greatly simplifies our problem. Next, since the rule of law entails eliminating private uses of coercive force, we need to only measure how successfully this has been done in a given country. Perhaps the homicide rate can serve as a rough proxy for the overall level of violence and physical restraint experienced in civic society.[4] Measuring the public use of coercive force would appear more difficult, since we must discount those cases in which it is used merely to support a legally valid prescriptive rule. Assuming, however, that most people prefer not to expose themselves to coercive force, and will therefore try to observe the laws, the relative size of the prison population might perhaps serve as another rough proxy: if one society has a much higher prison population than other, it seems reasonable to infer that it must be harder for ordinary citizens in the former to avoid public coercion than in the latter.[5]

Considered separately, of course, neither statistic would be a reliable indicator of the rule of law: one might achieve a low homicide rate through excessive authoritarianism, or a low prison population through excessive leniency. Considered together, however, they are much more informative: it is difficult to imagine how a country might achieve both of these simultaneously *without* having an effective rule of law. Conveniently, both statistics are widely reported in units per 100,000 population. Table B.1 displays them for the OECD countries in 2010.

---

[4] While far from perfect, homicide rates have the advantage of being comparatively easy to measure and reliable across historical and cultural contexts. The homicide rate is less sensitive, for example, to changes in definition or reporting: what counts as rape or assault, for instance, might vary culturally or historically, and people might become more or less inclined to report such crimes as prevailing attitudes about them evolve.

[5] Barring, that is, any systematic differences in cultural attitudes toward prison time, of course. Note that we use the total prison population rather than the number of persons imprisoned in a given year because one continues to experience coercion for the duration of a prison term.

Table B.1: *The rule of law in OECD countries (2010)*

	Homicides per 100,000	Prisoners per 100,000	Index	Freedom House score
Japan	0.4	57	1.910	15
Iceland	0.6	52	1.928	16
Slovenia	0.7	64	2.043	14
Norway	0.6	74	2.079	16
Denmark	0.8	71	2.113	14
Switzerland	0.7	79	2.134	15
Sweden	1.0	74	2.176	16
Germany	0.8	85	2.190	15
Austria	0.6	102	2.217	15
Netherlands	0.9	92	2.247	15
South Korea	*0.9*	99	2.279	13
Finland	2.2	61	2.298	16
France	1.1	*98*	2.318	15
Ireland	1.2	94	2.320	15
Italy	0.9	112	2.332	12
Portugal	1.2	110	2.388	15
Belgium	1.7	97	2.423	15
Greece	1.6	102	2.428	11
Australia	1.0	135	2.435	14
Canada	1.4	*118*	2.456	15
Spain	0.8	165	2.475	14
United Kingdom	1.2	151	2.524	14
Hungary	1.3	163	2.577	12
New Zealand	1.0	198	2.600	15
Luxembourg	2.0	136	2.614	16
Czech Republic	1.0	209	2.623	14
Poland	1.1	210	2.647	13
Slovakia	1.6	186	2.687	12
Turkey	2.7	164	2.786	8
Israel	2.0	270	2.910	11
Chile	3.2	313	3.120	15
Estonia	5.4	266	3.233	14
United States	4.7	500	3.456	14
Mexico	21.8	194	3.648	6

Note: Italicized values estimated from neighboring years. Ranking index calculated by adding log(1+homicides) and log(1+prisoners).

Source: World Bank (worldbank.org); International Center for Prison Studies (prisonstudies.org); Bureau of Justice Statistics (bjs.org); and Freedom House (freedomhouse.org)

Table B.2: *Are homicide and imprisonment rates related in OECD countries?*

	Imprisonment Rate
Homicide Rate	7.87
	(4.17)
N	34
R-squared	0.10
p-value	0.068

Note: Ordinary least squares coefficient with standard error in parentheses.

Since neither homicide rates nor imprisonment rates are normally distributed, the ranking index in the third column has been generated by taking the log of each and adding them together. For comparison, column four shows the Freedom House rule of law score for each country. Notice that since imprisonment rates are uniformly higher than homicide rates, the former carries more weight in the ranking index. This is as expected, insofar as well-developed countries have largely succeeded in overcoming the problem of social order: in such countries, one is much more likely to experience coercive force at the hands of the government than at the hands of fellow citizens. In many other countries around the world, of course, this would not be true.[6]

It is also interesting to observe that although the two rates are positively related, the relationship is not statistically significant, and captures only a small amount of the overall variation (Table B.2). This supports our view that the two aspects of the rule of law are indeed independent: to achieve the rule of law, we argued in Chapter 4, societies must solve *both* the social order problem and the constitutionalism problem.

How does our index compare with the Freedom House rule of law scores? Since the latter are based on qualitative expert surveys, they serve as an interesting basis for contrast. As one would hope, they are indeed related in the expected direction, and to a statistically significant

---

[6] Furthermore, homicide rates would be insufficient in a context of serious civil or political unrest, since they do not include organized mass killings or combat deaths.

degree (Table B.3). Some striking individual differences are worth commenting on, however – most obviously, the low ranking of the United States. Though widely perceived as having a robust rule of law, one might argue this is true only for the relatively privileged: considering the abysmal state of the public defender system, the poorly controlled discretion of police and public prosecutors, the existence of noxious practices such as civil forfeiture, and so on, the law as experienced by poor and minority Americans is very different, perhaps amply justifying a low ranking. Other surprises might be the relatively high

Table B.3: *Relationship between two rule of law measures*

	Freedom House score
Rule of law index	−3.07
	(0.80)
N	34
R-squared	0.31
p-value	0.001

Note: Ordinary least squares coefficient with standard error in parentheses.

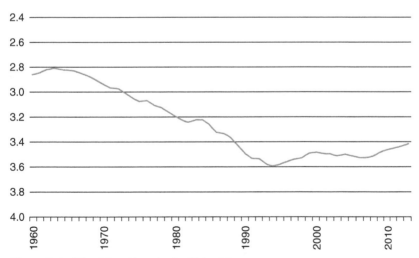

Figure B.1. The rule of law in the United States.
Source: Uniform Crime Reports (fbi.gov); Bureau of Justice Statistics (bjs.org).

ranking of South Korea, Italy, or Greece. Here the limitations of our exercise, which ignores strategic anticipation, corruption, and so forth, are no doubt evident.

Finally, we might be interested in changes in the degree of the rule of law over time. Figure B.1 charts the recent history of the rule of law in the United States, calculated in the same manner as earlier. As can be seen, the quality of the rule of law declined significantly in the 1970s and 1980s, and then again slightly (after some improvement) in the 2000s. At no point, however, would the United States have appeared near the top of the OECD ranking.

Bibliography

Abel, Richard L. 1999. "Legality Without a Constitution: South Africa in the 1980s," in *Recrafting the Rule of Law: The Limits of Legal Order*, David Dyzenhaus, ed. Hart Publishing.

Austin, John. [1832] 1998. *The Province of Jurisprudence Determined*, with an introduction by H. L. A. Hart. Hackett Publishing.

Barro, Robert. 2000. "Democracy and the Rule of Law," in *Governing for Prosperity*, Bruce Bueno de Mesquita and Hilton L. Root, eds. Yale University Press.

Barros, Robert. 2003. "Dictatorship and the Rule of Law: Rules and Military Power in Pinochet's Chile," in *Democracy and the Rule of Law*, José María Maraval and Adam Przeworski, eds. Cambridge University Press.

Bellamy, Richard. 2007. *Political Constitutionalism: A Republican Defense of the Constitutionality of Democracy*. Cambridge University Press.

Bentham, Jeremy. 1970. *Of Laws in General*, H. L. A. Hart, ed. Athlone Press.

    [1843] 1987. "Anarchical Fallacies," in *'Nonsense upon Stilts': Bentham, Burke, and Marx on the Rights of Man*, Jeremy Waldron, ed. Methuen & Co.

Berman, Harold J. 1983. *Law and Revolution: The Formation of the Western Legal Tradition*. Harvard University Press.

Bingham, Tom. 2010. *The Rule of Law*. Allen Lane.

Blackstone, William. [1765] 1979. *Commentaries on the Laws of England*, 4 vols. University of Chicago Press.

Bourdieu, Pierre. [1980] 1990. *The Logic of Practice*. Richard Nice, trans. Stanford University Press.

Bratman, Michael. 1987. *Intentions, Plans, and Practical Reason*. Harvard University Press.

    1999. *Faces of Intention: Selected Essays on Intention and Agency*. Cambridge University Press.

Brown-Nagin, Tomiko. 2011. *The Courage to Dissent: Atlanta and the Long History of the Civil Rights Movement*. Oxford University Press.

219

Calvert, Randall L. 1995. "Rational Actors, Equilibrium, and Social Institutions," in *Explaining Social Institutions*, Jack Knight and Itai Sened, eds. University of Michigan Press.

Campbell, Tom. 1996. *The Legal Theory of Ethical Positivism*. Dartmouth Publishing.

Chesterman, Simon. 2008. "An International Rule of Law?," *American Journal of Comparative Law* 56: 331–361.

Clark, Thomas S. 2011. *The Limits of Judicial Independence*. Cambridge University Press.

Coleman, James S. 1990. *Foundations of Social Theory*. Belknap Press.

Coleman, Jules L. 1982. "Negative and Positive Positivism," *Journal of Legal Studies* 11: 139–164.

   2001. *The Practice of Principle: In Defense of a Pragmatist Approach to Legal Theory*. Oxford University Press.

   2007. "Beyond the Separability Thesis: Moral Semantics and the Methodology of Jurisprudence," *Oxford Journal of Legal Studies* 27: 581–608.

Coleman, Jules, and Brian Leiter. 2010. "Legal Positivism," in *A Companion to Philosophy of Law and Legal Theory*, 2nd ed., Dennis Patterson, ed. Wiley-Blackwell.

Cover, Robert M. 1993. *Narrative, Violence, and the Law: The Essays of Robert Cover*. Martha Minow, Michael Ryan, and Austin Sarat, eds. University of Michigan Press.

Craig, Paul. 1997. "Formal and Substantive Conceptions of the Rule of Law: An Analytical Framework," *Public Law* 20: 467–487.

Davidson, Donald. 1980. *Essays on Actions and Events*. Oxford University Press.

Davis, Kenneth Culp. 1969. *Discretionary Justice: A Preliminary Inquiry*. University of Illinois Press.

Diamond, Jared M. 2005. *Collapse: How Societies Choose to Fail or Succeed*. Viking.

Dicey, A. V. [1915] 1982. *Introduction to the Study of the Law of the Constitution*. Liberty Fund.

Downs, Anthony. 1957. *An Economic Theory of Democracy*. Harper and Row.

Dworkin, Ronald. 1977. *Taking Rights Seriously*. Harvard University Press.
   1985. *A Matter of Principle*. Harvard University Press.
   1986. *Law's Empire*. Belknap Press.
   2002. "Thirty Years On," *Harvard Law Review* 115: 1655–1687.

Dyzenhaus, David. 2000. "Positivism's Stagnant Research Program," *Oxford Journal of Legal Studies* 20: 703–722.

   2006. *The Constitution of Law: Legality in a Time of Emergency*. Cambridge University Press.

2010. *Hard Cases in Wicked Legal Systems: Pathologies of Legality*, 2nd ed. Oxford University Press.

Ehrlich, Eugen. [1913] 1936. *Fundamental Principles of the Sociology of Law*. Walter L. Moll, trans. Harvard University Press.

Elster, Jon. 1982. "Marxism, Functionalism, and Game Theory," *Theory and Society* 11: 453–482.

1986. "The Market and the Forum: Three Varieties of Political Theory," in *The Foundations of Social Choice Theory*, Jon Elster and Aanund Hylland, eds. Cambridge University Press.

1989. *The Cement of Society*. Cambridge University Press.

2000. *Ulysses Unbound: Studies in Rationality, Precommitment, and Constraints*. Cambridge University Press.

Epstein, Richard A. 2011. *Design for Liberty: Private Property, Public Administration, and the Rule of Law*. Harvard University Press.

Eskridge, William N., Jr., and John Ferejohn. 1994. "Politics, Interpretation, and the Rule of Law," in *Nomos 36: The Rule of Law*, Ian Shapiro, ed. New York University Press.

Estlund, David M. 2008. *Democratic Authority: A Philosophical Framework*. Princeton University Press.

Fallon, Richard H. 1997. "'The Rule of Law' as a Concept in Constitutional Discourse," *Columbia Law Review* 97: 1–56.

Finnis, John. 1980. *Natural Law and Natural Rights*. Clarendon Press.

Friedmann, Wolfgang. 1951. *Law and Social Change in Contemporary Britain*. Stevens.

Fuller, Lon L. 1958. "Positivism and Fidelity to Law – A Reply to Professor Hart," *Harvard Law Review* 71: 630–672.

1969. *The Morality of the Law*, revised ed. Yale University Press.

Galanter, Marc. 1974. "Why the 'Haves' Come Out Ahead: Speculations on the Limits of Legal Change," *Law and Society Review* 9: 95–160.

Galligan, D. J. 2007. *Law in Modern Society*. Oxford University Press.

Gardner, John. 2001. "Legal Positivism: 5½ Myths," *American Journal of Jurisprudence* 46: 199–227.

Gibbons, Robert. 1992. *Game Theory for Applied Economists*. Princeton University Press.

Gigerenzer, Gerd. 2008. *Rationality for Mortals: How People Cope with Uncertainty*. Oxford University Press.

Gilmore, Grant. 1977. *The Ages of American Law*. Yale University Press.

Ginsburg, Tom. 2008. "Administrative Law and the Judicial Control of Agents in Authoritarian Regimes," in *Rule by Law: The Politics of Courts in Authoritarian Regimes*, Tom Ginsburg and Tamir Moustafa, eds. Cambridge University Press.

Gowder, Paul. 2013. "The Rule of Law and Equality," *Law and Philosophy* 32: 565–618.

Green, Leslie. 1985. "Authority and Convention," *The Philosophical Quarterly* 35: 329–346.

　1999. "Positivism and Conventionalism," *Canadian Journal of Law and Jurisprudence* 12: 35–52.

Greenberg, Mark. 2014. "The Moral Impact Theory of Law," *Yale Law Journal* 123: 1288–1342.

Habermas, Jürgen. 1988. "Law and Morality," Kenneth Baynes, trans. *Tanner Lectures on Human Values* 8: 217–279.

Hadfield, Gillian K., and Barry R. Weingast. 2014. "Microfoundations of the Rule of Law," *Annual Review of Political Science* 17: 21–42.

Haggard, Stephan, Andrew MacIntyre, and Lydia Tiede. 2008. "The Rule of Law and Economic Development," *Annual Review of Political Science* 11: 205–234.

Haggard, Stephan, and Lydia Tiede. 2010. "The Rule of Law and Economic Growth: Where Are We?," *World Development* 39: 673–685.

Harrington, James. [1656] 1977. "The Commonwealth of Oceana," in *The Political Works of James Harrington*. J. G. A. Pocock, ed. Cambridge University Press.

Hart, Henry M., Jr., and Albert M. Sachs. 1994. *The Legal Process: Basic Problems in the Making and Application of Law*. Foundation Press.

Hart, H. L. A. 1955. "Are There Any Natural Rights?," *Philosophical Review* 64: 175–191.

　1958. "Positivism and the Separation of Law and Morals," *Harvard Law Review* 71: 593–629.

　1965. Review of Lon Fuller's *The Morality of Law*, in *Harvard Law Review* 78: 1281–1296.

　1994. *The Concept of Law*, 2nd ed. Clarendon Press.

Havel, Václav. 1992. "The Power of the Powerless," in *Open Letters: Selected Writings 1965–1990*, Paul Wilson, ed. Vintage Books.

Hayek, Friedrich A. [1944]. 1994. *The Road to Serfdom*. University of Chicago Press.

　1960. *The Constitution of Liberty*. University of Chicago Press.

　1973. *Law, Legislation, and Liberty,* vol. 1: *Rules and Order*. University of Chicago Press.

Hershovitz, Scott. 2015. "The End of Jurisprudence," *Yale Law Journal* 124: 1160–1204.

Hobbes, Thomas. [1651] 1998. *Leviathan*. J. C. A. Gaskin, ed. Oxford University Press.

Hoebel, E. Adamson. 1954. *The Law of Primitive Man: A Study in Comparative Legal Dynamics*. Harvard University Press.

Holmes, Oliver Wendell. [1897] 1997. "The Path of the Law," *Harvard Law Review* 110: 991–1009.

Holmes, Stephen. 2003. "Lineages of the Rule of Law," in *Democracy and the Rule of Law*, José María Maraval and Adam Przeworski, eds. Cambridge University Press.

Holton, Richard. 2009. *Willing, Wanting, Waiting*. Oxford University Press.

Hutchinson, Allan C., and Patrick Monahan. 1987. "Democracy and the Rule of Law," in *The Rule of Law: Ideal or Ideology*, Allan C. Hutchinson and Patrick Monahan, eds. Carswell.

Jackson, Frank, and Philip Pettit. 1990. "In Defense of Folk Psychology," *Philosophical Studies* 59: 31–54.

Kahn, Jeffrey. 2006. "The Search for the Rule of Law in Russia," *Georgetown Journal of International Law* 37: 353–409.

Kahneman, Daniel. 2011. *Thinking, Fast and Slow*. Penguin Books.

Kelsen, Hans. [1960] 1967. *Pure Theory of Law*, 2nd ed. Max Knight, trans. Peter Smith.

Kennedy, Duncan. 1997. *A Critique of Adjudication: Fin de Siècle*. Harvard University Press.

Knight, Jack, and James Johnson. 2007. "The Priority of Democracy: A Pragmatic Approach to Political-Economic Institutions and the Burden of Justification," *American Political Science Review* 101: 47–61.

Kramer, Matthew H. 2004. "On the Moral Status of the Rule of Law," *Cambridge Law Journal* 63: 65–97.

Kripke, Saul. 1982. *Wittgenstein on Rules and Private Language*. Blackwell.

Krug, Peter. 2002. "Prosecutorial Discretion and Its Limits," *American Journal of Comparative Law* 50: 643–664.

Krygier, Martin. 2011. "Four Puzzles About the Rule of Law: Why, What, Where? And Who Cares?" in *Nomos 50: Getting to the Rule of Law*, James E. Fleming, ed. New York University Press.

Kutz, Christopher. 2001. "The Judicial Community," *Philosophical Issues* 11: 442–469.

Laborde, Cécile. 2009. *Critical Republicanism: The Hijab Controversy and Political Philosophy*. Oxford University Press

Lamond, Grant. 2001. "Coercion and the Nature of Law," *Legal Theory* 7: 35–57.

Lax, Jeffrey R. 2003. "Certiorari and Compliance in the Judicial Hierarchy," *Journal of Theoretical Politics* 15: 61–86.

   2007. "Constructing Legal Rules on Appellate Courts," *American Political Science Review* 101: 591–604.

Legomsky, Stephen H. 2007. "Learning to Live With Unequal Justice: Asylum and the Limits to Consistency," *Stanford Law Review* 60: 413–474.

Leiter, Brian. 2007. *Naturalizing Jurisprudence: Essays on American Legal Realism and Naturalism in Legal Philosophy*. Oxford University Press.

Lewis, David. 1969. *Convention*. Harvard University Press.

List, Christian. 2006. "Republican Freedom and the Rule of Law," *Politics, Philosophy, and Economics* 5: 201–220.

List, Christian, and Philip Pettit. 2011. *Group Agency: The Possibility, Design, and Status of Corporate Agents*. Oxford University Press.

Locke, John. [1690] 1980. *Second Treatise of Government*. C. B. Macpherson, ed. Hackett Publishing.

Lovett, Frank. 2002. "A Positivist Account of the Rule of Law," *Law and Social Inquiry* 27: 41–78.

   2010. *A General Theory of Domination and Justice*. Oxford University Press.

   2012. "Harrington's Empire of Law," *Political Studies* 60: 59–75.

Lowi, Theodore J. 1969. *The End of Liberalism: Ideology, Policy, and the Crisis of Public Authority*. W. W. Norton and Co.

MacCormick, Neil. 1985. "A Moralistic Case for A-Moralistic Law?," *Valparaiso University Law Review* 20: 1–41.

Machiavelli, Niccolò. [1532] 1998. *The Prince*. Harvey C. Mansfield, trans. University of Chicago Press.

Malinowski, Bronislaw. 1926. *Crime and Custom in Savage Society*. Routledge and Kegan Paul.

Maltzman, Forrest, James F. Spriggs II, and Paul J. Wahlbeck. 2000. *Crafting Law on the Supreme Court: The Collegial Game*. Cambridge University Press.

Maravall, José María, and Adam Przeworski. 2003. "Introduction," in *Democracy and the Rule of Law*, José María Maravall and Adam Przeworski, eds. Cambridge University Press.

Marmor, Andrei. 2001. *Positive Law and Objective Values*. Clarendon Press.

   2010. "The Ideal of the Rule of Law," in *A Companion to Philosophy of Law and Legal Theory*, 2nd ed., Dennis Patterson, ed. Wiley-Blackwell.

Marx, Karl. [1843] 1978. "On the Jewish Question," in *The Marx–Engels Reader*, 2nd ed. Robert C. Tucker, ed. W. W. Norton.

Maynor, John W. 2003. *Republicanism in the Modern World*. Polity Press.

McAdams, Richard H. 2005. "The Expressive Power of Adjudication," *University of Illinois Law Review* 2005: 1043–1121.

McClennen, Edward F. 1990. *Rationality and Dynamic Choice: Foundational Explorations*. Cambridge University Press.

Michelman, Frank. 1988. "Law's Republic," *Yale Law Journal* 97: 1493–1537.

Milgrom, Paul R., Douglass C. North, and Barry R. Weingast. 1990. "The Role of Institutions in the Revival of Trade: The Law Merchant, Private Judges, and the Champagne Fairs," *Economics and Politics* 2: 1–23.

Mnookin, Robert H., and Lewis Kornhauser. 1979. "Bargaining in the Shadow of the Law: The Case of Divorce," *Yale Law Journal* 88: 950–997.

Montesquieu, Charles de Secondat. [1748] 1949. *The Spirit of the Laws.* Thomas Nugent, trans. Haffner Press.

Murphy, Walter F. 1964. *Elements of Judicial Strategy.* University of Chicago Press.

Neumann, Franz L. [1937] 1996. "The Change in the Function of Law in Modern Society," in *The Rule of Law Under Siege*, William E. Scheuerman, ed. University of California Press.

Nicholas, Barry. 1962. *An Introduction to Roman Law.* Clarendon Press.

North, Douglass C., John Joseph Wallis, and Barry R. Weingast. 2009. *Violence and Social Orders: A Conceptual Framework for Interpreting Recorded Human History.* Cambridge University Press.

Nozick, Robert. 1974. *Anarchy, State, and Utopia.* Basic Books.

Peerenboom, Randall. 2005. "Human Rights and Rule of Law: What's the Relationship?," *Georgetown Journal of International Law* 36: 809–945.

Pereira, Anthony W. 2008. "Of Judges and Generals: Security Courts Under Authoritarian Regimes in Argentina, Brazil, and Chile," in *Rule by Law: The Politics of Courts in Authoritarian Regimes*, Tom Ginsburg and Tamir Moustafa, eds. Cambridge University Press.

Perry, Stephen R. 1989. "Second-Order Reasons, Uncertainty, and Legal Theory," *Southern California Law Review* 62: 913–994.

   1995. "Interpretation and Methodology in Legal Theory," in *Law and Interpretation: Essays in Legal Theory*, Andrei Marmor, ed. Clarendon Press.

Pettit, Philip. 1990. "Virtus Normativa: Rational Choice Perspectives," *Ethics* 100: 725–755.

   1991. "Decision Theory and Folk Psychology," in *Foundations of Decision Theory: Issues and Advances*, Michael Bacharach and Susan Hurley, eds. Basil Blackwell.

   1993. *The Common Mind.* Oxford University Press.

   1997. *Republicanism: A Theory of Freedom and Government.* Clarendon Press.

   2008. "Freedom and Probability: A Comment on Goodin and Jackson," *Philosophy and Public Affairs* 36: 206–220.

   2009. "Law and Liberty," in *Legal Republicanism: National and International Perspectives*, Samantha Besson and José Luis Martí, eds. Oxford University Press.

   2012. *On the People's Terms: A Republican Theory and Model of Democracy.* Cambridge University Press.

Pettit, Philip, and Michael Smith. 1990. "Backgrounding Desire," *Philosophical Review* 99: 565–592.

Pogge, Thomas W. 1989. *Realizing Rawls*. Cornell University Press.

2002. *World Poverty and Human Rights*. Polity Press.

Posner, Eric A. 2000. *Law and Social Norms*. Harvard University Press.

Posner, Richard A. 2007. *Economic Analysis of Law*, 7th ed. Aspen Publishers.

Postema, Gerald J. 1982. "Coordination and Convention at the Foundations of Law," *Journal of Legal Studies* 11: 165–203.

Radin, Margaret. Jane. 1989. "Reconsidering the Rule of Law," *Boston University Law Review* 69: 781–819.

Rawls, John. 1971. *A Theory of Justice*. Belknap Press.

Raz, Joseph. 1979. *The Authority of Law: Essays on Law and Morality*. Clarendon Press.

1985. "Authority, Law, and Morality," *The Monist* 68: 295–324.

1986. *The Morality of Freedom*. Clarendon Press.

1999. *Practical Reason and Norms*, 2nd ed. Oxford University Press.

2009. *Between Authority and Interpretation: On the Theory of Law and Practical Reason*. Oxford University Press.

Reenock, Christopher, Jeffrey K. Staton, and Marius Radean. 2013. "Legal Institutions and Democratic Survival," *Journal of Politics* 75: 491–505.

Richardson, Henry S. 1999. *Democratic Autonomy: Public Reasoning About the Ends of Policy*. Oxford University Press.

Rodriguez, Daniel B., Mathew D. McCubbins, and Barry R. Weingast. 2010. "The Rule of Law Unplugged," *Emory Law Journal* 59: 1455–1494.

Rosenberg, Gerald N. 2008. *The Hollow Hope: Can Courts Bring About Social Change?*, 2nd ed. University of Chicago Press.

Rousseau, Jean-Jacques. [1762] 1987. "On the Social Contract," in *The Basic Political Writings*, Donald A. Cress, trans. Hackett Publishing.

Rubin, Edward L. 1989. "Law and Legislation in the Administrative State," *Columbia Law Review* 89: 367–426.

Scalia, Antonin. 1989. "The Rule of Law as a Law of Rules," *University of Chicago Law Review* 56: 1175–1188.

Schauer, Frederick. 1991. *Playing by the Rules: A Philosophical Examination of Rule-Based Decision-Making in Law and in Life*. Clarendon Press.

2010. "Was Austin Right After All? On the Role of Sanctions in a Theory of Law," *Ratio Juris* 23: 1–21.

Schelling, Thomas C. 1960. *The Strategy of Conflict*. Harvard University Press.

1985. "Enforcing Rules on Oneself," *Journal of Law, Economics, and Organization* 1: 357–374.

Scheuerman, Bill. 1994. "The Rule of Law and the Welfare State: Toward a New Synthesis," *Politics and Society* 22: 195–213.

Schwartzberg, Melissa. 2009. *Democracy and Legal Change*. Cambridge University Press.

Sebok, Anthony J. 1998. *Legal Positivism in American Jurisprudence*. Cambridge University Press.

Segal, Jeffrey A., and Harold J. Spaeth. 2002. *The Supreme Court and the Attitudinal Model Revisited*. Cambridge University Press.

Shapiro, Martin. 2008. "Courts in Authoritarian Regimes," in *Rule by Law: The Politics of Courts in Authoritarian Regimes*, Tom Ginsburg and Tamir Moustafa, eds. Cambridge University Press.

Shapiro, Scott J. 1998. "On Hart's Way Out," *Legal Theory* 4: 469–507.

   2000. "Law, Morality, and the Guidance of Conduct," *Legal Theory* 6: 127–170.

   2006. "What Is the Internal Point of View?," *Fordham Law Review* 75: 1157–1170.

   2008. "How Rules Affect Practical Reasoning," in *Reasons and Intentions*, Bruno Verbeek, ed. Ashgate.

   2011. *Legality*. Belknap Press.

Simmonds, N.E. 2007. *Law as a Moral Idea*. Oxford University Press.

Skaaning, Svend-Erik. 2010. "Measuring the Rule of Law," *Political Research Quarterly* 63: 449–460.

Skinner, Quentin. 1998. *Liberty Before Liberalism*. Cambridge University Press.

Solum, Lawrence B. 1994. "Equity and the Rule of Law," in *Nomos 36: The Rule of Law*, Ian Shapiro, ed. New York University Press.

Stewart, Hamish. 2006. "Incentives and the Rule of Law: An Intervention in the Kramer/Simmonds Debate," *American Journal of Jurisprudence* 51: 149–164.

Stone, Martin. 2011. "Legal Positivism as an Idea About Morality," *University of Toronto Law Journal* 61: 313–341.

Strauss, David A. 2010. *The Living Constitution*. Oxford University Press.

Strotz, R. H. 1956. "Myopia and Inconsistency in Dynamic Utility Maximization," *Review of Economic Studies* 23: 165–180.

Summers, Robert S. 1993. "A Formal Theory of the Rule of Law," *Ratio Juris* 6: 127–142.

Tamanaha, Brian Z. 1997. *Realistic Socio-Legal Theory*. Clarendon Press.

   2004. *On the Rule of Law: History, Politics, Theory*. Cambridge University Press.

   2008. "The Dark Side of the Relationship Between the Rule of Law and Liberalism," *NYU Journal of Law and Liberty* 3: 516–547.

   2010. *Beyond the Formalist–Realist Divide: The Role of Politics in Judging*. Princeton University Press.

Taylor, Charles. 1995. *Philosophical Arguments*. Harvard University Press.

Thompson, E. P. 1975. *Whigs and Hunters: The Origins of the Black Act.* Pantheon Books.

Twining, William. 2009. *General Jurisprudence: Understanding Law from a Global Perspective.* Cambridge University Press.

Unger, Roberto M. 1976. *Law in Modern Society: Towards a Criticism of Social Theory.* Free Press.

Vinx, Lars. 2007. *Hans Kelsen's Pure Theory of Law: Legality and Legitimacy.* Oxford University Press.

Viroli, Maurizio. 2002. *Republicanism.* Antony Shugaar, trans. Hill and Wang.

Waldron, Jeremy. 1989. "The Rule of Law in Contemporary Liberal Theory," *Ratio Juris* 2: 79–96.

  1994. "Why Law – Efficacy, Freedom, or Fidelity?," *Law and Philosophy* 13: 259–284.

  1999a. "All We like Sheep," *Canadian Journal of Law and Jurisprudence* 12: 169–186.

  1999b. *Law and Disagreement.* Oxford University Press.

  2002. "Is the Rule of Law an Essentially Contested Concept (in Florida)?," *Law and Philosophy* 21: 137–164.

  2007. "Legislation and the Rule of Law," *Legisprudence* 1: 91–123.

  2008. "The Concept and the Rule of Law," *Georgia Law Review* 43: 1–61.

  2011. "The Rule of Law and the Importance of Procedure," in *Nomos 50: Getting to the Rule of Law*, James E. Fleming, ed. New York University Press.

Waluchow, W. J. 1994. *Inclusive Positivism.* Clarendon Press.

Ward, Kenneth. 2002. "Looking for Law in All the Wrong Places: A Critique of the Academic Response to the Florida Election," *University of Miami Law Review* 57: 55–99.

Watson, Alan. 2001. *The Evolution of Western Private Law*, expanded ed. Johns Hopkins University Press.

Weber, Max. [1922] 1978. *Economy and Society: An Outline of Interpretive Sociology.* Guenther Roth and Claus Wittich, eds. University of California Press.

Weingast, Barry R. 1997. "Democratic Stability as a Self-Enforcing Equilibrium," in *Understanding Democracy: Economic and Political Perspectives*, Albert Breton et al., eds. Cambridge University Press.

Wittgenstein, Ludwig. 1958. *Philosophical Investigations*, 3rd ed. G. E. M. Anscombe, trans. Prentice Hall.

Zinn, Howard. 1971. "The Conspiracy of Law," in *The Rule of Law*, Robert Paul Wolff, ed. Simon and Schuster.

Index

adjudication, theories of
  activist model, 163–164, 169–170
  defined, 160, 168
  legal officials and, 168
  legal positivism and, 160–161
  republican model, 165–167,
    171–173
  restraint model, 164–165, 170–171
  social justice and, 161–163,
    166–167
administrative lawmaking. *See* legal
  change
Americans with Disabilities Act, 183
antitrust law, 125
arbitrary power, 115–116
asylum adjudication, 198
attitudinal model, 12
Austin, John, 20, 90

basic legal community, 79–81
Bentham, Jeremy, 20, 90, 118
best response correspondence, 53
Blackstone, William, 118, 203
Bowers v. Hardwick, 23
Bratman, Michael, 49
Brown v. Board of Education, 170,
  172, 184
Bush v. Gore, 130

Calvert, Randall, 47
coercive agent, defined, 66. *See also*
  public coercive agents
coercive force, defined, 65
common knowledge, and rule of law,
  131–132
conscription, military, 195
coordination
  authority and, 103, 105
  bargaining and, 103, 106, 118

coercion and, 105–106
convention and, 29, 61, 104, 106,
  177–180
deliberation and, 103, 105, 118,
  180
failure of, 101–103
methods of, 103–105
coordination conventions
  asymmetric, 46
  impure, 45–46
  symmetric pure, 43–44
  v. law, 68
  v. social norms, 57, 145–146
corporations, law of, 88
Corpus Iurius Civilis, 65
critical legal studies, 12
critical reflective attitudes, 39
critical theory, 121
custom, 42–43, 48
  defined, 43
  social order and, 61
customary law, 90

Davidson, Donald, 33
deliberative democracy, 13
desuetude, 78
Dicey, A.V., 101, 133–134, 198
difficult cases, 156, 173–174
discretionary authority
  rule of law and, 196–197, 199–200
  types of, 197–199
Downs, Anthony, 49
Dworkin, Ronald, 21, 30
  hard cases and, 156–158
  plain facts view and, 153
  semantic sting and, 58

Eighth Amendment, 189
Enabling Act of 1933, 112

equality, legal. *See* legal equality
Eskridge, William, and John
　Ferejohn, 5
exclusionary reasons. *See* second-order
　preferences

Fallon, Richard, 5, 209
family law, 88, 111
fidelity to law, 149, 159
Finnis, John, 5, 209
Flanders, Chad, 90, 202
Frank, Jerome, 11
freedom, from domination, 1, 114,
　125–126, 206. *See also* arbitrary
　power; republicanism
　independent judiciary and, 162
　rule of law and, 116–118
freedom, from interference, 118–119
Friedmann, Wolfgang, 4
Fuller, Lon, 6, 14–17, 112, 124,
　204

Green, Leslie, 30
Greenberg, Mark, 21
Guantánamo Bay, 130

habits, 33–34
　defined, 33
　v. personal rules, 35
　shared, 42
　social order and, 61
Hadfield, Gillian, and Barry Weingast,
　134–135
hard cases
　defined, 155–157
　legal positivism and, 157–158
　rule of recognition and, 158
　theories of adjudication and,
　169–173
Harrington, James, 2, 108
Hart, H. L. A., 10, 12, 18, 20–21, 30,
　85, 91, 204
　critical reflective attitudes and, 39
　internal point of view and, 48–49,
　97
　normativity of law and, 91–94
　practice theory and, 55–61
Havel, Václav, 122
Hayek, Friedrich, 5, 133–134, 192,
　196, 200

Hobbes, Thomas, 20, 66, 90, 95, 105,
　118
Hoebel, E. Adamson, 70
Holmes, Oliver Wendell, 48, 139
human action
　purposeful, 31–32
　rational, 32–33

ideology, and rule of law, 121–123
incentive compatibility, 83
indeterminacy, legal. *See* rule skepticism
internal point of view, 48–49
　possibility of law and, 96–99
international law, 206–207
interpretivism, 21

judicial lawmaking. *See* legal change
judicial review, 164–165, 173
jurisprudence, normative v. analytic,
　18–19
justice, economic, 192–196, 202
justice, global, 205–207
justice, social
　defined, 1, 204
　domination and, 116
　independent judicary and, 162–163
　rule of law and, 1–2, 119, 176,
　201
　theories of adjudication and, 161–163,
　166–167
justice, transitional, 126, 204–205

Kahn, Jeffrey, 114, 152
Kelsen, Hans, 4, 20, 89, 109
　rule of law and, 111–113
Kennedy, Duncan, 12
Korematsu v. United States, 69, 84,
　110

law and economics, 12–13
law, legal system. *See also* basic legal
　community; legal validity; rule of
　recognition
　defined, 68, 70–71
　functional accounts, 70, 74, 84
　legal change and, 184–185
　normativity of law, 91–96
　possibility of, 82–85, 94, 96–99
　public coercive agents and, 68–70,
　72–74

published legal texts and, 87–88, 109
sanctions and, 74–79
social order and, 68–70
social rules and, 68–74, 81
varieties of, 85–87
Lax, Jeffery, 151
legal authorization, 109, 111
legal change
administrative lawmaking, 187–188
endogenous, 177–180
exogenous, 180, 185–192
forms of, 181
judicial lawmaking and, 189–192
legal validity and, 184–185
legislation and, 186–189
rule of law and, 178, 182–184
legal equality, 132–135
legal formalism, 153
legal obligation, theories of, 95
legal officials
defined, 168
and difficult cases, 173–174
legal pluralism, 106
legal positivism, 17–21. *See also*
separability thesis; social fact thesis
classical v. modern, 90–91
hard cases and, 157–158
inclusive v. exclusive, 25, 189–191
indeterminacy and, 153–155
legal realism and, 140–141
theories of adjudication and, 160–161
legal realism, 11–12, 139–140. *See also*
rule skepticism
legal positivism and, 140–141
rule of law and, 141–143
legal validity
defined, 83
legal change and, 83–84, 184–185
rule of law and, 109, 111–113
separability thesis and, 20, 23–25
legality, principles of. *See* principles of legality
legislative authority, defined, 186
legislative due process, 187
liberty. *See* freedom

Llewellyn, Karl, 11
Locke, John, 203

MacPherson v. Buick Motor Co., 179, 189
Magarian, Greg, 70
Marshall, John, 3
Marx, Karl, 121
McLoughlin v. O'Brian, 156, 158
medieval law, 88–89
methods of coordination. *See* coordination
Mill, John Stuart, 140
Mojave Desert, 22–23
Montesquieu, Charles de Secondat, 3
moral impact theory, 21
Moses, Robert, 201

Nash equilibrium
defined, 53
social rules and, 46–47, 49–51
sub-game perfect, 54, 83, 91
sub-optimal, 57
natural law jurisprudence, 19, 21, 118

Obergefell v. Hodges, 172
organized crime, 89–90
Osborn v. Bank of United States, 3

Peirce, Charles Sanders, 3
Pogge, Thomas, 206
practice theory, 30, 55–61, 93–94
legal obligation and, 95–96
principles of legality, 26, 113, 128–132, 209–211
derivation of, 13–14, 126–128
disagreement over, 5–7
Fuller on, 15–17
privity of contract, 179
problem of constitutionalism, 107, 216
problem of social order, 106, 216
prosecutorial discretion, 198
public coercive agents
defined, 66
effective range of, 67, 82
group agency and, 66–67, 82–83
law and, 68–70, 72–74
subject community of, 82–83

Rawls, John, 6, 194
Raz, Joseph, 5, 8, 30, 107, 209
    exclusionary reasons and, 39
    service account and, 95
realism, legal. *See* legal realism
republicanism, 1, 116. *See also* freedom
        from domination
    independent judiciary and, 162
    rule of law and, 118–119
    theories of adjudication and, 165–167,
        171–173
Restatement of Contracts, 64
Riggs v. Palmer, 157–158
Roe v. Wade, 170, 172
Rousseau, Jean-Jacques, 132
rule of law
    common knowledge and, 131–132
    defined, 106
    discretionary authority and, 196–197,
        199–200
    economic justice and, 192–196,
        202
    evil regimes and, 120–121
    formal v. substantive accounts, 7–9,
        113
    freedom from domination and,
        116–118
    global justice and, 205–207
    hard cases and, 158–160
    ideology and, 121–123
    judicial lawmaking and, 192
    legal authorization and, 109, 111
    legal change and, 178, 182–184
    legal equality and, 132–135
    legal positivism and, 21–26
    legal realism and, 141–143
    legal validity and, 109, 111–113
    legislation and, 185–189
    limits of, 124–126
    measuring, 212–218
    normative ideal of, 108
    rule skepticism and, 146–148
    service activities of the state and,
        200–202
    social justice and, 1–2, 119, 176, 201
    transitional justice and, 204–205
    two dimensions of, 106–107
rule of recognition
    defined, 83
    hard cases and, 158

    possibility of law and, 84–85,
        97–99
    written constitutions and, 85–86
rule skepticism, 12–13. *See also* legal
        realism
    appeals process and, 148–149
    efficacy, 143–147
    final courts and, 150–152
    indeterminacy, 144, 152–155
rules
    v. commands, 129
    bright line v. standards, 115, 197–198
    prescriptive v. descriptive, 34–35
    Wittgenstein challenge and, 36–38,
        58–60
rules, personal, 35–36, 41–42
    commitment and, 39–41
    v. habits, 35
    obligation and, 95
    shared, 43
rules, social, 43–47. *See also*
        coordination conventions; law,
        legal system; practice theory;
        social norms
    v. competative equilibria, 49–51
    defined, 43
    disagreement and, 58–61
    internal point of view and, 48–49
    joint intentional activities and,
        49–50
    legal change and, 181
    as Nash equilibria, 46–47
    normativity of law and, 92–93
    social order and, 61–62

sanctions, and law, 74–79
Scalia, Antonin, 5
second-order preferences, 38–39
separability thesis, 20–21, 190
slavery, law of, 88, 111, 125
social fact thesis, 19–21, 30, 141, 190
social formations, 9–11
social norms, 54–55, 141–142
    v. coordination conventions, 54,
        145–146
    defined, 54
    v. law, 68
stability, of judicial institutions, 163,
        168–169
stare decisis, 172

strategic situation, defined, 46
strategies
  defined, 51–52
  social rules and, 52–54

Tamanaha, Brian, 2, 70
Tedla v. Ellman, 171–172
theories of adjudication. *See*
  adjudication, theories of

Unger, Roberto, 12
Uniform Commercial Code, 64, 190
utility function, 32

Waldron, Jeremy, 130–131
Weber, Max, 43, 46, 70
*Williams v. Walker-Thomas Furniture
  Co.*, 190
Wittgenstein, Ludwig, 7, 37, 58